Feminist Methodologies for Critical Researchers

The Gender Lens Series

Series Editors

Judith A. Howard
University of Washington

Barbara Risman
North Carolina State University

Joey Sprague
University of Kansas

The Gender Lens Series has been conceptualized as a way of encouraging the development of a sociological understanding of gender. A "gender lens" means working to make gender visible in social phenomena, asking if, how, and why social processes, standards, and opportunities differ systematically for women and men. It also means recognizing that gender inequality is inextricably braided with other systems of inequality. The Gender Lens Series is committed to social change directed toward eradicating these inequalities. Originally published by Sage Publications and Pine Forge Press, all Gender Lens books are now available from AltaMira Press.

BOOKS IN THE SERIES

Feminist Methodologies for Critical Researchers

Bridging Differences

JOEY SPRAGUE

ALTAMIRA
PRESS

A Division of
ROWMAN & LITTLEFIELD PUBLISHERS, INC.
Walnut Creek • *Lanham* • *New York* • *Toronto* • *Oxford*

ALTAMIRA PRESS
A Division of Rowman and Littlefield Publishers, Inc.
1630 North Main Street, #367
Walnut Creek, CA 94596
http://www.altamirapress.com

Rowman and Littlefield Publishers, Inc.
A Member of the Rowman and Littlefield Publishing Group
4501 Forbes Blvd., Suite 200
Lanham, MD 20706

PO Box 317
Oxford
OX2 9RU, United Kingdom

British Library Cataloguing in Publication Information Available

Library of Congress Cataloging-in-Publication Data

Sprague, Joey, 1947–
  Feminist methodologies for critical researchers : bridging differences / Joey Sprague
    p. cm. — (The gender lens series)
  Includes bibliographical references and index.
  ISBN 0-7591-0902-8 (cloth : alk. paper) — ISBN 0-7591-0903-6 (pbk. : alk. paper)
  1. Women's studies—Methodology. 2. Sociology—Research—Methodology.
  3. Sociology—Statistical methods. I. Title. II. Series
  HQ1180.S65 2005
  305.4'072—dc22

                                                                        2005008429

Printed in the United States of America

∞™ The paper used in this publication meets the minimum requirements of American
National Standard for Information Sciences—Permanence of Paper for Printed Library
Materials, ANSI/NISO Z39.48-1992.

Contents

Series Editors' Foreword

It is now more than twenty years since feminist sociologists identified gender as an important analytic dimension in sociology. In the intervening decades, theory and research on gender have grown exponentially. With this series, we intend to further this scholarship, as well as ensure that theory and research on gender become fully integrated into the discipline as a whole.

In their classic edited collection *Analyzing Gender: A Handbook of Social Science Research* (1987), Beth Hess and Myra Marx Ferree identify three stages in the study of women and men since 1970. Initially, the emphasis was on sex differences and the extent to which such differences might be based on the biological properties of individuals. In the second stage, the focus shifted to the individual sex roles and socialization, exposing gender as the product of specific social arrangements, although still conceptualizing it as an individual trait. The hallmark of the third stage is the recognition of the centrality of gender as an organizing principle in all social systems, including work, politics, everyday interaction, families, economic development, law, education, and a host of other social domains. As our understanding of gender has become more social, so has our awareness that gender is experience and organized in race- and class-specific ways.

In the summer of 1992, the American Sociological Association (ASA) funded a small conference organized by Barbara Risman and Joey Sprague to discuss the evolution of gender in these distinctly sociological frameworks. The conference brought together a sampling of gender scholars working in a range of substantive areas with a diversity of methods to focus on gender as a principle of social organization. The discussions of the state of feminist scholarship made it clear that gender is pervasive in society and operates at multiple levels. Gender shapes identities and perception, interactional practices, and the very forms of social institutions, and it does so in race- and class-specific ways. If we did not see gender in social phenomena, we were not seeing them clearly.

The participants in the ASA-sponsored seminar recognized that although these developing ideas about gender were widely accepted by feminist sociologists and many others who study social inequalities, they were relatively unfamiliar to many who work within other sociological paradigms. This book series was conceived at that conference as a means of introducing these ideas to sociological colleagues and students and of helping to develop gender scholarship further.

As series editors, we believe it is time for gender scholars to speak to our other colleagues and to the general education of students. There are many sociologists and scholars in other social sciences who want to incorporate scholarship on gender and its intersections with race, class, and sexuality in their teaching and research but lack the tools to do so. For those who have not worked in this area, the prospect of the bibliographic research necessary to develop supplementary units or transform their own teaching and scholarship is daunting. Moreover, the publications necessary to penetrate a curriculum resistant to change and encumbered by inertia have simply not been available. We conceptualize this book series as a way of meeting the needs of these scholars and thereby also encouraging the development of the sociological understanding of gender by offering a "gender lens."

What do we mean by a *gender lens*? We mean working to make gender visible in social phenomena, asking if, how, and why social processes, standards, and opportunities differ systematically in women and men. We also mean recognizing that gender inequality is inextricably intertwined with other systems of inequality. Looking at the world through a gendered lens thus implies two seemingly contradictory tasks. First, it means unpacking the assumptions about gender that pervade sociological research and social life in general. At the same time, looking through a gender lens means revealing how central assumptions about gender continue to be the organization of the social world, regardless of their empirical reality. We show how our often unquestioned ideas about gender affect the words we use, the questions we ask, the answers we envision. The Gender Lens Series is committed to social change directed toward eradicating these inequalities. Our goals are consistent with initiatives at colleges and universities across the United States that are encouraging the development of more-diverse scholarship and teaching.

The books in the Gender Lens Series are aimed at different audiences and have been written for a variety of uses, from assigned readings in introductory undergraduate courses to graduate seminars and as professional resources for our colleagues. The series includes several different styles of books that address these goals in distinct ways. We are excited about the series and anticipate that it will have an enduring impact on the direction of both the pedagogy and the scholarship in sociology and other related social sciences. We invite you, the reader, to join us in thinking through these difficult but exciting issues by offering feedback or by developing your own project and proposing it for us in the series.

ABOUT THIS VOLUME

Joey Sprague offers a nuanced and engaging analysis of why and how methodologies matter: they shape the kinds of influence social science research has on society. After evaluating the epistemologies available to social researchers at this historical moment—positivism, postmodernism, critical realism, and standpoint theory, Sprague argues that a sociological perspective leads to a preference for standpoint epistemology. She explores discussions about relationships among researchers' social power, their power in the research process, and their authority as knowledge producers, and argues that a sociological reading of standpoint theory leads not to simple transfers of authority to some select group but rather to approaches that bridge standpoints.

In chapters 4 and 5, she takes up quantitative and qualitative methods, respectively, arguing in chapter 4 that although quantitative methods are vulnerable to certain kinds of biases, feminists have found ways to use them to forward critical feminist scholarship. In chapter 5, she challenges the common assumption that qualitative methods are freer from distortions of power and privilege, and evaluates a range of strategies feminists have developed in using these methods to respond to standpoint epistemology. The message of these parallel chapters is that no method is free of bias, and either set of methods can be used to promote a less biased and more socially useful scholarship.

The last two chapters take up issues that are rarely covered in discussions of methodology. Chapter 6 examines both conventional and experimental ways of reporting research findings and proposes some strategies for developing research questions that serve social justice. In the final chapter, Sprague calls for a transformation in the social organization of social research, from collaborative research agendas to changing the terms of evaluation of scholarly productivity.

Dr. Sprague takes on many historically dichotomized positions—between qualitative and quantitative methods, relativism versus positivist perspectives, subjectivity versus objectivity—and resists the tempting or seemingly obvious choices, instead laying out the reasons for, histories, and implications of these choices. In short, to cite Dr. Sprague herself, this book is intended to increase our "methodological mindfulness." She accomplishes just that, offering a beautifully reasoned strategy for conducting carefully crafted research that furthers the twin causes of better social science and a better society.

Acknowledgments

In one sense, this book began at a session on the sociology of gender at an annual meeting of the American Sociological Association in 1988. The story carries a moral for critical scholars that I think is general enough to share it here. My paper was the only one among the four that drew on quantitative methods—I used structural equation models to show how we could measure gender as a social variable. The discussant, a famous feminist, had interesting things to say about the other papers on the panel, but when it came to mine, she turned to me and said that she had nothing to say about it. I was shocked and embarrassed.

Fortunately, the other panelists did find things to ask about or comment on, so I managed to make it through the session without breaking into tears. One of the other panelists walked out of the room with me after the session, gave me a pep talk about the quality of my work, invited me to send her a copy of the paper, and returned it with helpful comments and lots of support. I will always be grateful to Patricia Yancey Martin for her compassion and work for a junior scholar who was a stranger to her. By the time I got home, my embarrassment had turned to anger, and Mary Zimmerman called my attention to a call for papers for a special issue of *American Sociologist* on feminist transformations of knowledge. Together we turned my anger at the unfairness of the discussant's lack of respect for quantitative work into a paper critiquing feminist assumptions about feminist methodology, which the editors accepted enthusiastically. Paula England, who also had a paper in that issue, read ours and invited us to write something for *Theory on Gender/Feminism on Theory*, an anthology that she was putting together. The stream of work that led to this book had begun.

The moral? It is not easy to be a truly critical scholar, one who does not accept unquestioningly the assumptions of one's peers. On the other hand, it is possible to be a critical scholar because you are not really alone. There are others willing to support you, give you chances, help you do your best. So recognize the anger behind your fears, use that anger to direct you toward work that needs to be done, and reach out to support others who are also struggling to push boundaries.

The community of critical scholars keeps social science vibrant. I have benefited from the sisterhood and brotherhood of many other researchers who have listened to or read my words and have given me the gift of supportive criticism. In particular, Jennifer Glass, Judy Howard, and Barbara Risman have been my "feminist troika," the go-to group when I need advice on the whole gamut of work and life concerns. I value their intelligence, ethics, and commitment to good scholarship more than they know. One of the wonderful things about teaching is that it brings a regular stream of smart and idealistic people with fresh insights and impatience regarding the status quo into a scholar's life—just thinking about all the terrific people I have first met as students makes me feel incredibly fortunate. I hesitate to name any because it would be hard to know where to stop, but if you have been my student, I have probably learned at least as much from you as you have learned from me, so thanks.

Many people made direct contributions to this book. I particularly want to thank all those researchers who are reflecting on research practices and thoughtfully experimenting with ways to improve them, including all the folks I cite in this book and the many others I did not have time or space to cover. Invitations to speak to the sociology department at North Carolina State and the women's studies program at Indiana University, South Bend, gave me the chance to get valuable feedback on material when it was in early stages of development. Mitch Allen is a publisher who is smart, thoughtful, collegial, and feminist—and I have benefited from all of these qualities during the process of creating this book. Jennifer Glass, Shirley Hill, and Barbara Risman read drafts of specific chapters and helped me strengthen them. Marjorie DeVault and Don Tomaskovic-Devey read the whole manuscript and gave perceptive and very helpful feedback.

The Gender Lens book series assigns to each book project a *madrina* who offers editorial support, and mine has been Judy Howard. *Madrina* is Spanish for godmother, but Judy has been more like a fairy godmother to me—always there to help think through a conceptual issue, find a citation, ease my panic, or smooth out my prose. I know that her contributions, while seemingly magical, took a lot more effort than simply waving a wand. Those who have written a book know that it is a long slog with plenty of frustration and confusion. I am so lucky and grateful to have had Judy on this walk with me.

Through the many years it took to write this book, Gary Brunk has been my *compañero*—my colleague, my lover, my comrade, and my best friend. He has read many drafts of these chapters with his sharp pencil, giving me the benefit of his considerable editorial skills and his gift for clear, direct writing. Few of our almost daily long walks together have been free of discussions of some theoretical issue or organizational challenge. At times when I have been under deadlines, and particularly in the last few months of writing, Gary has done way more than his share of domestic work—all the shopping, cooking, and cleaning—and he's done it with such good cheer that he almost had me convinced that he enjoyed it. And most importantly, he has taken me seriously and believed in the value of my ideas; there is simply no greater gift to a scholar.

Our two children, Jessica and Amanda, have drawn me away from the work of sociology to remind me of the joys and struggles of lived experience. Their love, passion, talent, and trust strengthen my commitment to making sure that their generation has at least as good a world to live in as mine has had, and hopefully a better one. I hope this book will, in some small way, help critical social scientists to more effectively understand how to make a better world for all people's kids. Jessica and Amanda, this is for you.

1

The Field of Vision

I believe that many who are attracted to sociology, and to social science more broadly, are motivated to learn about society and how social processes work so that they can help make our world more fair, and thus more peaceful and rewarding for all of us. However, few researchers have had the time, the opportunity, or even the inclination to systematically think through how standard research practices contribute to making our society more just, much less to consider the possibility that the way they do their work might even, if unintentionally, undermine this goal. I think this is as true of those who identify themselves as critical researchers engaged in a project of increasing justice as it is of those who think of themselves as nonpolitical.

Part of the problem is that only the truly hard-core feel a rush of excitement when they encounter the word *methodology*. For most of us, the word conveys either boredom or intimidation. I suspect the two responses are often related—we are bored because we are intimidated. Whether the primal force is boredom or intimidation, the consequence is the same: each leads to avoidance behaviors. In spite of all advice, undergraduate majors tend to put off those required methods courses until the last possible semester. Faculty members show no more enthusiasm for the topic—they do not typically line up to teach those courses. It is the rare social scientist who can claim he or she approaches reading the methods sections of articles in scholarly journals with enthusiasm. I wonder how many could honestly deny skipping those sections altogether, at least occasionally.

Would this avoidance be so common if more people saw that those methods courses and sections of articles are saturated with issues of philosophy, politics, and core values? I suspect not, and getting the reader to see it that way is a major goal of this book. The argument I will present here is that all knowledge develops out of specific social contexts and sets of politically relevant interests, and that mainstream social science, like mainstream knowledge more generally, tends to assume the position of privileged groups, helping to naturalize and sustain their privilege in the process. To create knowledge that is more complete and less systematically biased toward elite views, therefore, we need to ground each view of the social world in the standpoint from which it is created, and foster dialogue among those developing the picture from different social positions.

This book offers a step in moving that dialogue forward, by organizing and critically evaluating feminist writing about how to take standpoints and interests into account when conducting social research. I offer what I see as the key debates and most promising resolutions to others who may not be reading or thinking about this literature. I want to help those who do social research to look systematically at the "in order to" part of the connection between social research and progressive social change: how should we do our research *in order to* increase the likelihood that it will actually help make the world a better place?

WHY FEMINISTS?

Why do I limit my attention to feminists? After all, many social scientists have come to agree that the production of knowledge in social science is very much a social enterprise, shaped by the culture and society in which we do it. I have three reasons for writing this book from the perspective of feminism. First, perhaps because feminists have for so long been excluded from or, when included, marginalized within the academy (Collins 1986; Oakley 2000; Sherman and Beck 1979; Stacey and Thorne 1985), they have a long track record of linking questions of how to best do research with critiques of prevailing assumptions about what knowledge is and who is a trustworthy source of information. I see this integration of methodology with epistemology as an essential part of moving the dialogue forward.

Second, feminists have been experimenting with alternatives for quite a while through several different streams of conversation. Many of their experiments have emphasized shifting the point of view of the research to the formerly marginalized. They have accumulated a rich literature, vast and complex, and even most feminists are not familiar with all of it, let alone other critical researchers struggling to stay on top of their own research literatures. I hope to make it easier for all who want to do critical research to get a sense of the issues and alternatives being considered from specifically feminist standpoints.

Finally, I am a feminist, and while feminists are a very heterogeneous group and we disagree on many issues, there are two things on which we have consensus: (1) gender,[1] in interaction with many other areas like race/ethnicity, class, ability, and nation, is a key organizer of social life; and (2) understanding how things work is not enough—we need to take action to make the social world more equitable. That is, the call to progressive social change is a central commitment of feminism. These two points of agreement are both what make me a feminist and what make feminist discussions about how to best do research particularly important for my central goal in writing this book: I want to help social scientists to generate research that will be more useful to progressive social change.

WHO AM I?

Because a key argument of this book is that knowledge is socially and historically grounded, the reader should know that I am operating from a specific social position, biography, and agenda, which helps me see some things and makes me overlook or even be completely wrong on others.

I am one of the many who entered social science because I believed that improving our knowledge about society would help make the world a better place. When I decided to go to graduate school to become a sociologist, I had been working for several years in the insurance industry as a claims investigator. My job often put me face-to-face with the conflict between the interests of capitalism and of people—between the makers of products and the consumers who sustained injuries from them, between employers and the workers who sustained illness or injury at their jobs or were merely totally demoralized by them. I had grown up in a working-class, union family, which is probably a big part of the reason I felt more sympathy for the regular working people I got to meet than I did for the corporations it was my job to represent.

I had majored in anthropology as an undergraduate, fascinated by the discovery of alternative ways of organizing and making sense out of social life, and this led me to a cultural curiosity about what I was seeing on the job. I went back to school to try to understand why people in our society seemed much more likely to blame themselves or other individuals for their bad outcomes rather than questioning the way our economy and laws were organized, the system of corporate capitalism. Because the culture in which I was now most interested was my own, I chose to study sociology. I discovered an answer to my question in the sociology of knowledge, and in its analysis of the way social structure influences the contents and form of common sense and culture, and thus our understanding of ourselves and the world.

As a white, heterosexual U.S. citizen and a professor with tenure at a research-intensive institution in the United States, I have a very privileged position in many ways. However, as a woman from the working class and a mother, in many ways I am still an outsider within the academy (Collins 1986; Tokarczyk and Fay 1993). As I labored in the trenches of sociology, I began to turn the lens of the sociology of knowledge onto first the content of the knowledge we and others produce about social phenomena, and eventually onto the social organization of my working conditions, that is, onto the production of sociology itself. Those efforts eventually led to this book. I am a sociologist, which is both a great advantage and a disciplinary blinder. I hope that what I have to offer will be useful to other social scientists, and that some of them can then help to adjust the picture from their own disciplinary perspectives.

WHAT IS METHODOLOGY?

Discussions about methodology have tended to be narrowly technical. They focus on the details of how to conduct a kind of research—how to select what to observe, how to measure and code, how to apply an analytic strategy—all of which, taken in isolation, can be pretty tedious stuff. We can blame our boredom with this fixation on details on the predominance of positivism in scientific discourse. Positivist epistemology has dominated scientific discourse so completely that its specific way of connecting beliefs about knowing with research practices appears seamless. We tend to assume that a method and an epistemology are identical, and many even use terms that elide the two, like "positivist methods." This collapsed conception of science reduces methodology to a seemingly endless discussion of the trivially technical.

But methodology becomes a much more interesting terrain if we walk through the door that Sandra Harding (1987) opens when she distinguishes three elements embedded in how we do research: epistemology, methodology, and method. An *epistemology*, Harding says, is a theory about knowledge, about who can know what and under what circumstances knowledge can be developed. A *method*, she says, is a technique for gathering and analyzing information. We can gather information by listening, watching, and examining documents; we organize our observations by counting instances of preconceived categories and/or by looking for unanticipated patterns. Researchers' choices of *how* to use these methods constitute their methodology. For example, one can pose questions, collect evidence, and analyze the data in different ways. Each methodology is founded on either explicit or, more often, unexamined assumptions about what knowledge is and how knowing is best accomplished; together, these assumptions constitute a particular epistemology. That is, a methodology works out the implications of a specific epistemology for how to implement a method.

When we decouple the elision of epistemology and method, methodology emerges as the terrain where philosophy and action meet, where the implications of what we believe for how we should proceed get worked out. Reflecting on methodology—on how we do what we do—opens up possibilities and exposes choices. It allows us to ask such questions as: Is the way we gather and interpret data consistent with what we believe about how knowledge is and should be created? What kind of assumptions about knowledge underlie our standards for evaluating claims about how things are or what really happened? We can even pose questions rarely considered in relation to methodology, questions about how knowledge fits into the rest of social life: Whose questions are we asking? And to whom do we owe an answer? Thinking about methodology in this way puts the technical details into a social and political context and considers their consequences for people's lives. It gives us a space for critical reflection and for creativity.

More critical reflection and creativity are exactly what social science needs—at least that's the argument of many feminist and other critical social scientists. Social science has traditionally claimed to be value-free, or at least has operated as though values and politics are irrelevant side topics at best, and pose unresolvable dilemmas at worst. Yet an increasing number of critical scholars find fault with the assumption that any knowledge is value-free.

Feminists have made perhaps the most compelling case that conventional practices for the production and distribution of knowledge show patterns of systematic bias that keep sociology from fulfilling its promise.

WHAT'S KEEPING SOCIOLOGY FROM ITS PROMISE?

German sociologist Claus Offe (1985) argued that, once Enlightenment philosophers had successfully made the case for human equality as a core value, the critical edge moved to sociology, because sociology has the potential to reveal where we as a society are not achieving the goal of equality. Many sociological researchers have taken up that mantle, and they have generated a huge and valuable research literature exposing the existence of inequalities and the dynamics creating them, such as those based on gender, race, class, disability, age, and nation. However, feminists who have entered the academy have complained that some conventional practices in sociological research limit the discipline's ability to expose and help reduce inequality. They have identified biases in scholarly norms and standards throughout the stages of the research process, including (1) the kinds of questions researchers value the most; (2) the analytic frames they tend to use to interpret findings; and (3) the practices by which they communicate the results of research. There is a problematic pattern to these biases: they tend to work toward the interests of the privileged and against the interests of the rest, that is, of most people.

The Questions Researchers Tend to Ask

While methodology books devote attention to techniques for making questions more specific and researchable, the notion that research questions come from someplace is underdeveloped at best. It is common to identify some likely sources of questions, social theory, prior research, or, less often, personal experience. But the flavor of the discussion is that the source of the researcher's question is either rational and impartial, or it is individual and idiosyncratic. Feminists disagree.

Harding has observed that "there isn't such a thing as a problem without a person (or groups of them) who have this problem: a problem is always a problem for someone or other" (1987: 6). Feminists have found that traditional social scientists tend to ask questions from the perspective of the privileged, the powerful, those who manage people and strive to minimize the consequences of discontent (cf. Fine 1994; Harding 1991; Smith 1990). To begin with, not all kinds of researchable questions are equally valued—a scholar's evaluation of a research question varies with both its goal and its topic.

Hierarchy of Basic over Applied

Mainstream academic standards distinguish two major goals of research: "basic" and "applied." Basic research is research that furthers the body of scientific knowledge; its questions emerge from and contribute to the ongoing scholarly discourse. Applied research is directed toward producing knowledge that can be used to address a specific question or problem generated in specific communities. Academics conventionally hold basic research to be more important and more valuable. For example, when *Contemporary Sociology*, the field's leading journal of book reviews, commissioned essays by five sociologists on the topic of "What Is Sociology?" only one even referred to the fact that sociologists do not all work in colleges and universities, even though at least 30 percent of all sociologists work outside the academy.[2]

The norm valuing basic over applied research is particularly ironic in sociology, given its beginnings. The canonized forefathers of sociology, Marx and Weber, were deeply engaged in the politics of their time. The founders of American sociology, including the first chair of the first department (Albion Small at the University of Chicago, in 1892), were very interested in putting their science into the service of social reform (Oakley 2000). But over the course of its history, sociology as a profession has been relatively disengaged from policy debates. Its ranks have provided few public intellectuals, particularly in the United States. Contemporary sociological researchers have been more likely to see their intellectual projects as individual quests to maintain, develop, and extend the stream of ideas in a scholarly literature than to feel responsible to the needs of or questions from their communities (Sprague 1997, 1998). Sociologists committed to producing scholarship that is more directly engaged in social policy debates or that serves specific communities have found it necessary to develop their own networks of intellectual and professional support, for example, the Society for the Study of Social Problems (www.sssp1.org/index.cfm?tsmi=1) and the Sociologists for Women in Society (newmedia.colorado.edu/~socwomen/).

Supporters of a more engaged sociology have gradually increased their presence in the profession. The American Sociological Association has engaged in some public policy debates where sociological research is relevant.

Under the leadership of Michael Burawoy, the profession's key organization has been taking steps to create a more visible space in the discipline for "public sociology," arguing for its value, pointing to the ways many sociologists already do work in and for the public, and even organizing an annual meeting around that theme (cf. Burawoy 2004). While exciting, the very fact that the effort is required is testimony to the degree to which prevailing norms and values still construct sociology as isolated from the public arena.

Many feminists reject the mainstream ideal of a disengaged, "value-free" science, arguing instead that the goal of research must be to understand how oppression works and to provide knowledge that will help fight against injustice (Cancian 1992; Cook and Fonow 1986; Harding 1987; Mies 1993; Smith 1987). Some argue that applied research is more important than basic research. For example, Cancian (1992) submits that engaging in problem-solving research actually produces better data, by providing localized knowledge about a topic, and can generate evidence that approaches experimental, or at least quasi-experimental, research. In a similar vein, Oakley (2000) calls for the reinstitution of the social experiment as a way for critical scholars to develop solid evidence that will make a convincing case for social policy reforms. The point is not that we should reverse the conventional hierarchy and say that applied research is preferable to basic, but rather that we should call both the hierarchy and the dichotomizing into question.

What Counts as Social

Even within "basic" sociological research, feminists have found that the discipline creates a hierarchy of value among potential research topics. Mainstream sociology tends to employ a pattern of selective attention in selecting and evaluating research topics, creating a systematic stratification of social life. O'Brien (1981), for example, observes that we have social theories that address nearly all of the major aspects of our biological existence: providing for our physical needs (Marxism), sexuality (psychoanalysis and social constructionism), and death (theology and secular philosophy). The stark omission in that array, before feminists came onto the scene, was a serious consideration of the social arrangements and philosophical issues concerning human reproduction.

Feminists coming onto the scene complained that conventional social science had adopted uncritically the idea that the public and the private are two distinct realms of social life. Sociologists in particular have placed a relatively low priority on understanding the nurturance and development of people, and on emotions and intimate relationships in general (cf. Aptheker 1989; Hillyer 1993; hooks 1990; Ruddick 1980; Smith 1987). Their accounts essentially ignore what Aptheker (1989) calls "the dailiness" of ordinary lives, the struggle to preserve quality of life for one's family in the face of exploitation and oppression, to hold on to and nurture a positive sense of self in a culture that demeans and devalues one's kind.

Social science has operated as though the official institutions of the public sphere—the official economy, the polity, and related institutions—are the whole of what is social, or at least the most important part of it (cf. Fraser 1989; Mies 1986; Pateman 1983; Sprague 1997, 1988; Ward 1993). Ironically and tellingly, this version of society has then been constructed in such a way that it often appears to be unpopulated. Interpersonal relationships at work and emotional aspects of work itself are excluded from view; the persons who are acting as citizens and leaders have no bodies that locate them in specific social relationships (cf. Fraser 1989: chapter 6; Hochschild 1983).

The notion of the public and the private as distinct spheres of social life is possible to maintain only at a high level of abstraction, but it took the entry of feminists into the academic discourse to expose this. Feminists were the first to show that the personal is not just social; it is political. They began the analysis of power structures and struggles within a family. Feminists continue to show how family power relations shape their members' positions in relations of power at work and in public arenas, and how social power influences personal life. The dichotomous, hierarchical opposition of public to private represents relationships as if they did not occur within and were not constrained by social structures. It makes structures seem as though they have more reality than the daily relationships among people that actually constitute them and keep them going (Smith 1990). Even conventional terminology seems to suggest a hierarchy of value: social analyses that address large-scale social institutions as abstract structures are labeled "macro," while those that focus on individuals and the relationships among them, with an attention to process, are "micro," too often with the connotation of substantive and intellectual triviality.

The Form of the Question

Although scholars talk of basic research as an idealized notion of the dispassionate, disengaged pursuit of problems that emerge from the ongoing scholarly discourse, feminists have identified some systematic patterns in the kinds of questions scholars ask, and about whom we ask them. These patterns emerge in considering which social distinctions are most salient, how questions vary depending on the social category under study, the tendency to study those at the bottom of social hierarchies, and the tendency to approach social problems as individual rather than the outcome of social context.

Social science has exerted a great deal of collective effort to explore the differences between some groups that are hierarchically related to each other, notably those between men and women, or whites and nonwhites, or heterosexuals and homosexuals, or those with average to above-average intelligence and those with cognitive impairments (cf. Epstein 1999; Fausto-Sterling 1985; Hauser et al. 1995; Howard and Hollander 1997; Sprague and Hayes 2000). While research on the differences among members of these hierarchically related social categories abounds, there is a much smaller inventory of research testing the hypothesis that cross-group differences are small compared to within-group variation. For example, we see many fewer studies asking about the similarities between men and women than we do about the differences between them.

Questions posed about class differ markedly from those concerning gender and race/ethnicity. There is a substantial research literature on the itinerary by which people achieve a class position. On the other hand, until critical scholars became involved, social researchers treated gender and race as ascribed positions. There was very little analysis of the process by which individuals achieve gender or race, that is, how people decide which gender and race categories a person falls into, or the work individuals do to achieve recognition from others about the appropriateness of their classification (Howard and Hollander 1997). While social researchers ask how traits differ across gender and race, they rarely ask whether the affluent are a different kind of people than those with more modest means (Howard and Hollander 1997). In general, class seems to have lost ground as a salient social variable (Fine and Gordon 1989). Even among feminist researchers there is more focus on race and gender than on class.

Social researchers also tend to ask different kinds of questions about the privileged than they do about the dominated. Research questions are more likely to explore the deficiencies of those in disadvantaged social positions than of those with social power. It has been much more common to ask, for example, why women have so little self-confidence than why men have so little modesty. We have much more research asking why women value work outside the home so little than why men place such a high priority on it (Tavris 1992). Asking why white men are in elite positions is not nearly as common as asking why so many women or men of color are not (Morgan 1981). There is almost no research on the selves of people with cognitive disabilities; the implicit assumption is that people with developmental disabilities have no internal lives (Sprague and Hayes 2000).

In general, social researchers tend to "study down," that is, direct their attention to those who have less power. Anthropologist Laura Nader observed that books on American society through the 1960s "made no mention of the advertising, insurance, banking, realty, or automobile industries, which most people on the street know have played a major role in forming modern American society" (1969: 292). Psychologist Michelle Fine (1994) reports that when her graduate students wanted to study upper-class white women, they could not find much literature on them. Unlike poor women, affluent women do not come under the surveillance of law enforcement or social service agencies, and thus there is no "scholarly discourse on their dysfunctionality" (Fine 1994: 73).

Until sociologist Ruth Frankenberg (1993) undertook her pathbreaking work, there was very little scholarship on "whiteness" as a cultural construct, or on the traits and practices of white people. There is not much social psychological research on the degree to which individualism and individualistic conceptions of the self are unique to privileged peoples in the West (Howard and Hollander 1997). Research abounds on people who have sex too young or with others of the same sex, or who engage in sexual violence, but research on sexual practices and preferences of adult married heterosexuals has been much less common (Sprague and Quadagno 1989).

No doubt questions about social problems are usually posed by scholars who feel sympathy for the plight of those who suffer from them. Without a parallel concentration of research focusing on the problematic character of elites and the social institutions bolstering their privilege, the focus on what's wrong with disadvantaged people creates a picture in which those on the downside of hierarchies have, *and thus are*, problems. Researchers "studying down" make the relatively powerless even more visible to observation. Posing questions in this way implies that those with power are normal; their traits, behaviors, and social position require no justification.

Questions that address a social problem tend to be framed in terms of what is wrong with the person who is experiencing the problem, rather than in terms of what it is about the current social order that makes the problem likely. For example, a list of common research questions in the social sciences reads: What kind of people are likely to abuse drugs? Do women have different communication patterns than men? Why is the working class so weak and disorganized? What characteristics of individuals explain their sexual behavior? What is the influence of families and peers on discouraging African American children from succeeding in school? How can we teach people with developmental disabilities to have more self-determination?

Compare those questions to how some critical scholars have posed questions on the same issues: What is it about the form of social organization and circulating discourses in the United States that tends to make drug use so attractive to many of those who live there (Sprague and Zimmerman 1993)? Are women's communication patterns their strategies to responding strategically to situations in which they have less social power than others (Kollock, Blumstein, and Schwartz 1985; Sherif 1979)? Does the strong support that the U.S. capitalist class gets from the state, up to and including the use of violence against protestors, explain the relative lack of working-class power in that country (Vanneman and Cannon 1987)? What social and historical forces shape individuals' sexual desires and constrain their choices (Callero and Howard 1989)? What is it about the culture in schools that makes it easier for white children to succeed than African American children (Ferguson 2000)? How do we organize our communities to make it difficult for people with disabilities to be independent (Sprague and Hayes 2000)?

In sum, the kinds of questions posed tend to emphasize and even naturalize gender and racial/ethnic differences. Research questions are more likely to focus on members of disadvantaged groups and explore their deficiencies, while the attributes and practices of those with social power are much less likely to be exposed to social science surveillance. And in addressing social problems, the emphasis is more on the attributes of those experiencing the problem than on considering what it is about the current social order that makes the problem likely. In other words, there is a tendency to ask questions that make inequality seem either natural or the responsibility of those on the downside of social hierarchies.

Overall, the research questions that have traditionally earned the most respect in academic sociology are more likely to come out of the interests of
scholars than out of the everyday struggles of groups working for social
change, to focus on the areas of concern to privileged white men rather than
those typically assigned to women, and to ask what is wrong with those who
are at the bottom of social hierarchies rather than with those who are at the
top. These are not questions that are likely to challenge existing power
arrangements.

Our Frameworks for Interpreting Observations

Another line of feminist critique has been to challenge the interpretive
frameworks that dominate mainstream social science discourse. Among the
most problematic ways of organizing our observations are the reliance on logical dichotomy and the tendency to conceptualize individuals in abstraction
from their social context. Taken together, these conceptual practices facilitate
a third: objectification.

Logical Dichotomy

The framing device that has drawn the most criticism from feminists is the
logical dichotomy, which makes sense of a phenomenon by opposing it to another in a construction that is represented as mutually exclusive and exhaustive
(Jay 1981). The logical dichotomy runs through the history of hegemonic Western European social thought: mind/body, city of god/city of man, capitalist/
worker, nature/culture, nature/nurture, macro/micro, structure/agency (Alway
1995; Harrison 1985; hooks 1994; O'Brien 1981; Tuana 1983).

Logical dichotomies do not emerge out of empirical observation. They are
difficult to find in nature, Nancy Jay (1981) notes, in which everything is in
the process of becoming something else—acorn to oak tree to humus. Most of
the dualisms we use to describe everyday life are not logical dichotomies, but
rather refer to points on some form of a continuum—sick to well, bad to
good, night to day. Even a dichotomy that seems as basic as me/not-me does
not necessarily describe human existence. It is transcended in the experience
of a pregnant woman in relationship to the fetus developing within her, which
is both part of her and increasingly a different being, both live and not yet
alive (Rich 1976).

The artificiality of these dichotomies is exposed when one tries to identify the line that demarcates them empirically. Consider the dichotomy that has organized much social science research about human behavior: nature versus nurture. Asking whether some human skill or trait is due to nature or to nurture, to biological or to social causes, makes little sense when considering some of the many ways that biologies and social circumstances interact, for example, in nutrition, the amount and type of exercise, access to basic medical care, and the stimulation in and responsiveness of the social environment.

Similarly, the artificiality of the demarcating line between public and private is exposed when considering state-imposed policies that seek to control some aspects of intimate life while staying out of others (Sprague 1988). Recall that the second wave of the women's movement in the United States emerged out of a challenge to the public/private dichotomy under the banner of the saying "the personal is political." States impose restrictions on sexual acts involving people of the same sex that they do not intend to restrict among people of different sexes. States impose all kinds of limitations on the choice to terminate a pregnancy, but refuse to require drug-insurance providers to cover birth control.

Many of our most contentious political struggles can be seen as debates over where to draw the border between public and private in a particular domain of life. When should the state intervene in parents' child-rearing practices (e.g., discipline, feeding) and decisions (e.g., immunization, schooling, medical care)? Should those who personally believe in a particular religious tradition be able to pray in public school? When a person helps a loved one or patient commit suicide, is that the private act of suicide or the public act of murder?

Seeing the social world through logical dichotomies has generated conceptual distinctions that distort the lived experience of many people. Consider these examples:

- As a discipline, sociology dichotomizes the "Sociology of Work" and the "Sociology of the Family." Yet caring for a family is more than an emotional response; it takes a great deal of work. Many jobs involve taking care of individuals and families, and many workers put effort into nurturing their coworkers, whether by choice or because it is part of the gendered expectations of adequate job performance (Cancian 1985; Cancian and Oliker 1999; De-Vault 1991; Oakley 1974).

- The sociological distinction between work and leisure is not applicable to daily lives of the vast majority of women who work the double shift of paid work and unpaid domestic labor (Hartmann 1981; Hochschild 1989).
- The distinction between paid and domestic labor is not adequate to describe the lives of many women, particularly women of color, who for many years were blocked from any waged work other than paid domestic labor and child care (Collins 1986; Glenn 1992).

In each of these cases, the dichotomy describes a contrast that is possible only in the lives of the relatively privileged.

The following examples show even more clearly how dichotomies in social science that are used without reflection can mask the workings of power.

- Social psychology constructs altruism and aggression as opposites, yet Judith Howard and Jocelyn Hollander (1997) argue that these behaviors are intimately linked through the operation of social power. Power determines who has the resources to offer help, who needs help, and who cannot turn down help. Cultural power determines what gets defined as help (e.g., public assistance is, but big tax subsidies are not), and what gets defined as aggression (e.g., stealing bread is, but allowing one in six children to lack an adequate diet is not).
- The distinction between "first world" and "third world" hides the relationships that mutually construct them—the underdevelopment of the third world is the product of exploitation by powers in the first world, and the level of consumption in the "advanced nations" is dependent on continuing that exploitative relationship (Mies 1986; Ward 1993).

Notice how in each of these cases, dichotomies hide social relations that allow members of one social category to benefit at the expense of those in another. The point is not that dichotomies do not exist, but rather that they are ways of constructing social relationships that facilitate social domination. Using dichotomies to organize understanding without being mindful of the way they hide power unwittingly serves the interests of the powerful.

Abstract Individuation

Another common framing device organizing social science interpretations is a way of conceptualizing people that I call *abstract individuation*. That is, we talk of the individual in isolation from and unconnected with its interpersonal, historical, or physical context (Sprague 1997). A prime instance of the use of abstract individuation in social science is the notion of rational man [*sic*]. Rational man is an actor who establishes priorities and sets out to achieve them, evaluating options along the way in terms of an abstract value system or their utility to goal attainment (e.g., Coleman 1992). The image hides from us the degree to which most of us, especially women and men with responsibilities for the care of others, find daily life to be an ongoing juggling of competing responsibilities emerging from the complex web of our most important relationships (England 1989; Risman and Ferree 1995; Smith 1987).

Abstract individuation enables social scientists to conceive of social phenomena like race, class, gender, sexual preference, or limitation in ability in isolation from one another. Libraries are filled with books and articles about one or another class, one or another race or ethnicity, one or another disability, and even men or women, where little or no attention is given to systematic variation among members of these social categories created by their membership in other social categories. Like the logical dichotomy, we social scientists do not derive the frame of the abstract individual from empirical observation. Most individuals would not feel they were adequately described by just their gender, race, or class, because all people live their lives within a complex of intersecting social relationships (Collins 1989; Dill 1983; hooks 1981; King 1988).

The expectations and constraints that men and women must negotiate differ markedly depending on their race/ethnicity and on whether they are affluent, middle-class, or poor. For example, all women are held more responsible for doing domestic work, but affluent women can hire poorer women to do the work for them; those poorer women will, after doing their employer's housework, have to go home and do their own (Glenn 1992, 1999). Women in the working class have to contend with two shifts of work, paid and unpaid, and get little respect for either (Shelton 1992). As another illustration, men who immigrated to the United States from Asia in the nineteenth century faced gendered immigration laws preventing their wives, mothers, and sisters from joining them, and an employment market that often forced them into "women's work" in cleaning, cooking, and personal service (Espiritu 1997).

The same interactive dynamic applies no matter where we start. Race is organized in gendered ways and is experienced differently by women and men (Collins 1991/2000; hooks 1981). For example, while slavery was a horrible exploitation of both men and women, women's very bodies were subjected to rape and used to breed more slaves (Davis 1993). Class works in race- and gender-specific ways. For example, the African American middle class is more vulnerable than the white middle class in economic, political, and ideological power (Collins 1991/2000). Even racially and economically privileged women encounter a "glass ceiling" of limitations on how far they can go in achieving economic and political power (Acker 1999a; Reskin and Padavic 2002).

Abstract individuation creates systematic biases in knowledge. When mainstream scholars simply talk about class, without specifically paying attention to how it works in race- and gender-specific ways, they tend to generalize from the experience of men (King 1988). Similarly, abstract talk about race, divorced from gender and class variation, tends to assume a reference to men. Universalistic analyses of gender tend to fall back on the situation and needs of privileged whites (Combahee River Collective 1982; Dill 1983; hooks 1981; King 1988).

Representing individuals outside the context of the social relations in which they are embedded encourages us to assume the needs and priorities of the privileged party in the relationship, and to attribute problems to the disadvantaged. In fact, whether or not you think of yourself as having a gender, race, sexual preference, and so on, is likely to depend on whether you are on the privileged or the disadvantaged side of the social relationship that the label signals. Mainstream accounts of the practices of men, for example, typically operate as though men did not have a gender. Feminists have shown how even something as apparently gender-neutral as foreign economic and military policy is actually thoroughly gendered, built on the assumed needs, priorities, and practices of a particular form of masculinity (Connell 1995; Enloe 1990; Mies 1986).

Abstract individuation entails focusing on one part of a complex system and leads researchers into a kind of mistaken identity. We attribute outcomes to what is really a part of a system, when it would be more accurate to think of these outcomes as aspects of the way the system is organized (Stacey and

Thorne 1985). That is, words like "woman" or "Black" or "poor" or "Third World" point to positions in social relationships, relationships in which the researcher and the reader are also embedded. "Woman," for instance, has social relevance only because it is "not-man" in a social order that is based on that distinction. Talking about other people as a homogeneous mass and separate from their social context, while at the same time hiding one's own stake in the situation, amounts to constructing them as Other (Fine 1994).

Even something as apparently individual as a physical disability is actually the outcome of the way people's own abilities interact with the presumptions guiding the organization of the society in which they live (Sprague and Hayes 2000). For example, we think of the disability associated with deafness as the attribute of an individual. However, the *social significance* of deafness is created by a system of social relationships that relies heavily on oral communication. In communities in which everyone speaks sign language, deafness has much less social significance—some people still cannot hear, but that makes very little functional difference in their lives (Groce 1985). Similarly, what makes "Black" socially relevant is that we live within a society and a history in which presumptions about people's race organize their biographies, histories, life chances, entitlement, representation in cultural stories, and personal expectations. What makes Black socially relevant is the long history over which it has been defined in opposition to White, and the degree to which White cultural practices, preferences, history, and current situation are assumed as normal in our society.

Objectification

When interpretive frameworks rely on both logical dichotomy and abstract individuation, it becomes easy to objectify those we study. Objectification is the tendency to talk of and treat people as though they were objects, devoid of subjectivity, the opposite of agents who are developing analyses of their situations and working to cope with them. Mainstream scholars tend to objectify their subjects, to turn people into data, particularly those at the bottom of social hierarchies—women, the poor, oppressed racial/ethnic groups, postcolonial nations, people with disabilities (Collins 1989, 2000; Friere 1970; hooks 1981, 1994; Smith 1990; Sprague and Hayes 2000).

Feminists have warned that there is real danger in the practice of objectification—it has a distancing effect that can lead to justifying exploitation and abuse. Western societies' relationship to the environment provides an example. Prior to the modern era in the West, and continuing to the present in some other cultures, people understood the earth as alive, part of the human identity, even sacred (Merchant 1980; Mies 1993). Such an orientation dimly echoes in expressions like "mother earth." The dawn of the modern era is marked by a move to seeing the earth as an inanimate storehouse of resources, a framework that facilitates the development of technologies that "remove" those resources. Seeing seeds and livestock as commodities allows for the scientific decimation of the natural diversity in plant and animal life through hybridization and genetic manipulation (Shiva 1993).

The same principle applies to how researchers understand the human subjects of their research, which, as Ann Oakley shows, happened in Western gynecology. The founder of American gynecology, J. Marion Sims, practiced surgery on African American slaves whom he kept in a hut in his backyard; with the development of anesthetics and antiseptic procedures, he started operating on white women, using poor Irish immigrants as guinea pigs (Oakley 2000). Between 1955 and 1976, New Zealand's Dr. Herbert Green didn't want to remove cancerous ovaries in young women because it would also have been a form of birth control. With hospital permission, he failed to treat large numbers who had some precancerous cervical cells, to see, in a macabre sort of experiment, if it would lead to cancer. His subjects died at a much higher rate than women who had hysterectomies. None of the participants knew she was in an experiment. Green's research subjects were disproportionately Maori and poor—he continued to offer surgery to his private patients.

There are many other examples of heinous treatment of human subjects enabled by their objectification. Defining Jews, people with mental retardation, Gypsies, and others as less than human made human experimentation on them in Nazi concentration camps thinkable (Mies 1993). Researchers let syphilis develop among the patients in Tuskegee, even though they already knew about the severe consequences of the disease and after a cure had been discovered, just to see how seriously it would ravage their bodies (Oakley 2000).

However, even in research that is generally held to be ethical, interpreting data in objectifying ways can have deadly consequences, as Paula Treichler's (1993) analysis of the scientific response to what became known as AIDS demonstrates. As the Centers for Disease Control was collecting data on early

AIDS cases, the organizing framework was based on the kind of person who got AIDS, not on the kind of practices that made one vulnerable to it. The result was the "4 H's" typology of risk: homosexuals, hemophiliacs, heroin addicts, and Haitians. Further, in developing the list, some codes were more salient than others: gay or bisexual men who injected drugs were coded by their sexuality, not by their intravenous drug use. Marking sexual minorities as a different kind, as other than normal human beings, led to analyses that no doubt created a false sense of invulnerability to this deadly disease in people who were excluded from the typology, notably women, a group whose rates of HIV infection have skyrocketed more recently.

The process of objectification seems to be gaining in popularity in the scientific as well as public discourses, where the human subject of research is increasingly decomposed into fragments in interpretations of data. People living their lives in particular social relationships, within contexts of opportunity, constraint, and social expectations, disappear behind a flurry of abstract attributes and syndromes (e.g., ADHD, alcoholism, chronic fatigue syndrome, social anxiety disorder). Behavior that is not functional in contemporary social arrangements is isolated from those contexts and their history; rather, it is conceptualized as symptomatic of something about the person, an illness or genetic abnormality (Conrad 1975; Conrad and Potter 2000; Haraway 1993; Szasz 1971).

Reducing human beings in concrete social relationships down to a set of attributes or a consequence of a genetic pattern makes it hard to see social and environmental conditions that give rise to or exacerbate behavior that we find problematic. It leads to a search for how to change the individual, rather than a consideration of how we might change the situation. Thus, it protects those who most benefit from the status quo.

The Way We Report Our Findings

The conventional approach to scientific publication is that it is not political in either style or publication format. The writing is supposed to be transparent; the facts and their theoretical framing alone convey the message (Gusfield 1976; Richardson 1994). Yet scholarly writing conventions involve a specific set of preferences and practices that constitute an analyzable form of rhetoric (Gusfield 1976). Scientific reports rely on narrowly specialized language, stay at a high level of abstraction, hide the personhood of the researcher, and favor a dispassionate and often passive voice. The most highly valued form of publication is through hierarchically ranked scholarly journals. Each of these reporting norms has political implications that serve to sustain the status quo.

Jargon

Academic writing has earned its reputation for being tedious and laden with complex grammatical constructions. Scholarly publications use language so dense with specialized jargon that colleagues often cannot read one another across subspecialties within the same discipline, much less across disciplines (Sprague 1997; Sprague and Zimmerman 1993). The intelligent and interested non-scholar is many times barred altogether. Within academic culture, the accessibility of a text is often taken as indicating a less scholarly content. For example, one indication of accessibility is that a text can be used in a college classroom, which is to say that reasonably intelligent people with a high school education can read it without difficulty. Texts that are usable in a classroom are often redefined as teaching materials, a downgrade in the prevailing hierarchy of academic work (Sprague 1998).

Quantitative researchers are particularly vulnerable to complaints of inaccessibility. Even sociologists with backgrounds in research often find themselves struggling with jargon in descriptions of techniques and findings. Descriptions of technical procedures tend to assume that the reader has familiarity with specialized techniques. Little bits of folk wisdom circulate among sociologists that suggest the consequences for scholarly discourse. For example, there's the one about how many people subscribe to the top-ranked journal, *American Sociological Review*, and how few actually read it. There's also the one about how often readers skip the methods section when reading quantitative papers.

Abstraction

Another feature of scholarly rhetoric is its tendency to be highly abstract. Abstracting from observations, creating categories and labeling them, is an important aspect of intellectual work. But it is also one that can lead to reification of researchers' terms and objectification of the people they are used to describe. As Ellen Langer (1989) notes, we tend to become unreflective about the categories we adopt, forget they are somewhat arbitrary and necessarily flawed. Not only do we tend to reify categories, those individuals whose lives we sort into these cubbyholes tend to disappear behind the labels and become objects.

Quantitative research is particularly vulnerable to critiques of excessive abstraction. While virtually all research involves abstracting from data, quantitative methods require researchers to move to a fairly high level of abstraction—designing survey instruments or experimental conditions, taking measurements, constructing variables, specifying models that can be subjected to statistical tests, interpreting coefficients. Too often quantitative reports fail to come back from that abstract journey, speaking in terms of coefficients, variables, and models without translating the implications into the concrete terms of daily life. Conventional quantitative rhetoric transforms human beings into the invisible bearers of attributes and sources of variation.

Hiding the Researcher

Research is supposed to be discussed deductively. The text is represented as a completed analysis, blanketing over the long period of searching, even confusion, the dead-ends, the debates, and the selection processes that preceded it (Charmaz and Mitchell 1997). Quantitative reports represent the data and the analysis as speaking for themselves: "the author's activity is displaced in methods, which act on the data for the author" (Paget 1990: 158). The constructedness of qualitative research reports can be even more hidden than that of quantitative ones. Because these reports use people's words, describe their actions, and give a sense of place, they convey the impression of authenticity, of things exactly as they are. Yet researchers have been active constructors of these texts, too. They have reconstituted the people they interviewed and whose lives they observed into selected quotes from transcripts and field notes (DeVault 1990; Riessman 1993).

Authors are supposed to represent themselves as neutral, which is to say, not represent their selves at all. The norms of traditional scholarly writing call for the writer to "be seen (in the credits) but not heard (in the text)" (Charmaz and Mitchell 1997: 193). Instead of "I found," the norm is to write "the author found," or even "it was found" (DeVault 1999: 105). It is rare to read about the motivations of quantitative researchers in pursuing the topics they choose. It is more common for qualitative researchers to make personal statements about the research experience, but these are still segregated from the research report: "Personal experiences, anxieties, and fears are marginalized, written about in introductions, appendices, memoirs, and 'reflections' sections of qualitative journals" (Richardson 1988: 203).

Reporting styles that hide the researcher are particularly deceptive in the case of qualitative research, which is developed through sometimes intimate and sometimes extended relationships between the researcher and the researched. However, the tradition in qualitative publications is for authors to disclose little information about the relationship between the researcher and the researched. For example, the researcher's feelings, the quality of the interaction, and the informant's attempts to build a relationship by asking about the researcher or providing hospitality to him or her and/or other indications of social closeness or distance go unreported (Oakley 1981). Thus the reader gets little insight into subjects' choices and strategies in offering information or the researcher's reasons for pursuing certain topics and not others. Instead, the reader must rely almost exclusively on the researcher's subjective interpretation of what went on. In qualitative research, the investigator is the primary, and often the only, "measuring instrument," yet the reader receives little indication of how to assess the reliability of the investigator or the interactions that produce much of the data.

Tone and Voice

The tone generally considered appropriate for academic writing is something that Marianne Paget (1990) calls "disinterested discourse." Scientific writing should express rationality without emotion or humor, speaking plainly so that the unvarnished "facts" and "truths" will be obvious (Gusfield 1976; Richardson 1989). This emotional flatness not only helps to hide the researcher in the text, it creates emotional distance in the reader, too. The audience is supposed "to think and not to feel" (Gusfield 1976: 21). The scholarly norm that discredits speakers who show feelings like caring, anger, or outrage within the context of scholarly communication distances the reader from caring about the situation under discussion, much less feeling compelled to do something about it (Paget 1990). Arlie Hochschild (1983) draws the parallel between the emotion work of creating a dispassionate text and the steps taken in an autopsy to make sure medical students will be distanced from the humanness of the corpse so as not to be disturbed by what is being done to it. The scholarly norm of disinterested discursive style conflicts with the goal of communicating about knowledge, which is to persuade (Paget 1990).

Although many would agree that good writing limits the use of the passive voice, it is a practice that continues to thrive in research reports. Passive voice does not just hide the agency of the researcher; explanations in the passive voice hide social power. June Jordan (1985) argues that the voice of verbs communicates political meanings. In passive voice, people are fired or impoverished, or rebellions are crushed. There may be victims, but there are no clear agents, no one to whom we can assign responsibility for outcomes. In active voice, Jordan (1985) observes, someone is doing something to someone else—someone fires someone—and can be held accountable for the consequences of their actions. In the passive voice, our attention is drawn to the victims; in the active voice, we are at least as likely to be aware of the perpetrators. Using passive voice when there are clear agents amounts to hiding the exercise of power.

Publication Outlets

In addition to *how* scholars talk about research findings, consider *where* they talk about them (Sprague 1998). There are many channels through which sociologists do or could communicate about research findings: teaching classes to undergraduate and graduate students, publishing in the popular media, giving talks to community groups, as well as publishing in scholarly journals and books. Standards of evaluation in the academy, however, are sharply, and often explicitly, hierarchical. These various channels of publication are first trichotomized into research (e.g., journal articles or scholarly books), teaching (textbooks or classroom lectures), and service (articles in the popular media, trade books, or speaking to the public). Publications are valued in that order— the publications recognized with the most prestige and professional rewards are those in refereed scholarly journals or in books published by academic presses. Publication in popular outlets, on the other hand, can even diminish scholarly prestige. Within each category, forms of publication are also ranked. For example, journals and book publishers are hierarchically ordered. Similarly, research institutions that have graduate programs traditionally value graduate-student teaching more than undergraduate education.

The writing and publishing standards and norms in mainstream research reporting conflict with the goals of critical scholarship. Using jargon and highly technical language restricts the scope of critique of the work. People who are working in a somewhat different substantive terrain or using a different method may not read the work at all, or at least not read it as carefully as they might if it were written accessibly. Thus researchers lose the chance for feedback from those colleagues who have a different perspective on the social phenomena in question. Needless to say, these writing practices sharply reduce the chance of getting the perspective of the everyday social actors who are actually engaged in the social practices under study.

Even if authors manage to minimize the use of jargon and talk about their analyses in more accessible ways, as long as they maintain the dispassionate tone of disinterested discourse, Paget (1990) says, researchers are protecting themselves from what might be the most politically telling avenue of criticism. Standard writing conventions do not compel them to consider their own material and political interest in the questions they ask and in the interpretations they prefer.

Perhaps the most deadening consequence of standard academic rhetoric is that it keeps scholars from caring about the substance of scholarship (Paget 1990). The concepts, the measures, the data, the findings, and the subjects of research appear as objects to writers as well as to readers. No one is engaged as an impassioned potential actor. Yet who is it that will make the social change to which critical scholarship points, if not impassioned social actors?

In summary, writing conventions make researchers disappear, and hide their agendas, biases, and doubts. Mainstream practices for providing answers to research questions deflect criticism, limit the size and scope of audiences, hide the workings of power, and deaden potential emotional responses to irrationality or injustice. In these ways, traditional standards of academic discourse serve the interests of the powerful.

Looking across all three phases of research, from asking questions through doing the analysis to publishing the findings, mainstream social scientists have been, however unintentionally, asking the questions of the powerful, developing analyses that make existing inequalities seem natural, and creating knowledge within a context that is highly elitist and hierarchical. The knowledge being produced by scholars, many of whom have been committed to the goal of value-free science, has bolstered the system of social domination. Primarily elites have benefited from the knowledge produced, the form in which it appears, and the restriction of conversations about knowledge to very small and elite circles. The question is: How should critical social scientists respond?

KNOWING CHOICES

Contemporary critiques of mainstream knowledge have fed a kind of methodological schizophrenia in the social sciences. On one side are a legion of committed practitioners of quantitative methods who, aided by the rush of technological developments, are pursuing ever-increasing levels of technical precision, mostly untouched by the swirl of doubt about the validity of their product. On the other side, many critical researchers are rejecting quantitative methods because of their skepticism about assumptions of objectivity, impartiality, and control. Instead, they are relying on qualitative methods, believing that these have more potential for avoiding some of the major pitfalls of the past.

This latter pattern describes much of the feminist conversation about research methodology. Feminist researchers have displayed great creativity in the development of qualitative strategies for responding to the critiques of mainstream knowledge. By comparison, they have left quantitative strategies largely untouched. Quantitative scholars who want to be responsive to feminist and other critiques of positivism have little to go on, and the prospect of confronting a broad literature densely cast in specialized jargon can be immobilizing. Goals on which most sociologists could agree—developing the best possible understanding of social dynamics and enhancing public conversations about social policy—are not well served by qualitative-quantitative methods wars.

Those who take the position that one class of methods is good and another is bad are committing the same logical error that conventional scholars do—they fail to distinguish among method, methodology, and epistemology. They are collapsing a technique for gathering evidence with the logic and philosophy that guides how it is to be implemented (Sprague and Zimmerman 1989).

But simply rejecting a whole class of methods is not just a logical error—it is a political one as well. Anyone who cares about society, about social and environmental justice, about peace, and who is committed to democracy, cannot give up on the idea of science. Humans are intentional and social actors. If we do not accept some standard for valid knowledge, we cannot agree on how to proceed. If those critical of existing social arrangements reject any basis for valid knowledge, they cannot make politically effective claims about where and how change needs to occur. If critical researchers say that science is nothing but ideology, why should we bother to listen to any social scientist, including them?

So we have real reason to distrust "social science as usual," and yet we have even more pressing reasons to need social science. This dialectic has a resolution: we need to look at our methodology carefully. We need to be mindful of our ideas about how knowledge is produced and of the implications of the choices available to us in implementing any method. This book is an effort to increase our methodological mindfulness. The central argument is that *what distinguishes critical from uncritical research is not the method used, but how the method is used, both technically and politically.*

An Overview of What Is to Come

In the next chapter, I attempt to clarify these issues by giving careful attention to the choice of epistemologies available at this point in history and their implications for research methodology. I cast light on the assumptions underlying positivism and argue that they are untenable, given what sociology has demonstrated about human subjectivity and human social institutions. Postmodernism and other strong versions of social constructionism have made it clear just how untenable assumptions of objectivity and value-freedom are, but postmodernism, in the end, is also unsatisfactory to critical scholars, because it is weak in terms of serving social change. Critical scholars are left with two epistemological choices: critical realism and feminist standpoint epistemology. I argue that both a sociological perspective and the patterns of bias in traditional sociological knowledge should prompt us to adopt standpoint epistemology.

Any epistemology besides positivism raises questions about the relationship between authority and power. All research is organized and conducted through relationships—relationships between researchers and the researched, relationships among researchers, and relationships between researchers and other members of the society. Like other forms of human relationships, research relationships happen in a milieu of interpersonal and social power, in societies and a world order in which power is distributed unequally. In chapter 3, I draw on standpoint theory to explore discussions about the relationships among researchers' social power, their power in the research process, and their authority as knowledge producers. Out of this discussion, I develop some preliminary elements of a feminist methodology.

Feminist scholars have, like many other critical scholars, been understandably distrustful of the use of quantitative methods. In chapter 4, I consider biases embedded in standard practices for using quantitative methods. Since there is little written reflecting on the application of quantitative methods from a feminist standpoint, I pursue a different strategy: going to the trenches. I asked highly respected quantitative scholars who are also feminists which papers represent the best in feminist quantitative scholarship in their areas. An analysis of those projects reveals patterns in design and implementation of research that provide insights into more critical methodologies.

Critical scholars tend to assume that qualitative methods are relatively free from the distortions of power and privilege. In chapter 5, I outline some problems with that assumption. At the same time, feminists have developed some interesting, and even exciting, innovations in the practice of qualitative research. I describe strategies that feminists have used to adapt interviewing and ethnography to meet feminist epistemological and political concerns, evaluating them in light of the implications of feminist standpoint epistemology.

Earlier in this introduction I identified some crucial problems with the kinds of questions sociologists tend to ask and the ways they have traditionally reported their research findings. Feminists have developed many creative alternative forms of research reporting, and I describe these and reflect on their effectiveness in chapter 6. I also review and reflect on the much smaller literature on how sociologists might more systematically develop research questions that better serve the interests of social harmony and justice.

Finally, in chapter 7, I try to make the case for methodological connections. Practitioners of quantitative and qualitative approaches to research, especially as feminists have developed them, have a lot to teach one another. Each method has its own limitations, so an adequate representation of any social phenomenon would require integrating strategies. Because these methods require skill, some specialization makes sense. In order to build better understandings, I argue, we need to stop treating the development of knowledge as a collection of individual projects, and work toward collaborative research agendas. Finally, I maintain, doing social research the way it should be done, given a feminist standpoint perspective, will make this a job that critical researchers will love to do.

Methodology is a way of implementing a research method given a specific epistemology. Thus the first task is to figure out which epistemology is most consistent with a sociological worldview and a critical orientation. We have epistemological choices. Describing and evaluating them is the topic of the next chapter.

NOTES

1. I understand gender to be far more than the simple dichotomy of male and female. Gender is a whole set of social relations that organize us into different social positions with different advantages and constraints based on our sexual preferences and our parental status (cf. Sprague 1996). When I use the term *gender*, please understand it in this much broader way.

2. A fairly stable rate of 70 percent of sociology Ph.D.s were employed in colleges and universities over the period 1991 to 2001. Thanks to Roberta Spalter-Roth, Ph.D., Director, Research Program on the Discipline and the Profession, American Sociological Association, for compiling the data.

2

Seeing through Science: Epistemologies

Most researchers think of epistemology as a nonissue—or, more precisely, do not think of epistemology at all. We have learned to equate science with positivist epistemology and, for most people, the assumptions of positivism do not appear to be assumptions—they seem like common sense. Yet a major contribution of feminist and other critical scholarship has been to raise questions about epistemology. These scholars have questioned the assumptions underlying conventional research practices and have found that prevailing ideas about what knowledge is and how it is best produced emerge from relations of social domination and help to continue that domination.

An epistemology is a theory of knowing. It directs us in how to go about understanding a phenomenon. It spells out the grounds on which we can choose one account of that phenomenon over another (Alcoff 1989). Every epistemology, Anthony Genova (1983) says, involves assumptions about three things, which he describes as distinct points of a triad: the knower, the known, and the process of knowing (cf. Hawkesworth 1989). Genova describes the history of epistemological debates over the course of Western philosophy as revolving around this triad, focusing sometimes on the nature of the knower, other times on the nature of reality, and still other times on the process of knowing.

Feminists writing about epistemology identify the same three elements—the knower, the known, and the process of knowing—but in feminist analysis, the focus tends to be on how they are connected (Ring 1987; Smith 1990).

Epistemologies, from this perspective, are accounts of the knowing subject, the object of study, and the relationship between them.

First I will present two extreme positions in the current discourse on epistemology—on the one hand, the idea that the facts speak for themselves, and on the other, the idea that systematic knowledge of the social world is impossible. I will argue that while both positions have made important contributions, at this point in history they pose false choices, and critical researchers should be satisfied with neither. Later I will turn to two epistemological alternatives that have more potential usefulness for critical social science researchers because each accepts that knowledge is socially constructed and provisional but attainable: critical realism and standpoint theory.

POSITIVISM: DO THE FACTS SPEAK FOR THEMSELVES?

Almost every child who goes to elementary school in the United States encounters positivist epistemology; it permeates early science education and science fairs. Positivism could be described as an epistemology of the fact. Positivists generally believe that the world of experience is an objective world, governed by underlying regularities, even natural laws. Empirical observations, the "facts," are outcroppings of these underlying regularities. Positivists hold that if, and only if, we systematically and dispassionately observe the data of the empirical world, we can detect the lawful patterns of which they are evidence.

At the heart of positivist epistemology is an emphasis on objectivity. Positivism assumes that truth comes from eliminating the role of subjective judgments and interpretations. Good science, from this perspective, can and should be value-free. According to positivist epistemology, subjectivity is an obstacle to knowledge: the observer's personality and feelings introduce errors in observation. The practices of research are designed to minimize, and hopefully erase, any impact of the subjectivity of the researcher on the collection and interpretation of data. Observations are conducted systematically, through the use of precise instruments and countable measures. Interpretations are developed through applying statistical analyses and theories of probability to the quantities into which the data have been organized. Following these systematic procedures makes data collection and interpretation open to replication, and testing by others, a further assurance of objectivity (Barzun and Graff 1970: 222–29).

Thus, in terms of the three elements of epistemology—the knower, the known, and the process of knowing—positivism assumes the possibility of a sharp dichotomy between the knower and the known, and focuses attention on strategies that researchers might use to enforce that dichotomy (Ring 1987).

Sociologists know positivism well—this philosophy of science has been linked with sociology from its beginning. Auguste Comte, the mathematician often credited with founding the discipline, and Emile Durkheim, who played a major role in establishing the new discipline's credibility, were enthusiastic about the promise of the precise use of quantitative methods to reveal the natural laws underlying social phenomena. The founders of American sociology were oriented to sociology as a science, as a systematic collection and analysis of data (Oakley 2000). From the beginning many social scientists, both mainstream and critical, have equated positivist epistemological beliefs with quantitative methods. A key argument of this book is that this equation is inaccurate.

The development of positivism offered some clear advantages over the epistemology that prevailed prior to it, an epistemology based on faith and divine revelation, which grounded authority in tradition (Lovibond 1989). Positivism's reliance on empirical evidence and clear, replicable procedures for collecting and interpreting evidence opens up the production of knowledge to many more than a chosen—even literally anointed—few. The emphasis on systematic procedures presents knowledge claims within a context that is open to critique and argument, even refutation. Thus positivist epistemology has generated methods with democratic potential. However, positivism does have its problems, as has been shown by scholars from Mannheim (1936) to contemporary social constructionists who have argued that official knowing as we have inherited it is not the objective, unbiased, apolitical process it represents itself to be.

Observers See through a Cultural Lens

Scholarly paradigms, like other forms of human consciousness, are the expression of specific worldviews. The central criticism of positivism is directed at the notion that scientists can occupy an Archimedean point outside the ongoing swim of the social world, escaping its influence as they develop hypotheses, make their measurements, analyze the data, and draw conclusions (Smith 1987). The "facts" that are the raw material of scientific analysis are themselves the outcome of specific social practices. What we know about the process of human perception undermines the notion that we can detect pure facts outside some theory (see Bechtel 1988). The very first step in the practice of what we usually think of as scientific objectivity involves a social construction: scientists use some framework to carve up the continuity of lived experience to identify objects, or facts, that they then proceed to investigate (Shiva 1993; Smith 1990). Making any observation requires the acceptance of some background assumptions, some system of beliefs to organize what one is seeing. This is why Helen Longino says scientific data are "theory laden" (1989).

For example, the scientific research literature is filled with hypotheses about sex differences, for example, in brain organization, conceptual ability, and ethical development (Bleier 1984; Eagly 1995; Fausto-Sterling 1985; Gilligan 1982; Tavris 1992). All of this research is premised on the background assumption that sex is a naturally occurring dichotomy—that there are two and only two sexes. Yet there seems to be no consistent set of biological criteria by which we can divide the human population into two mutually exclusive and exhaustive categories (Fausto-Sterling 1985; Kessler 1998; Kessler and McKenna 1978). Further, other cultures have apparently observed the "facts" and reached different conclusions on the topic: a number of other cultures accept as natural the existence of three genders, each of which is accorded distinctive characteristics and social roles (Kessler and McKenna 1978; Lorber 1994). Because our culture assumes dichotomous sex, this has been an unquestioned background assumption guiding scientific research. That research has then been used to demonstrate the "naturalness" of dichotomous sex.

Harding (1998) asserts that even the positivist assumption of underlying natural laws governing phenomena is an expression of the imagery of divine law and purpose in European Judeo-Christian religious traditions. Developments like chaos theory in the natural sciences reveal that, even in physics, the idea that there are natural laws is a background assumption that is open to serious challenge.

The Data Do Not Confess

In addition to positivism's failure to recognize the "theory-laden" quality of the data themselves, Longino (1989) identifies another flaw in positivist logic: the assumption that the data directly support the hypotheses. Drawing on the empiricist philosopher Willard Quine, she argues that the data do not say which hypothesis for which they are evidence; that is, theories are "empirically under-determined" (cf. Alcoff 1989). The same data can be used to support contradic-tory hypotheses, and which connection gets made depends, again, on the background assumptions being made by the analyst (Longino 1989).

For example, African Americans tend to score lower on intelligence tests than do European Americans. These data can be used to support hypotheses about race inferiority, as the authors of one highly publicized book, *The Bell Curve*, did. However, this conclusion requires that one also make a whole string of other assumptions, including that what the tests measure is intelli-gence, that test instruments are not class- or race-biased, that race is unrelated to access to decent nutrition, health care, and education, to region, or to ex-posure to toxic substances in the environment, and that these social and envi-ronmental factors have no bearing on performance on intelligence tests (cf. Fisher et al. 1996; Hauser, Taylor, and Duster 1995). Each and every one of those assumptions is vulnerable to serious challenge.

In summary, when testing any one hypothesis, a scientist is also testing that set of other hypotheses embedded within it—all the background assumptions contributing to the worldview that supports the hypothesis in the first place. Scientific practices are deeply social. Yet, in the conventions of mainstream scientific interpretation and reporting, findings are represented as indepen-dent of the context in which they were generated. The social processes that "uncover" scientific facts are hidden from our view (Latour and Woolgar 1979).

The Practice of Science

The Quine-Duhem thesis in the philosophy of science literature illustrates another flaw with positivist assumptions about objectivity. These assumptions are undermined in the way scientists actually do science. If a test of the re-search hypothesis fails to achieve the expected results, the scientist does not necessarily reject that hypothesis, but rather can and often does tinker with the background assumptions, arriving at a way to make sense of the data while maintaining the original thought or expectation.

For example, early sex-difference researchers believed that men were more intelligent than women and developed a theory that brain size correlated with intelligence, which led them to predict that men would have larger brains.

When subsequent research on brain size revealed that women, on average, had larger brains in relation to their body size than did men, researchers did not reject the background assumption that men were more intelligent than women, or even consider the idea that men's and women's brains were essentially comparable. Rather, they moved on to other aspects of the brain that might show a systematic sex difference in the direction that would support the hypothesis of male superiority (cf. Bleier 1984; Fausto-Sterling 1985).

Thus the vision of a pure empirical test of scientific ideas is not realized in practice. As these examples illustrate, we always rely on background assumptions, and these assumptions are based in values, so science is not value-neutral (Alcoff 1989). In ignoring the cultural embeddedness of the knower, and in concentrating instead on the most accurate procedures for detecting the known, positivism is in a sense hiding the relationship between the knower and the known.

Assuming that science is value-free—and that science should be value-free—has serious consequences, according to Harding (1998). By refusing to consider the relationship between science and broader social phenomena, we preclude discussion about the connection between what we do in science and potential benefits or costs to broader communities. Instead, our discussions about science are radically narrowed into purely technical issues. And, as I argued in chapter 1, the "findings" tend to make the current relations of privilege and disadvantage seem natural.

RADICAL SOCIAL CONSTRUCTIONISM: IS KNOWLEDGE ILLUSION?

Most of the critiques of positivism reflect the position that knowledge is socially constructed (see Jussim 1991). Any order or perceived regularity in phenomena is not "out there" in the empirical world. We give order to our perceptions through the application of a cultural framework (Mehan and Wood 1975; Weedon 1987/1997). Thus the object of knowledge, the truth, is the creation of the very process that "discovers" it (Alcoff 1989; Foucault 1972; Fraser 1989; Haraway 1988).

Many social constructionists have been influenced by the writing of Michel Foucault (1972, 1975/1979, 1976/1978). Foucault uses the term "Power/Knowledge" to convey the idea that in the modern world, the two are inextricably linked: power is enacted through the organization of knowledge, and knowledge is constructed as a form of domination. For Foucault, even our subjectivity is a social construction: our values and our very sense of having a self are aspects of the way modern power/knowledge works (cf. Fraser 1989). Older forms of power, says Foucault (1975/1979), were directly enacted on people's bodies at intermittent times. The lord of the manor could impose his will on serfs by threatening or actually administering physical punishment, and when the lord was away, the serfs could engage in small acts of resistance. Newer forms of power operate through discourses that circulate through our daily lives and the way these discourses prompt us to construct certain forms of self-awareness and to manage our own behavior, that is, to discipline ourselves.

Social science, according to Foucault, has been an important part of the development of power/knowledge. The social sciences and their practices of classifying, labeling, diagnosing, and treating groups and individuals constitute a system of intensive surveillance. Social scientists turn the diversity of humanity into linearly distributed characteristics with measurable means and standard deviations. Each individual can now be classified in terms of where they fall on multiple distributions of traits. Social sciences create official standards of normality, feeding a whole set of discourses that circulate through the culture, from professional manuals to self-tests in popular magazines. Notions of normality prompt all of us to monitor and discipline one another and, perhaps especially, ourselves to try to conform to those standards (see Fraser 1989).

Intelligence is one example. In an earlier time in U.S. culture, intelligence was a multifaceted concept. People were diverse in their combinations of skills and limitations, and some were "slower" than others in cognitive processing speed (Bogdan and Taylor 1976). With the invention of the IQ test, scientists focused on a specific kind of intelligence—speed and facility with abstract reasoning—making it visible and measurable. Implementation of the IQ test gave us a distribution of scores interpretable in terms of their deviations from the mean, and a mechanism for assigning each individual a place in that distribution. Those who diverge significantly from the center of this distribution were assigned into categories for "special" attention—mentally retarded at one end, and gifted at the other (Wolfensburger 1983). A person's categorization is used to determine his or her opportunities and experiences, and, as a consequence, his or her sense of self (Sprague and Hayes 2000). Scientific conceptualization and measurement of intelligence is a key part of a power/knowledge system through which we manage one another and ourselves.

Social constructionism contributes to our understanding of the production of knowledge in at least three ways. First, it keeps the social character of knowledge production in the foreground, providing an analysis of the connection between the organization of knowledge and social domination. Second, it raises important questions for scholars to address, questions about their own embeddedness in a culture and about their own social role in the institutions that produce and distribute official knowledge. Third, social constructionism has developed useful methods for deconstructing ideas, theories, and practices, methods that can reveal the often complex and even contradictory meanings embedded in cultural "facts." However, there are significant divergences among those who would agree with the basic idea that knowledge is socially created, and some significant limitations with the most extreme positions.

Relativism as a Dead End

In the most radical version of constructionist epistemology, every object of knowledge—each phenomenon, every experience—is a text, a bearer of multiple and conflicting meanings (cf. Hawkesworth 1989). "All actual experience is understood as a surface/screen upon which fantasies are projected and displaced, even while experienced in reality" (Clough 1993: 176). It is not that mass-mediated discourses impose ideologies on the reader or writer; they engage and shape "unconscious mechanisms of wish-fulfillment, denial . . . and resistance" (Clough 1993: 178). The very idea that we have a distinct self that can observe and interpret anything is a creation of discourse. Thus we cannot talk about the discourses and people's subjectivities separately—they are inextricably bound up together and are "all but indistinguishable in the subject position of discourse" (Clough 1993: 178). Knowledge, then, is itself a narrative, another text, even an act of faith based on cult membership (Haraway 1988). Each person's interpretation of the text that is experience is an equally valid and equally limited reading—there is no privileged or definitive interpretation (Fraser 1989).

Ironically, this most radical form of social constructionism's construction of the knower, the known, and the process of knowing is in a sense the mirror image of positivism's. While positivism dissolves the subject into the object, radical social constructionism dissolves the object into the subject. If positivism is the epistemology of fact, then this radical version of constructionism is an epistemology of fiction.

The timing and popularity of this radical form of constructivist response to positivist epistemology are worth considering. In an earlier day when the institutions that organize official knowledge production were homogeneously white, male, and upper-class, the dominant epistemology claimed an objective observer, who disinterestedly pursued the discovery of naturally existing laws. Just when increasing numbers of those previously marginalized or even excluded from the ranks of knowledge producers—women, people from the working class, and people who are not white or from the West—begin to enter these institutions and demand a voice in creating knowledge, another epistemology emerges and gains substantial support, one that asserts that no one has a claim to the truth.

It is easy to imagine the effects of such a relativist stance on struggles to overcome personal and collective oppression. As Mary Hawkesworth notes, when things are unequal, "relativist resignation reinforces the status quo" (1989: 557). Intentional action is premised on an analysis of what is and what might be. Social change takes social action, usually coalitions among diverse groups who recognize mutual interests and shared goals. When analyses of experiences are considered mere texts or individual readings, the potential for supporting meaningful social change is eroded (Fraser and Nicholson 1988; Mascia-Lees, Sharpe, and Cohen 1989). Scholarship separated from action can devolve into a form of intellectual game conducted by a privileged class of knowledge producers with no relevance to most everyday actors. Haraway's term for the impact is "epistemological electro-shock therapy" (1988: 578).

But the choice between a blind trust in the facts and a radical rejection of them is a false choice, one that would be rejected by many of those who believe in science and/or social constructionism. There are two approaches to epistemology that take as a given that knowledge is socially constructed, without losing the possibility of developing knowledge at all: critical realism and standpoint theory.

CRITICAL REALISM

Critical realist epistemology holds that the world exists independently of our thinking about it, there are patterns to the way it works, and our perceptions of it are varied (Bhaskar and Norris 1999; Collier 1994; Cook and Campbell 1979). The world is complex: an effect may be the consequence of multiple causes, some causal links are two-way, and both natural and social systems are open and changing (Cook and Campbell 1979). This means that "science . . . [is] a process in motion attempting to capture ever deeper and more basic strata of a reality at any moment of time unknown to us and perhaps not even empirically manifest" (Bhaskar and Norris 1999). Thus causal laws are imperfect; they leave things out and have to be understood as probabilistic (Cook and Campbell 1979). Even if we will never be able to develop a perfect knowledge of the world, through science and the application of human rationality we can approximate the regularities in phenomena (Bhaskar and Norris 1999).

Sylvia Walby (2001), a feminist proponent of this approach, suggests that we see science as a loosely integrated collection of networks of scholars who often disagree, thus pushing the process of knowledge-building forward through a continual quest for further information and better understandings. Scientific understandings change over time, and, in the process, knowledge is improved, Walby asserts. Sometimes change happens in dramatic ways, with a complete shift of paradigms, as when Einstein's theory of relativity overthrew Newtonian physics. But much more often, change in knowledge is gradual, the result of continued rational and empirical effort—gathering more evidence, reexamining what evidence exists, and reconsidering interpretations in dialogue with other researchers. In Walby's words, "Science is not a mirror of nature, but neither is it a mirror of culture" (2001: 485).

Thus, Hawkesworth says, we should adopt "a minimalist standard of rationality that requires that belief be apportioned to evidence and that no assertion be immune from critical assessment" (1989: 556). On these grounds, she maintains, we will be able to claim superior knowledge "from the strength of rational argument, from the ability to demonstrate point by point the deficiencies of alternative explanations" (Hawkesworth 1989: 557).

For critical realists, the knower is socially constructed, shaped by the discourses of culture and science. The known is complex and changing, including in response to social action. Thus the relationship between the knower and the known is mediated by discourse but amenable to adjustment and increasing refinement, though the known will never be more than an increasingly accurate approximation of reality.

Critical realist epistemology is appealing. It steps back from positivism's most problematic assumptions by recognizing that the data do not speak for themselves, that some person is using an interpretive framework to organize them. And, unlike more radical forms of constructionism, critical realism retains an epistemological grounding for doing science, for working to maximize the adequacy of our understandings, and thus a basis for taking informed action. For critical realists, the relationship between the knower and the known is culturally organized, but every knower has the same potential access to the known, or at least there is nothing systematically organizing the relationship of groups of knowers to the known. This last point is the main source of disagreement between critical realists and the other important application of social constructionism to epistemology, standpoint theory.

STANDPOINT THEORY

Standpoint epistemology argues that all knowledge is constructed in a specific matrix of physical location, history, culture, and interests, and that these matrices change in configuration from one location to another (Harding 1998). A standpoint is not the spontaneous thinking of a person or a category of people. Rather, it is the combination of resources available within a specific context from which an understanding might be constructed. Standpoint theorists reject positivism's pretense of creating a view from nowhere in favor of the postulate that subjects are specific, located in a particular time and place. This locatedness gives access to the concrete world. Thus a knower has a particular vantage point with regard to the object. Knowing is not relative, as radical constructivists maintain; it is partial, local, and historically specific (Haraway 1988; Harding 1998; Hartsock 1983).

In most versions of standpoint theory, there are certain social positions from which it is possible to develop better understandings. Marxist epistemology generally privileges the standpoint of an undifferentiated working class (Bar On 1993; Lukacs 1971). In feminist standpoint theory, epistemic privilege is often accorded to the standpoint of women, who are themselves diverse in location in systems organizing race, class, nation, and other major relations of social domination. I will outline the arguments of four standpoint theorists who have had a major impact on feminist social science: Nancy Hartsock (1983, 1985), Donna Haraway (1978, 1988, 1990, 1993), Dorothy Smith (1979, 1987, 1990), and Patricia Hill Collins (1986, 1989, 2000). Not all of these scholars agree on every point, but they do give a good sense of the general logic of the argument and several ways it can be applied to reveal systematic biases built into the way mainstream knowledge is constructed.

Nancy Hartsock: Standpoints on Power

Nancy Hartsock (1983, 1985), a political scientist who pioneered the notion of standpoint, carefully distinguished a standpoint from the spontaneous thinking of social actors. A standpoint, she says, is "achieved rather than obvious, a mediated rather than immediate understanding" (1985: 132). To illustrate the contrasts in the kinds of knowledge that are accessible from distinct standpoints, Hartsock uses the example of varying ways political scientists have developed a conceptualization of power.

Beginning with the experience and interests of capitalists, those who own the means of production, leads scholars to focus on exchanges in the market because capitalists are removed from the concrete circumstances of producing goods and services, including their relationship with workers. Taking the standpoint of capitalists, Hartsock says, provides resources for understanding power as a thing, a commodity that a person has more or less of, something that can be exchanged, taken, or given away. The predominant notion of power in political science, and in our culture more broadly, Hartsock says, is developed by taking the capitalist standpoint.

On the other hand, scholars who begin from the practical experience of workers are more likely to foreground the capitalist/worker relationship. Workers must sell their labor to capitalists, do their work in coordination with the labor of other workers, and earn wages that are lower than the market value of the goods that they produce. The workers' standpoint offers resources for understanding power as a relationship of domination, in which one party, by virtue of its control over wealth, is able to take advantage of and extract compliance from, that is, has "power over," the other. Marxists, for example, have built their analysis of power from the standpoint of workers.

But, Hartsock argues, there is a third construction of power, one that becomes available by taking the standpoint of women. The sexual division of labor in our culture makes women responsible for domestic labor in the home, doing the work of transforming commodities into food, clothing, and other things that meet people's needs. Beginning from the position of those who do the work of nurturing makes it possible to develop a notion of power as capacity or potential, as in the word *empower*. Hartsock argues that the standpoint of women offers unique resources for developing the notion of power as "power to."

Donna Haraway: Vision Is Embodied

Donna Haraway (1978, 1988, 1990, 1993), an anthropologist, criticizes positivism for violating one of its own assumptions. Positivism is based, Haraway notes, on the primacy of data, that is, information that is detectable directly through the senses. Positivist epistemology is, then, logically grounded in the materiality of people's bodies. Yet positivism denies the presence of these bodies in making its claims to validity. For example, the bodies of those dominating the production of knowledge have for the most part been in specific social locations in systems of race (white), class (privileged), gender (male), and nation (Western), and yet there is no consideration of how their observations might have been shaped by their social position. Haraway agrees with positivist and critical realist arguments that it is through our sensory experience, our bodies, that we have access to the world; however, she maintains that this empirical grounding is both the basis of valid knowledge and a limit on it. She uses the term "embodied vision" to emphasize that our vision is located in some specific social and physical place, that our knowledge is "situated," and thus partial.

How can we compensate for the partiality of any perspective? Haraway says that the best way to gain a critical perspective on one's situated view is to get a sense of how things look from a different position. Access to contrasting perspectives on a phenomenon reveals the limits and constructedness of each view. Because each of us experiences life and our selves in multiple facets that are "stitched together imperfectly" (586), we can partially identify with another, empathy is possible, and through it, two knowers can make a partial connection. By translating across distinct perspectives and connecting ever-shifting situated knowledges, it is at least theoretically possible to rationally build some collective, if provisional, agreement on the whole. Of course, differences in social power can obstruct such collaboration, as I discuss in chapter 3.

Dorothy Smith: Sociology versus Everyday Life

Dorothy Smith (1979, 1987, 1990), a sociologist, analyzes the standpoint of sociology and of knowledge institutions more broadly. Like Foucault, Smith argues that social science has been part of the practices by which we are all organized and managed. She agrees that knowledge is socially constructed, but in contrast with radical constructionism Smith argues that society has material, knowable reality. What is real is people acting in concert, taking one another's practices into account, within webs of social power and domination that Smith calls "relations of ruling." The sexual division of labor in our society has created a bifurcation of human experience: those who develop knowledge about society are separated from the actual practices that sustain everyday (and everynight) life. The result, Smith says, is a sociology (and by extension, a social science) that is alienated from social life.

The men who dominate the conceptual realm in knowledge institutions are free, if they choose, to almost ignore their bodily existence in every sphere of their lives. This has been possible only because women have been taking care of the practical activities for them: providing for their human needs and for those of their children outside the workplace, and doing the material work of implementing their abstract conceptualizations—clerical work, interviewing, taking care of patients, and so on—in the workplace. The better these women are at their work, the more invisible that work is to the men who benefit from it, allowing them to take women's work for granted and to have their own authority and contribution bolstered in the process.

While Smith draws a sharp male/female division here, in actuality race and class interact with gender in sorting people on both sides of this divide. Racially and economically privileged men are most likely to be in positions of power in the realm of the conceptual, but some privileged women, particularly those who are not directly engaged in the practices of sustaining life, gain significant power. On the other hand, women with children, and/or women who are not from racially and economically privileged backgrounds, are the most likely to do the most hands-on practical activities, though some men are also engaged in these activities.

Mainstream scientific research only superficially overcomes the split between official knowledge and practical existence, because scholars work from the standpoint of the managers, the powerful. Researchers reach out through their conceptual frameworks to pluck bits of the empirical world, and retreat to their offices to organize the data to fit their abstract frameworks. Then they cycle this ordering through what Smith describes as a "textually-mediated virtual reality," creating a new order. They reassemble the facts into a construction of their view of "what actually happened," and use that reconstructed version as a lens through which to reexamine lived experience. Sociological practices like these "convert what people experience directly in their everyday/everynight world into forms of knowledge in which people as subjects disappear and in which their perspectives on their own experience are transposed and subdued by the magisterial forms of objectifying discourse" (1990: 4).

Smith argues that sociologists need to make everyday/everynight life our problematic, the place from which we start, the puzzle for us to solve. We need to unpack the "facts" and the conventional abstractions describing them and see what lies behind them, because the concerted activity of specific people in concrete circumstances sustains these "facts" on a daily basis.

Women sociologists, especially those with caretaking responsibilities for children or relatives, tend to cross and recross the boundary between the conceptual and the practical realms. They experience on a daily basis both the sociological virtual reality and the concrete work of meeting human needs, coordinating with child care and schools, finding medical resources, and so on. The standpoint of women within sociology provides an opportunity to drive a wedge through the breach between the means by which we develop our understandings of social life and the concrete work of keeping social life going. It gives us the opportunity to discover ways that sociology constructs a knowledge that mystifies lived experience, thereby playing a role in the relations of ruling.

Patricia Hill Collins: Black Feminist Epistemology

Patricia Hill Collins (1986, 1989, 2000) argues that anyone who reflects on his or her practical experience is an intellectual, a creator of knowledge. She analyzes how the social construction of Black women's standpoint offers a distinctive basis for developing knowledge. First of all, Black women have the experience of oppression and an interest in struggling against it. Second, their work has brought them into contact with dominant groups, but in a marginalized way, for example, as domestics in the households of the affluent and, more recently, as outsiders within the academy.

This marginalization is an epistemic advantage because it distances Black women from hegemonic thought and practices, facilitating the development of a critical attitude. Further, segregation brought Black women together (although these days, class divergences are breaking that up a bit), giving them safe spaces in which to construct their own analysis of their experiences. Black women have also historically had access to alternative discourses to use to interpret their situations, including West African traditions, and even though they were blocked from participating in formal knowledge production, they found other channels to communicate with one another, including blues music. Thus, while Black women have been subjected to and have internalized the derogating images of them in the dominant culture, they have also found collective ways to resist.

Black women's knowledge has been systematically invalidated, because the validation of knowledge, Collins argues, is a political process involving epistemological gatekeeping, influenced by the standpoint of the existing community of experts applying their standards of credibility, and also by the way the larger culture defines certain groups as more credible than others (2000: 203–4). She uses positivism to illustrate epistemological gatekeeping (2000: 205). The goal of positivist criteria is to decontextualize the observer to produce objective observations via certain rules of method. These include distancing the researcher/subject from the "object" of study, suppressing emotions, defining considerations of values and ethics as outside the process, and preferring the use of adversarial debates in order to choose among contending claims to the truth. Each of these rules, Collins observes, gives the advantage to those with social privilege.

The standpoint of Black women presents alternative criteria for validating knowledge claims, criteria that contrast starkly with those that dominate the academy. First, Collins says, the hegemonic view constructs a dichotomy between science and common people's understandings, with the latter clearly discredited. In Black Feminist epistemology, on the other hand, concrete experience and the wisdom developed through it are valued as resources in evaluating knowledge claims. People's use of stories from their lives or of passages from the Bible to communicate some insight is a cue to the wisdom developed through practical everyday experience.

Second, the organization of official knowledge is hierarchically controlled by an elite and distributed to the populace. In Black Feminist epistemology, in contrast, knowledge claims are not hierarchically imposed by an elite, but rather are worked out through dialogue with everyday social actors. The validation of truth claims by the common people is crucial. Knowledge, in this perspective, is not the vision of individuals. It is rather a form of communication and connection, a search for harmony in a community.

Third, the official approach to knowledge constructs rationality as the opposite of emotionality. Black Feminist epistemology, on the other hand, incorporates emotions such as empathy and attachment into the notion of intellect, holding that feeling and caring can usefully guide knowers in asking and answering questions. Further, because each individual is unique, emotional identification with and empathy for the other is an important vehicle for understanding another's position.

Finally, in hegemonic knowledge, claims to truth stand on their own, to be judged independently of their human source. On the other hand, Collins says, in Black Feminist epistemology the character and biography of the person advancing an idea are legitimately used to interpret and evaluate the truthfulness of the idea. "Every idea has an owner and . . . the owner's identity matters" (Collins 2000: 218). For example, Collins tells of how students in a class discussion of the work of a Black scholar wanted to know about his life before deciding how to evaluate his claims regarding Black feminism. A biography that reveals a knower who is not living according to an ethic of caring undermines that knower's credibility.

Collins asserts that because all knowledge is situated, and thus partial, all knowledge claims should be open to critique, and this critique should integrate multiple perspectives. She quotes Alice Walker: "Each writer writes the missing parts to the other writer's story. And the whole story is what I'm after" (2000: 38–39). Collins's model for reaching the truth is based on dialogue and consensus building. We need to pivot the center from one standpoint to another, she says. In the process, people who don't own their own position when making knowledge claims are less credible. "Everyone must listen and respond to other voices in order to be allowed to remain in the community" (2000: 236–37). Those ideas that are validated by multiple standpoints "become the most 'objective' truths" (2000: 236).

In sum, standpoint epistemology integrates assumptions about the socially constructed character of subjects and also of the things we seek to understand with the materiality of the world and people's practical activity in it. Knowers are specifically located in physical spaces, in systems of social relations, within circulating discourses. Knowing, the relationship between the knower and the object of knowledge, is, as Jennifer Ring (1987) says, dialectical.

THE CHOICE: CRITICAL REALISM OR STANDPOINT THEORY?

Both critical realists and standpoint theorists see the relationship between the knower and the known as socially mediated. They disagree over whether there is anything systematic in the biases created in the way that relationship is organized, depending on the social location of the knower. Do we think of the knower as a universal human subject, as multiple individual subjects, or as categories of subjects? Do some knowers relate to the known in qualitatively different ways than do others?

We do not have to resolve the choice between standpoint theory and critical realism in the abstract—there are data for us to consider. In chapter 1, I outlined some of the systematic biases in the construction of mainstream sociology. This corpus is predominantly the work of a fairly homogeneous group: official knowledge producers in the tradition of Western thought have been overwhelmingly racially and economically privileged men who are not engaged in the gendered (in race- and class-specific ways) work of nurturing life (Sprague 1996). We can compare what feminists have identified as distinctive in the worldview associated with this privileged social location to see if there are parallels with the patterns in the knowledge they produce.

Psychoanalysis and (Privileged) Male Consciousness

There are a variety of accounts of the ways that the experience of privileged men in the social organization of white-supremacist, capitalist, patriarchal society has prompted the development of a distinct form of consciousness. The analyses of Nancy Chodorow (1978, 1991) and Mary O'Brien (1981, 1989) operate within distinctly different theoretical traditions and methodological approaches—psychoanalysis and historical materialism. Yet they display a remarkably strong consensus about the object of analysis: the parameters of hegemonic masculine consciousness.

Psychoanalysis analyzes how our selves are formed in the process of trying to meet basic human needs, for example, the need to connect emotionally and physically with other people and the need to exercise some control over our lives, within the context of social constraints. The most pivotal relationships in the formation of the self are our earliest relationships. Chodorow (1978, 1991) observes that in contemporary Western society, these relationships are organized by gender in two crucial ways: men are relatively uninvolved in nurturing, and we learn to use a person's gender as a key indicator of how to treat one another. Thus the nature of these early relationships and their psychic consequences are qualitatively different for boys and for girls. Boys are likely to develop their selves in an "opposite-sex" relationship, while girls do so in a relationship defined as "same-sex." Distinctions in boys' and girls' early experiences lead to the development of gender differences in the sense of self and relationship to others: men develop a highly individuated sense of self in opposition to others and an abstract orientation to the world; for them, connection threatens the loss of identity. Women develop a connected sense of self embedded in concrete relationships; they see themselves in relationship to others.

Chodorow's analysis, like many in feminist theory, gives little attention to the dynamics of class. Her clinical data are heavily biased toward the affluent and highly educated clientele of psychoanalysis, which no doubt explains her analytic focus on the male breadwinner/female housewife nuclear-family form (see Fraser and Nicholson 1988 and Lorber, Coser, Rossi, and Chodorow 1981 for critiques). Though the limits of her analysis imply that caution should be used in extending it beyond the relatively privileged, those same biases make Chodorow's work particularly useful for identifying the consciousness of the privileged.

Her findings parallel those of researchers who study how class organizes consciousness. Scholars in this tradition also use words like *individualistic* and *abstract* to refer to the worldview of capitalists, in contrast with a more collective and concrete orientation in the working class (e.g., Bulmer 1975; Mann 1973; Mueller 1973; Ollman 1972). Integrating Chodorow's view with Marxist perspectives, we see an argument that the consciousness of economically privileged European American men is more likely to be abstract and individuated than the worldviews of men from less-privileged classes and races and most women.

Historical Materialism and Reproductive Consciousness

Mary O'Brien (1981, 1989) uses a historical materialist approach to argue that differences in consciousness are the product of differences in the ways men and women have historically taken intentional action regarding the material imperative to reproduce. To assert social control over a process in which they are marginalized biologically, men in the European traditions she is describing have historically dominated reproduction from the outside, by creating and controlling the public sphere. Men's flight from involvement in the work of reproduction poses a challenge to the legitimacy of their control over the process, a challenge that is addressed by according the male role as much social significance as possible. This, O'Brien argues, is why the dominant patriarchal worldview of reproduction emphasizes intercourse and male potency and overlooks the value of the work of nurturing.

Having distanced themselves from the concrete community of people who do the work of caring, O'Brien says, men have created an abstract community in the public sphere. Alienated from the concrete history of human continuity across generations, men have constructed and sanctified a history of abstractions and ideas. Maintaining privilege through constructing a public/private dichotomy, they tend to see things in terms of opposition and dichotomy. The cultural and social structure they have reproduced encourages the development of a consciousness that is abstract, oppositional, and discontinuous. O'Brien's analysis shares major themes with class-based studies of consciousness. The structuring of work under capitalism leads those in privileged class locations to be more individualized and to have a more abstract orientation to the world (Hartsock 1985; Lukacs 1971).

In summary, whether looking through the lens of psychoanalysis or historical materialism, feminist scholars identify a privileged masculine consciousness, at least in this narrow social historical window, that is highly abstract, individualistic, organized in terms of oppositions, removed from the concrete world of meeting people's needs, and oriented to control.

Social Science and the Standpoint of Privileged Men

Now recall the kinds of criticisms feminists have raised against mainstream social science research, as reviewed in chapter 1. They argued that sociology in particular and social science in general are detached, both intellectually and emotionally, from the daily work of keeping life going, from the people whose lives we study, and from popular political discourse. The organization of knowledge production, from their perspective, seems more oriented to manage people, particularly people on the downside of social hierarchies, than to nurture them. Conceptual frameworks depend heavily on dichotomy, operate at high levels of abstraction, and tend to be organized in framing devices that talk of dominance and control.

The terms of the feminist critique roughly parallel the description of contemporary Western privileged masculine consciousness. The emphasis on detachment and control is the expression of a specific kind of masculine psychology, one that is threatened by all things culturally defined as feminine, including empathy and emotional connection, and by the loss of individuality through connection with another. The hegemonic masculine response to this threat is to maintain control of relationships—to connect through domination (Hartsock 1985; Keller 1982). This is striking evidence in support of Smith's (1990) claim that if sociology has a subject, it has been a (privileged) male subject.

In the end, the choice between critical realism and standpoint theory has to do with how we understand the knower. Are we looking at knowers as abstract individuals sharing the same culture that shapes their paradigms, as critical realism implies? Or are we seeing knowers as people who are located in specific positions in the social relations, organizing inequalities by race, class, gender, and nation, with all that implies for conflicting material interests, access to interpretive frameworks, and admission to effective participation in the dominant discourses?

Critical realist epistemology accepts the notion that knowledge is not a perfect mirror of reality (Walby 2001), that the culturally informed subjectivity of knowers shapes their construction of knowledge. But, in my view, stopping there is just not being critical—or realistic—enough, at least at this moment in history. Standpoint theory calls us to ask if there is something systematic and social to the nature of the biases in knowledge. Many feminist scholars working in this tradition have shown us over and over again that if we actually consider the data—the kind of knowledge that gets produced and accepted as "good"—we find systematic biases toward the interests, experience, and forms of subjectivity of the privileged. Given the choice between critical realist and standpoint approaches, the more careful choice for now is to adopt a standpoint epistemology.

STANDPOINTS, KNOWING, AND TRUTH

The world, including humanity, is socially constructed, which is not to say that it is not real, but rather that it is the product of human activity. Human activity in the world is real, and so are the structures that humans devise to meet the challenges they face. If socially constructed categories are used to direct human social action, those categories are real because we are making them real: race, gender, class, and nation are real in their consequences (cf. Thomas and Thomas 1928). Nonetheless, if something is socially constructed, then it is not the durable, detached web of lawlike operations that positivism conjures up. It is—and we are—historically specific and changeable. Rational knowledge is open-ended because the world is open-ended.

Our methodology must center on "the dynamic between human experience and the material world" and must assume "constant change, that is, human history" (Ring 1987: 766). Truth, Ring (1987) argues, emerges out of the interplay between intentional, critical subjects and their social action in the world. We will attain truth, she says, when we have finally eliminated the conflicts between subjects and object, expressed as the oppositions of ideas to material reality, of consciousness to history, of thought to action. That is, truth is the outcome of people acting in concert in the world, freely, consciously, and intentionally. Since knowers are specifically situated in distinct locations, truth implies a working consensus on practical activity. Since human activity changes the world, truth is always historically specific and changeable.

Standpoint approaches raise the stakes of the discussion of epistemological choices by pointing to the political character of the project of making assumptions about the knower, the known, and the relationship between them. As Collins puts it, the concerns of epistemology are not "benign academic issues"—they are about "which version of truth will prevail and shape thought and action" (2000: 203). What does that mean for how sociologists should actually go about implementing research methods? Feminists have not yet agreed. The disagreement is based on two contrasting readings of standpoint theory: one that emphasizes the subjectivity of parties to research, and the other, which builds strategically on contrasting social locations. In the next chapter I will argue in favor of the latter, as I explore the implications of standpoint epistemology for responding to the relationship between knowledge and power, for allocating scientific authority, and for indicating how sociologists should go about doing research.

3

Authority and Power

Research is organized and conducted through relationships—relationships between researchers and the researched, relationships among researchers, and relationships between researchers and other members of the society. Like other forms of human relationship, research relationships happen within a milieu of interpersonal and social power, whereby one party to the relationship can exercise its will even in the face of opposition by another. Researchers are often relatively powerful vis-à-vis those they study, both in the research process and in the broader social structure.

Standpoint epistemology increases the salience of questions about how power interacts with authority to influence who is a legitimate creator of knowledge and what kind of knowledge is created. Feminist social science researchers who find standpoint epistemology persuasive have been centrally concerned with how to respond to the distortions created by power imbalances due to gender, race/ethnicity, class, and nation. This attention to power has generated a common stereotype of feminist methodology as entailing researchers transferring their authority as producers of knowledge to specific groups of "others."

In this chapter, I will argue that this stereotypical notion of feminist methodology as handing over authority to research subjects is not well considered and, in fact, results from a misreading of standpoint epistemology as making a subjectivist argument. I will describe the subjectivist reading of standpoint epistemology and two stereotypes of feminist methodology that follow from it: transferring authority completely over to research subjects, and/or privileging "insider" research. I will discuss the conceptual, pragmatic, and political limitations of these strategies, which are substantial. Then I will show how subjectivism is a misreading of the argument of standpoint epistemology and will argue that the primary texts are making a social rather than a subjective argument. From this perspective the epistemic advantage goes not to a specific group, but to a specific strategy: "boundary crossing." I will use Harding's elaboration of the components of a standpoint to analyze the standpoint of social researchers and will derive from that some implications of standpoint epistemology for how we can do research that is more sensitive to the biases associated with power.

POWER AND AUTHORITY, IDEOLOGY AND KNOWLEDGE

Feminists identify three ways in which researchers have power (D. Wolf 1996). First, the researcher has more control than the researched over the process of research and how their relationship is constructed in it. Second, the researcher has power over how the findings are interpreted and represented to others. Finally, researchers often have more social power than those whom they study, because of their relatively privileged positions in social structures of inequality such as those organizing gender, race, class, and nation.

Researchers' control over the process of research and its immediate product has received most of the attention in feminist and other critical discussions about research. Researchers' control is pervasive. Investigators determine the topic of research, that is, what is important and worthy of study and, by inference if not explicitly, what is not. They control how the issue will be addressed—what the salient data are and how information will be collected. For example, they determine what is and what is not a legitimate response to a survey question, or what is and what is not an irrelevant digression in a qualitative interview. Researchers conventionally decide how to analyze and interpret findings; they choose how to combine quantitative measures into a statistical model and which pieces of the transcript of an interview are interesting and interpretable. Finally, researchers choose the venue through which they will publish findings and what the text will look like. Researchers do not typically make these decisions alone; they do it in dialogue with one another through formal and informal peer review. However, in conventional social science practice the subjects of research have very little, if anything, to say about these decisions.

In contemporary Western society, scholarly research has a privileged position in determining the content of what people in the society accept as official knowledge. Research findings are covered by news and information media as the current state of what we as a society know. Scholarly research is the raw material from which textbooks are fashioned. Policy makers legitimate their decisions by citing research. Certainly journalists, talk show hosts, popular and textbook authors, and policy makers apply their own standards in selecting from a broad and somewhat diverse body of research. Yet researchers' decisions about what to study, how to study it, how to make sense of what they find, and what to do with their findings create limits on what is available for others to propagate. Scholarly research puts some constraints on what is thinkable and prompts us to think in certain ways.

It is researchers' social power that makes their control over the process and products of research something to be concerned about. Researchers have authority as legitimate producers of knowledge, an authority that is explicitly based on methodology—on the process by which claims about truth have been generated and presented. However, the authority of scholars also, at least implicitly, resides in their credentials as people with a certain kind of education and expertise who are affiliated with institutions with some level of credibility in the social organization of knowledge production.

Science, including social science, is a loosely organized institution of research institutes, universities, journals, funding agencies, the military, and for-profit research and development organizations that are given the resources and the authority in our society to be official producers of knowledge. These organizations are made up of individuals in definite social relationships to one another, through which resources crucial to knowledge production—the research grants, tenured positions, journals, book contracts—are distributed. Those who are in control of these resources have to apply a system of evaluative standards and judgments of quality; the ones they are likely to use are the standards on which their own prestige and privilege are based. Hidden behind the veil of the "important," "interesting," and "rigorous," then, are systematic selection patterns that reflect the evaluators' stake within the existing network of prestige and power.

That network of prestige and power, in turn, is a consequence of a social life that is organized by class, race, and gender (cf. Tokarczyk and Fay 1993).

Traditionally, the socially privileged, those of the dominant gender, class, race, and/or nation, have controlled the production of knowledge. The career path to becoming a scholar is based on educational attainment, and progress through the pipeline of educational attainment is significantly shaped by class in interaction with gender, race, and nation.

The problem then, given the assumptions of standpoint epistemology, is that the most influential scholars in scientific networks occupy a relatively privileged standpoint. The concern is that researchers' privilege can influence their choices and that as a result, the knowledge they produce will be ideological.

While the term ideology can be used to convey the generic notion of a meaning system, of any relatively organized way of making sense of some phenomenon, critical social scientists from Karl Marx to Dorothy Smith have argued for the importance of drawing a distinction between ideology and knowledge. Ideology, from this perspective, refers to a distinct subset of meaning systems, those that are in some important way deceptive and/or distorting, whether unintentionally or by design.

Drawing on Marx's analysis, Dorothy Smith (1990) argues that in a social context that is organized by unequal power relations, an important criterion for evaluating whether a truth claim is knowledge or ideology is how it deals with power. Frameworks for making sense of the world can either expose relations of unequal power, or they can obscure them. To the extent that truth claims obscure power relationships, they are ideological.

For example, Marx (1867/1976) analyzed the representation of commodities in the market independently of the social relations producing and distributing them, that is, capitalist domination and worker exploitation. In hiding this social relation of dominance, the fetishism of commodities obscures how power determines what gets produced by whom at what cost and with what benefit; thus, it is ideological. Or take the common statement that ours is a technologically driven society. Saying that technology is propelling us into a future outside human control is staying at the level of ideology; examining how specific powerful elites may be promoting specific technologies to maximize their social advantage and control is creating knowledge.

Knowledge constructed from a privileged place in social relations of inequality is more likely to resonate with the interests and worldview of the privileged than with those of the oppressed. Chapter 1 provided some evidence: traditionally, sociology specifically and social science more broadly have tended, however unintentionally, to ask the questions of the privileged, and to use analytic categories and forms of discourse that support continued privilege. Researchers' power as people in privileged positions in social relations organizing gender, race, class, and/or nation interacts with their power as people with legitimate influence over what the society takes to be knowledge.

How should critical researchers respond to their privilege and power? This question has pervaded the literature on feminist research methodology. Most of the methodological strategies feminists have developed attempt to diminish the power imbalances in aspects of the relationship between the researcher and the researched, working toward getting the subjects of research more involved in shaping that research. In addition, feminist investigators have worked on being reflexive about the impact of their own biographies and biases on their research, and have experimented with reporting styles that make the researcher's perspective obvious or cede more of the text to the voices of research subjects. I will describe some of these strategies in the next three chapters.

But choosing from among these strategies those that best respond to standpoint epistemology depends on whether one interprets standpoint epistemology as a subjectivist or a sociological argument. First I will describe a subjectivist reading of standpoint epistemology, some principles derived from it, and problems with implementing these. Then I will point to the conceptual heart of the problem: the subjectivist reading is in error. Later I will turn to a sociological reading of standpoint epistemology.

THE SUBJECTIVIST INTERPRETATION OF STANDPOINT EPISTEMOLOGY

Many feminists and other critical scholars tend to equate a standpoint with what individuals think and/or say; the focus is on subjectivity, on the worldview of a group or even of a particular group member. Some researchers who take this view argue that there is no basis for choosing among competing claims about the why and how of social phenomena. Others privilege the accounts offered by members of oppressed groups, reasoning that the powerful are deluded by their own ideologies, while the powerless have no interest in supporting ideologies that justify their oppression. Sylvia Walby sees this approach to standpoint theory as "premised on the presumption of a chasm between the knowledge of the oppressed and the oppressor in which the oppressed develop their own practices in order to develop better knowledge" (2001: 486).

These assumptions are pervasive, though certainly not universal, in the talk and writing about methodology among feminist researchers, and they have generated some common stereotypes about feminist methodology. One is that feminist methodology means transferring control over knowledge to research subjects. Another is that researchers who are "insiders," that is, members of marginalized groups, will produce better knowledge about those groups. Taking a critical look at each, I argue, reveals that such simple transfers of authority are inadequate responses to the problems associated with researcher power.

Problems with Simply Transferring Power to Research Subjects

One methodological strategy advocated by those who use a subjectivist reading of standpoint epistemology is that researchers should give all control over knowledge creation to those being studied. The researcher should serve as the mere conduit, the holder of the microphone, to "give voice" to research subjects (cf. Hertz 1997; McCall and Wittner 1989). This position has at least four shortcomings: (1) it fails to take into account how and where research subjects already have some power; (2) it ignores situations in which the researched have even more power than the researcher; (3) it is insensitive to the selection biases built into implementing this strategy; and (4) it can privilege hegemonic discourses over critical ones.

Subjects Already Have Some Power

Even in conventional methodologies, subjects of research retain some control over the research process. The investigator controls the questions and the analysis, but those being studied control what they will disclose (cf. Holland and Ramazanoglu 1994). Qualitative interviewees can and do at times refuse to be led by questions, continue to talk about what they want in spite of efforts to change the subject, and even correct the interviewers' verbalization of their meaning (Ribbens 1989). Respondents filling out a closed-ended questionnaire item are limited by the specific response alternatives, but they do get to choose from these options how they will be counted, and thus in some ways have more control over how their responses will be coded than do those who are answering open-ended questions (Risman 1993). The more the researched is invested in the research topic and thus motivated to participate in a study, the more relative power the researcher has. Thus, study participants who have been selected through a random sampling process are likely to have more power than those who have volunteered to participate (Ribbens 1989).

The balance of power between the researcher and the researched shifts over the course of the research (Phoenix 1994). The subjects of research have the most power at the initial contact—they can choose to participate or not and negotiate the terms of their participation. Investigators have the most control over the final write-up. Even then, though, researcher power is not total. When people with some social power object to the analyses developed about them and their lives, they have the ability to assert their authority and control over and against that of the scholar. Some experienced researchers have learned the power of those they study to create problems for them if they do not like the published account (Warren 1980). In one well-known example, the publication of Arthur Vidich and Joseph Bensman's classic study of a college town generated enough anger among townspeople to motivate the college's administration to reprimand one of the researchers (cf. Vidich and Bensman 1964).

Some Researchers Study the Powerful

Discussions among feminist researchers about transferring power to research subjects tend to assume that researchers are "studying down," that is, that they have more social power than those they study, probably because feminists tend to study the relatively powerless (Luff 1999). However, researchers vary in gender, race, class background, and national origin, and thus in their degree of social power. Some researchers study those who have as much or more social power than they do, and who enact that power interpersonally. Researchers studying the economically and politically powerful, women studying men, people of color studying whites, and younger people studying elders all can be in situations in which their ability to control the interaction is limited, particularly when it is face-to-face.

For example, Jennifer Pierce (1995) describes doing participant observation working as a paralegal in a law firm. As a woman working for mostly male attorneys, she had to deal with the usual forms of gender subordination in that employment relationship, such as expectations that she act deferentially, take care of the attorneys, and endure acts of sexual harassment. Similarly, Lorna McKee and Margaret O'Brien (1983) independently learned the dynamics of social status and situational power in separate interview studies, one on new fathers and the other on lone fathers. Although the researchers took pains to construct the situation as professional, they still had to deal with sexual innuendo and flirting on the part of some of their interviewees in both studies. Some men felt free to speak in sexist ways and even express hostility toward women. Lone fathers, who were older as well as male, had a tendency to dominate the interviews.

Other researchers have found that male friends or relatives of a woman interviewee can feel entitled to control the interaction, leaving the woman interviewer powerless to do anything about it (Phoenix 1994; Thapar-Björkert 1999). Even interactions that solely involve women are not always dominated by the researcher. Sondra Hale (1991) describes struggling to interview Fatma Ahmed Ibrahim, a woman who had for years been a leader in Sudanese leftist politics and with the Woman's Union there. Hale reports that Ibrahim needed no support in telling her story. Rather, Ibrahim's social position as a leader led her to expect to dominate the interview and pursue her strategic interests in establishing a certain public image for herself and her organization. She did not respond to questions she did not care about, and was highly selective, even deceptive, in her representations of the facts (Hale 1991).

Researchers Still Point the Microphone

The simple transfer of authority to research subjects is simply not possible empirically. Research subjects are not monolithic; they vary in experience, information, and sense-making strategies. There is a wide diversity of thinking among people in any social category—in any race, class, or gender or, for that matter, in any particular combination of these positions. Scholars who want to privilege the subjectivity of a particular group inevitably must choose the members to whom they will listen, that is, identify which members of a category are the "best" spokespersons for that category. Thus researchers retain the power to decide who has authority, and the bases on which they choose are sources of perhaps unexamined selection bias.

It is an empirical question, of course, but it may very well be that the less privilege a group has, the more diverse its members will be in how they make sense of their experience. After all, the wealthiest white men have the financial and institutional resources to allow them to identify their material interests and to develop an analysis that supports their social position if they choose. Further, the centralization of corporate control over the mass media means that analysis is likely to dominate in mainstream cultural discourses. For example, everyday social actors in the United States are much more likely to encounter discourses that describe capitalism as the only feasible economic system or assert that race or gender are biologically determined and inevitable than discourses that are critical of these positions. If it were true that the diversity of worldviews increases as privilege decreases, then the risk and degree of selection bias would be greatest when "giving voice" to the most marginalized.

Can We Privilege Hegemonic Discourses?

Differences in the discourses available to researchers and those they study shape their differential assessment of what is important and interesting. This can be a valuable counter to the limitations of scholarly discourse, but simply transferring authority to research subjects can also be a way to foreground hegemonic discourses to which they are subject. Miriam Glucksmann (1994) describes an experience that illustrates the problem. In her reading of the research literature, she discovered that while much had been made of women's labor force participation during World War II, little was known about women's economic participation earlier in the century. Thus she set out to do research on the work experiences of British women in the 1920s and 1930s. She conducted qualitative interviews, aiming to give her interviewees the ability to voice their own history. However, when she tried to get her interviewees to describe their work experiences prior to and around World War II, she found that these women were not interested in talking about it. What was really interesting and important to them was their experience of the war itself.

Suruchi Thapar-Björkert (1999) reports a similar experience. She interviewed women who had been active alongside men in India's struggle for independence in the early twentieth century. Even though they were deeply engaged in political activism, they were still expected to keep up with their domestic responsibilities at home. These women were proud that they were able to meet their double burden; they accepted uncritically their society's traditional gender beliefs and practices. In Thapar-Björkert's project, as in Glucksmann's research, subjects' organizing frames mapped those of the dominant discourses in their cultures: downplaying women's economic activity and emphasizing the war effort, not questioning their oppression at home, while fighting against it in the public arena.

A strategy of simply transferring authority to research subjects is taking a very limited view of research and romanticizes the oppressed. It inadequately considers how power works in more conventional research relationships, and it fails to take into account situations in which researchers are studying those with more social power than they. Even when studying less powerful people, the simple transfer of authority can result in selection biases and in privileging hegemonic discourses while marginalizing critical ones. Such a practice is likely to obscure power relations between the researcher and the researched, and may hide the workings of social power in popular discourses as well.

As Glucksmann (1994) puts it, those who want to simply transfer authority to subjects of research have tended to confuse the empowerment of those we study in the process of doing research with real social empowerment. We would never make this error, she says, if we were thinking of men interviewing women (Glucksmann 1994). And if we were thinking of women interviewing men, of Blacks interviewing Whites, or of poor people interviewing the wealthy, we would be less likely to jump to the conclusion that giving the researched the power to control the process and product of research would necessarily produce more valid knowledge (Bhavnani 1988; Patai 1991).

Problems with Privileging Insider Research

Another strategy that seems to presume a subjectivist reading of standpoint epistemology is to grant authority based on the social identity of the researcher, for example, their gender, race, or national origin. Some say that researchers should not study people over whom they have social privilege: only women can study women, only Blacks can study Blacks, and so on. Others would merely assign epistemic privilege to insider researchers, that is, assume that researchers who are members of the social category they are studying will develop more valid knowledge than will outsider researchers.

This argument has been made most powerfully by scholars from countries that are former colonies, and who have analyzed the role of social science researchers in creating knowledge about them. They find that often Western scholars have generated knowledge that, however unintentionally, legitimates Western domination over other countries. Ong, for example, says that when Westerners study groups that have not been formally recognized as "cultural producers in their own right," it is an act of betrayal (1995: 354). Outsider researchers are denying people "their political interests as narrators of their own lives" (Ong 1995: 354) when they should instead be acting as conduits for getting these excluded perspectives into mainstream spheres of discourse in which the analyses of the marginalized will constitute a challenge to hegemonic ideology.

Postcolonial critiques led to a large-scale withdrawal from their former fields of study abroad by U.S. anthropologists, feeding the current trend toward doing ethnography "at home," that is, in the United States (Behar 1995). However, staying "home" to do research does not avoid the sticky situation. Disadvantaged groups in the United States and in other Western nations also have a history of being systematically excluded from being legitimate analysts of their own situation (Aptheker 1989; Collins 1986; hooks 1981).

Insiders Have Disadvantages as Well as Advantages

Members of marginalized groups who have become researchers can point to some important advantages they have in conducting social research on those groups (see Wolf 1996 for an extensive review). Maxine Baca Zinn (1979) suggests that there are several ways in which insider researchers may gather more complete data than outsiders would. For one, potential study participants might see members of their own gender or race as more trustworthy. The history of research on marginalized groups includes some horror stories, such as the ones I described in chapter 1, which can make members of those groups suspicious of research in general (cf. Oakley 2000: Chapter 11). With some striking exceptions, the history of privileged researchers studying marginalized groups has contributed more to their own careers than to making visible improvements in the day-to-day lives of the people they study (Beoku-Betts 1994; Edwards 1990). Insider researchers are more likely to generate trust that the research will not harm and might somehow benefit their common community (Baca Zinn 1979).

Another advantage of insiders, Baca Zinn (1979) argues, is that they are likely to get more valid data. Marginalized groups have to deal with negative stereotypes pervasive in the dominant culture, and they are likely to avoid revealing to an outsider information that might be taken as confirming these stereotypes. Insider researchers, however, are more likely to put group members at ease about such revelations (Baca Zinn 1979; Beoku-Betts 1994). Also, to the degree that they are participants in a shared culture themselves, insiders can more easily see through any "performances" group members may put on for researchers' benefit (Baca Zinn 1979).

There are also times when an outsider researcher can be unintentionally dangerous. For example, a woman who is being battered by a male intimate is likely to be uncomfortable around another man, and such contact could even precipitate further abuse (Reinharz and Chase 2002). Similarly, a member of an ethnically identified political organization may suffer retribution if colleagues learn that he or she has been consorting with a researcher they associate with the ethnic opposition (M. Wolf 1996).

On the other hand, insiders to any group, marginalized or not, face specific obstacles precisely because of their connections to the group they are studying. Insiders may be held more accountable to community norms for personal behavior restricting where they can go, with whom they can be, and under what circumstances (Zavella 1996). For example, Thorne (2001) describes the social pressure she faced in doing ethnography in an elementary school classroom. The teacher expected her, as another adult, to help maintain order among the students, but as a researcher she felt she would get better data from observing their disorder. Similarly, Josephine Beoku-Betts (1994), doing fieldwork among the Gullah, who live on an island off South Carolina, had to observe the same norms limiting contact with men as did other unmarried women in the community. Insider researchers also report that they are expected to produce analyses that are not critical of their communities, being held to a higher standard of loyalty to the group because they share membership in it (Zavella 1996).

Insider Is a Misleading Category

But more importantly, the very distinction between insider and outsider may distract researchers from noting significant power dynamics in their relationships with research subjects. The experience of members of historically marginalized groups who enter the academy, become scholarly researchers, and then go back to study their group reveals any simple dichotomizing of insider and outsider to be misleading. Ann Phoenix (1994), a researcher who is a Black woman, found that her privileged class and institutional affiliation generated distrust among the poor Black women she interviewed, and that these aspects of her identity were sometimes more salient than the fact that they shared the same race (cf. Thapar-Björkert 1999). Beoku-Betts (1994) describes how shared "race was not enough" to create openness and trust on the part of the Gullah women she was studying. Her gender, educational level, and status as a single woman created obstacles. She could draw on her experiences growing up in rural Africa to negotiate across the class barrier in specific interactions but, being a single woman, she could not do much to transcend the social barrier constructed between her and the men of the community.

Baca Zinn (1979) tells about participating in a community education program in order to gain access to Latino/a families she could interview about family dynamics. Even though as a Chicana she shared the same ethnicity with program clients, she found it was more difficult to develop relationships with the parents in the program than with program staff, many of whom were, like she, working toward an advanced degree. That class was constructing a barrier between the researcher and the program participants becomes clear in considering what Baca Zinn says finally broke the ice. The parents discovered that she did not know how to sew, a vital skill for Mexican women, and they could begin teaching her. Once the imbalance in knowledge and cultural authority was adjusted, Baca Zinn reports, conversations became more relaxed and open.

Being in the same racial/ethnic group is no guarantee of achieving an insider understanding on the part of even the most sympathetic researcher, as Patricia Zavella (1996) describes from her own experience. As an academic and an activist in the Chicana/o political movement, Zavella had developed a strong identity as a Chicana. She describes how her assumption of a shared identity interfered with her research when she went into the field to interview women of Mexican descent living in New Mexico. Finding that her informants had no clear and consistent ethnic identity, Zavella interpreted this lack as a kind of false consciousness. She believed that her interviewees were engaging in avoidance behavior—trying to avoid being identified with a devalued group and to instead blend into the hegemonic group. She reports that it took her a long time to see that she was wrong and they were right. Their ethnic situations were much more complex than hers, teaching her that ethnic identity is more contextual than she had assumed.

Simplistic notions of insider advantage are inconsistent with widely accepted claims of feminist theorists who argue that multiple relations of domination interact in shaping life chances and consciousness (Collins 1991/2000; Glenn 1999; hooks 1981). That is, how gender works depends on an individual's class and race/ethnicity; how race/ethnicity works varies across different combinations of class and gender, and so on. Thus, sharing some aspect of identity, say, gender or race, with the researched does not assure "common experiences or interests" (Zavella 1996: 141). Certain commonalities in life experience can enhance empathy. For example, women who confront similar normative expectations, struggle with discrimination based on their sex, and deal with similar interpersonal issues in their relations with men and children can identify with the struggles of other women, even across divisions of race, class, or nation. However, when the investigator differs from the investigated in other significant dimensions of social inequality, researchers' assumptions of shared identity can be an exercise in self-deception. Rosalie Wax's (1979) findings in an early review on the impact of various statuses on fieldwork probably still hold more generally: each investigator embodies attributes that constitute a set of advantages and obstacles.

Epistemological and Political Costs

Restricting research to insiders would also be problematic epistemologically. While some cultural nuances may be better observed by an insider, some may be more accessible to a person who did not grow up within the discourses dominating that culture (Wolf 1992: 5–6). What the insider shares with group members—cultural assumptions, shared social practices and history—can easily slip into the taken-for-granted. Yet taking things for granted is the bane of good social research. David Morgan said it well: "The obvious deserves at least as much attention from the sociologist as the extraordinary. It is also more difficult to recognize" (1981: 88).

Beyond the question of exactly who is and who is not an insider in any particular situation, an idealization of insider-only research has troubling political implications. Much of the history of social science is a classic case of insider-only research, of men who feel that they should study only men; they have not as a rule taken as their project "deconstructing the patriarchy" (Mascia-Lees et al. 1989). If privileged researchers avoid studying disadvantaged groups, that omission serves to sustain their own hegemony (Edwards 1990). If Whites do not study Blacks, if men ignore the lives and experiences of women, if the affluent do not seek to understand the circumstances of the poor, we will have returned to the bad old days when the privileged could easily justify ignoring the lives and perspectives of the oppressed.

Simple transfers of epistemic privilege to researchers who have something in common with the subjects of research do not solve the problem of researcher privilege distorting knowledge. Insider researchers have some access to data and insights that outsiders do not, but the reverse is also true. Further, the very notion of the insider can hide important differences in privilege between researchers and those they study at the same time that it lets more privileged researchers "off the hook" from exploring the power relations that reproduce their privilege.

In general, implementing any research method assuming a subjectivist reading of standpoint epistemology creates empirical and conceptual problems that are submerged only by ignoring those with power, romanticizing the oppressed, and understating the researchers' own control over the process. However, the assumptions that the oppressed have a privileged access to knowledge and that those who are privileged cannot adequately understand and analyze the situation of the oppressed are not inherent in the logic of standpoint theory.

Subjectivism Is a Misreading of Standpoint Epistemology

The position that the knowledge of the oppressed is better than the knowledge of the oppressor, or that the insider researcher has privileged access to knowledge, results from conflating people's subjectivity with their social location. A standpoint is *not* necessarily how people in a particular social location think.

This point has been reaffirmed by many, if not all, of the major standpoint theorists. In her classic early article on standpoint epistemology, Hartsock took pains to specifically distinguish a standpoint from the spontaneous consciousness of a category of social actors. A standpoint, she said, is "achieved rather than obvious, a mediated rather than immediate understanding" (Hartsock 1985: 132). Collins reaffirmed the point when she emphasized that standpoint is not about individual experiences—it is about "historically shared, group-based experiences" (1997: 375). Smith talks about a standpoint as a strategic choice in doing research—a place from which to start, a door to open on some aspect of social practices. A standpoint is, rather, a way of making sense of social processes and structures that can be developed from the resources available to a particular social location. The argument of standpoint epistemology is not psychological; it is social.

SOCIAL STANDPOINT EPISTEMOLOGY

Standpoint epistemology argues that knowledge is grounded in specific social and historical contexts. Recall the arguments I described in chapter 2. Hartsock

(1985) analyzed how potential conceptualizations of power developed from variations in the lived experience of human labor and the social relations organizing it. From a capitalist standpoint, power can be seen as a commodity; from the standpoint of workers, power can be seen as a relationship of domination. From the standpoint of the caretaker, power can be understood as the ability to make possible. This is not to say that every capitalist thinks the same way about power, nor every worker, or every homemaker, but rather that organizing the evidence accessible via one of these locations can allow one to see power in a certain way.

Similarly, Smith argues for the standpoint of women not because of what women think, but because the sexual division of labor in Western culture assigns men and women to different locations in the social world. Collins (1986, 1989) argues for the value of African American women's standpoint because from that particular position in the racial division of labor, respect, security, and opportunity, one can see things that are not seeable from more habitual social science haunts. In the arguments of each thinker, it is a specific location in physical and social reality that provides an opening for developing knowledge about how the social world works. The idea of a standpoint as the view that can be constructed from a specific social location comes clearest in Sandra Harding's (1998) analysis of the elements of a standpoint.

Harding's Specification of a Standpoint

Harding (1998) identifies four elements that contribute to constructing a standpoint: (1) actual location in nature; (2) interests with regard to that location; (3) discourses that provide tools for making sense of the location; and (4) position in the social organization of knowledge production. She illustrates how these forces come together to inform a standpoint by using this framework to analyze how gender creates distinctive standpoints for constructing knowledge about nature, that is, science.

Physical Location

First, all people are located in specific places in a nature that is heterogeneous and socially organized. For example, women and men are "exposed to different regularities of nature" (1998: 96). Women are biologically different from men: they experience menstruation, lactation, and other sex-specific reproductive functions, they have more body fat, different skeletal structure and patterns of endurance, susceptibility to drugs, and so on, all of which give them different access to nature. Further, gendered social structures assign women to different activities with regard to nature: they are engaged in more domestic labor, care of the sick, sex industries, and so on, so that "heterogeneous nature is partly differently distributed in men's and women's lives" (1998: 97).

Other feminists have demonstrated how race/ethnicity, class, and nation, among other relations of domination, influence which women and men are located where in nature. In the United States, for example, the gender order assigns care of bodies—households, children, the sick and infirm—to women. However, those women who are in a class position to afford it can and often do delegate their gender burden to domestic workers, housecleaners, restaurant workers, child-care workers, launderers, nurses' aides, and other service workers: people who are disproportionately poor, immigrant, and other than white in addition to being predominantly female (Glass 2000; Glenn 1992; Sprague 1996). Similarly, race/ethnicity, class, and nation shape which men are most likely to do work in agriculture, dig into the earth for minerals, or hunt animals, on the one hand, and which are more likely to be in professional jobs in which their connection to nature is more abstract.

Interests

The second element of a standpoint, Harding says, is that different locations in nature—different bodies and different places in the environment—create partial differences in people's interests and desires. To the extent that women's and men's activities are segregated, that will generate differences in interest. For example, women's involvement with domestic work, child care, care of the sick, and maintenance of community enhances their interests in knowledge to support this activity. Men who are distant from home, either because they are at the office or because they have immigrated to another location to make money, have less interest in knowledge regarding the support of kin and community, according to Harding. This implies that men who are engaged in the work of child care will have more personal stake in knowledge about child development than will women who are not engaged in such work.

Access to Discourses

Third, people vary socially in their access to discourses that provide tools they can use to interpret their experience, what Harding refers to as "metaphors, models, and narratives" (1998: 99). Discourses are heavily influenced by power. Western feminist scholars, Harding notes, have shown how the discourse of natural science is masculine. Men's "fantasies of potency" shape and constrain their interaction with nature. The natural science discourse represents nature as a bountiful mother, as a wild "harridan" to be controlled, or as a "shy maiden" whose veil must be lifted to uncover her secrets (Harding 1998: 100; cf. Haraway 1993; Merchant 1980). Women are much less likely to be as well schooled in this discourse as men are so relatively unaffected by it. Those women who are exposed to natural science discourse may be more sensitized by their own interests to what these representations of the feminine imply for derogating women in general, and thus, Harding asserts, less likely to embrace its interpretive frames.

Social Organization of Knowledge Production

The fourth element of a standpoint relates to its position vis-à-vis the organization of the production of knowledge. The social organization of scientific work, Harding (1998) says, facilitates some kinds of knowledge and creates obstacles to others. Social science work on organizations and on personal relationships demonstrates that gender structures the organization of workplaces and work relationships (e.g., Biernat and Fuegen 2001; Martin 2003; Reskin and Padavic 2002). Harding shows how this happens in the natural sciences. For example, she says, men and women scientists organize their work differently. Men encourage competition among their research assistants, while women encourage cooperation. Also, men compete with one another by doing research on "hot topics," while women select a niche to work steadfastly within. Men generate more articles, but women more carefully craft articles so have fewer but more highly cited publications (Harding 1998: 101). Women's marginalization in local scientific organizations may lead them to develop alternative networks. For example, Japanese women physicists are marginalized in their own country, and as a result are more likely to maintain ties with graduate school friends in the United States. These connections can be a route to being more heavily embedded in the international scientific community and exposed to the discourses that circulate within it.

Harding's four-pronged specification of physical location, interests with regard to that location, discourses that provide tools for making sense of the location, and the social organization of knowledge production is a template for analyzing any standpoints as places from which to build an understanding of the social world. It is impossible to generalize about the standpoints of the research subjects of social scientists, because of their diversity. The major variables in social science—gender, race/ethnicity, class, sexual preference, nation, immigrant status, physical or mental limitations, age—are salient precisely because they interact to locate people in distinctive positions in the social world. Each intersection varies along the dimensions of physical location, political interests, access to discourses, and participation in the social organization of knowledge production. On the other hand, there are some regularities to the social locations of researchers so that some general observations about their standpoint are possible.

The Standpoint of Social Researchers

Researchers in wealthy countries occupy a fairly privileged class location, although this varies considerably depending on the prestige of the researcher and of his or her institution. Still, researchers in the West are likely to be able to afford to live in safe neighborhoods with good schools, drive reliable cars, meet their monthly expenses, enjoy considerable social prestige, evade domestic labor, take nice vacations, and take for granted other comforts of professional middle-class life. Those who come from privileged class backgrounds also have families who can transfer significant resources to them, who can help them out with major purchases or in emergencies, and who can be sources of significant inheritances.

Though traditionally much more homogeneous, researchers increasingly vary in gender, race/ethnicity, national origin, and physical limitations, and these and other systematic social variations constitute distinctive social locations. Researchers with caretaking responsibilities in their families must juggle their scholarly work with worrying about child care, planning meals, arranging medical appointments, arranging for school conferences, helping an elder run errands, and so on. Men and women who are scholars of color may have family and friends in communities of color outside the academy, crossing a racial and often a class line when they go to work. Researchers who come from more modest class backgrounds and/or are immigrants are also likely to have personal connections that locate them in more diverse communities outside their paid work lives.

Their location in systems of class, gender, and race/ethnicity shapes whether people have a stake in maintaining or challenging current systems, and this is as true of researchers as it is of other people. Researchers who are women or persons of color experience discrimination—both the old-fashioned form of explicit sexism and the newer form of subtle devaluation of one's work and potential (cf. Biernat and Fuegen 2001; Martin 1996, 2003; Tokarczyk and Fay 1993). Similarly, scholars of color may find that their relative scarcity creates more demands on their time for committee work and advising, and that their racial/ethnic "otherness" means that they get less social and informal support from their colleagues, both of which can interfere with their ability to do research and contribute to scholarly discourse. Further, scholars who are marginalized within their institutions and who retain strong links with less privileged communities may understand their interests as overlapping with the interests of those communities.

Researchers and those they study exist within their shared society's hegemonic discourses, through such key distributors of metaphors and theories as education, religion, and the media. However, one aspect of the standpoint of social researchers that is likely to be quite different from the standpoint of those they research is the other discourses at their disposal, and thus the frames available to them to make sense of their experience. Although as I described in chapter 1, academic discourses tend to be organized from relatively privileged standpoints, researchers increasingly have access to multiple critical discourses, including feminism, Marxism, critical race theory, postcolonial theory, and queer theory. Further, in a society in which the hegemonic ideology revolves around individualism, merely asking how the facts of an individual's biography might be the outcomes of social processes is engaging in critical discourse (cf. Mills 1959).

The social organization of the production of knowledge creates a gap between knowledge producers and most others. Researchers read a great deal of the research done by others in their field and have training and experience in data collection and analysis. Those who work in the academy, especially in research-intensive institutions, have many opportunities to participate in regular dialogues with colleagues and students and access to libraries and technical resources. Scholars are culturally ordained as knowledge producers. Training, time, resources, and a sense of entitlement are important advantages for knowledge production.

On the other hand, researchers are located in specific institutional settings, and within specific disciplines and subdisciplines. The priorities of their institutions and disciplines shape their interests with regard to their locations. The standards of evaluation that they employ constitute obstacles to producing certain kinds of knowledge. For example, normative standards of evaluation give much more credit to publications in relatively elite journals than in more broadly accessible sources like textbooks, and give very little credit at all for reporting findings through public speaking and popular media. These standards also tend to assign credit based on the quantity of publications, rather than, for example, on how much effort it took to complete a particular project, or how useful the research has been in enhancing scholarly understanding or the lives of community members (Sprague 1998).

Institutions that survive based on successfully garnering grant money impose different standards of evaluation than those that have significant revenue streams to support teaching. As public funding for higher education has decreased, those institutions have increasingly pressured researchers to secure external funding to support their research. Within grant-dependent contexts, the interests of funders in specific kinds of scholarship become institutional constraints that intersect with the interests of researchers in having adequate resources to generate research and in enjoying the esteem of their colleagues. In some cases, those who have the most money to fund the research exercise a great deal of power over research agendas and methodologies and, sometimes, over forms of publication.

The standpoint of researchers, then, is a specific set of social locations that share considerable economic privilege. Many also enjoy privileged positions in other relations of social inequality. Researchers' professional and institutional interests may or may not coincide with their other interests. On the other hand, researchers have access to multiple discourses and some degree of institutional support for reflection and new learning. The standpoints of researchers are, like all standpoints, grounded and limited. The privileged do not have to be intentionally trying to legitimate gender and other social hierarchies—they are simply not in a position for many forms of domination to be salient in their experience and primary in their political interests. Critical researchers can either accept their limitations with all that implies for humility and caution, or they can actively work to compensate for their limitations by actively working to cross boundaries.

Standpoint Methodology Calls for Boundary Crossing

The logic of standpoint epistemology implies that crossing boundaries dividing standpoints and addressing the differences between them is a strategy for building social knowledge. For example, Patricia Hill Collins (1986, 1991/ 2000) argued for the special insights accessible to Black Feminist theorists because they are *outsiders within* the academy, both trained and certified within the hegemonic discourse and marginalized as Other at work and other parts of their daily lives. My reading of Collins's argument is that epistemological value of Black Feminist thought emerges because it is developed by a group of people whose lives involve continual boundary crossing, people at *the intersection of two contrasting locations* in social relations—in this case, official knowledge producer and member of a racially oppressed group. Similarly, Dorothy Smith (1987, 1990) advocated for the standpoint of women in sociology because the demands of work and family in their daily experience require that they *continually cross the line* between those who do the work of keeping the social going and those who determine what sense will be made of the social. This social location, Smith says, provides the opportunity to see the "line of fault" between official accounts of social life and the everyday experience of most social actors.

The lives of social scientists who are caretakers and/or who are in other marginalized groups automatically place them in contrasting social locations, making crossing boundaries between the academy and another location a matter of daily experience. Graduate students who are just confronting the disjuncture between their private experience and the discourse of social science knowledge are also in a dual location, compared with those who have been thoroughly schooled in a discipline's worldview (cf. Edwards and Ribbens 1988: 5–6). Researchers in these boundary-crossing positions and who experience the lack of fit between social science accounts and their life experiences may be compelled to try to bridge the differences, to do the research that will develop more adequate accounts.

However, all scholars can make the conscious effort to cross boundaries in their research. We all, Donna Haraway (1988) reminds us, have the ability to be empathetic, to listen to and imaginatively put oneself in the position of another. We are none of us completely integrated unitary selves, Haraway observes, and the multidimensionality of our identities allows us to make partial connections with other knowers, to see things to some extent from their perspective. This is what Haraway means when she says "splitting, not being, is the privileged image for feminist epistemologies of scientific knowledge" (1988: 586). The ability to be empathetic—to see things from the other's perspective while at the same time retaining one's own—is a key mechanism in the intellectual work of crossing boundaries and bridging the differences.

What does all of this imply for how we should do research? The logic of standpoint epistemology suggests at least four provisional guidelines for how we might move forward, implementing every method with more caution about the distorting effects power can have on the kind of knowledge we produce. These are: work from the standpoint of the disadvantaged, ground interpretations in interests and experience, maintain a strategically diverse discourse, and create knowledge that empowers the disadvantaged.

Work from the Standpoint of the Disadvantaged

A flourishing of new analytic frames and avenues of research has followed the increasing entry of women, men of color, people from working-class backgrounds, scholars from formerly colonized countries, and explicitly identified gay and lesbian scholars into the academy. Feminism has prompted significant changes in social science scholarship over the last three decades (England 1999). Certainly part of the process creating this change in the known has been the entry of more women and people of color into the ranks of official knowledge producers. Many of those who have changed our understanding of basic social phenomena like work, family, health, violence, politics, race/ ethnicity, demographic patterns, and criminology have been women; some have been scholars of color. However, *some have also been white men.* Further, there have been some women and some men of color who have not pushed sociologists to challenge taken-for-granted ways of thinking, and who have instead operated within traditional frameworks.

That is, the transformations in social science knowledge have occurred not because of the changing identity of the scholars, but because scholars have been shifting the standpoints from which they develop scholarship. Change in our understanding of the social has come when knowers, diverse in race, gender, sexuality, and class origins, have taken previously marginalized standpoints as their gateway to developing questions, collecting evidence, and developing interpretations.

For example, our notion of violence changed when scholars started challenging the prevailing conceptualization of rape by asking if married women could be raped, and if unwanted sex with an acquaintance counted. They could not simply ask women if they had been raped—the dominant definition of the word in our culture made it very difficult to think of unwanted sex with an intimate as rape. Scholars had to reoperationalize various sexual behaviors from the perspective of women's interests and preferences (cf. Russell 1984).

Similarly, our ideas of the equity involved in how wages are determined in this economy changed when scholars started asking whether the work women were doing was adequately described and evaluated consistently with analogous masculine jobs in existing pay systems. These scholars, too, found they could not simply ask women and working-class men to describe their jobs, because they, like the rest of us, were blinded by elitist standards that hid large components of skill, stress, and/or responsibility in nonelite jobs (Steinberg 1995). What made it possible to ask the question was taking these workers and their contributions seriously.

The whole idea of sex/gender being a distinct social system emerged only in the 1970s, even though the social regularities that point to its existence have been empirically pervasive across the globe for all of recorded history (Harding 1983). This happened as a result of the women's movement, women coming together to analyze their lives, and scholars taking their analyses seriously. In all of these examples, knowledge has changed in critical directions when knowers have taken the experiences, the material interests, the descriptions, and the accounts of women and oppressed men into account.

Those on the downside of social hierarchies are often the frontline actors of society, their daily practices the fundamental building blocks of how things work (Smith 1987). Smith calls us to begin our research with everyday life as everyday social actors know it, and discover how it is shaped, constrained, and made irrational because of the operation of power relations that are not immediately visible. However, working from the standpoint of the disadvantaged does not preclude studying the powerful. Rather, it involves problematizing power and advantage, asking about the mechanisms that sustain privilege and about the consequences of privilege for the broader society. Men, for example, can be feminists, and whites, antiracists, and both can provide crucial insights if they undertake an analysis of the circumstances and practices that support their privilege (Harding 1993). Harding argues that a good way to begin to do that is to examine their own biographies from the standpoint of those over whom they have privilege.

Ground Interpretations in Interests and Experience

Privilege is a great blinder. White researchers are more likely to think race is not significant in their projects, men to assume gender is irrelevant, heterosexuals to assume the social organization of sexuality is not in play, and so on. All are treading on risky ground from the perspective of standpoint epistemology. The best way to avoid the bias in dominant frameworks is to begin with the conceptual categories of the marginalized, with their ways of organizing what is relevant about experience (Smith 1990). Starting from the discourse of the marginalized makes it more likely that we will see the cultural assumptions embedded in scholarly interpretive frameworks.

Those at the downside of social hierarchies have some epistemological advantages. Their daily practices and the constraints within which they struggle are the basic stuff of how social power and domination work. They have much less material or ideological interest in continuing forms of social organization that place them at serious disadvantage, and so less reason to deny the flaws and injustices in those forms. As outsiders in relation to official knowledge construction, they may pick up on the gap between their experience and the conceptual frameworks that are distributed to make sense of it (Collins 1990; Harding 1991; Smith 1987, 1990). Some members of a disadvantaged group have experiences that lead them to develop critical perspectives on their circumstances.

Still, there are marked differences in the time and resources available to those who want to construct knowledge inside and outside the official institutions for doing so. The more oppressed a group of people is, the less likely the members are to see an analysis that identifies their situation as unjust or exploitative in high school textbooks, in popular magazines, or on the evening news. In fact, the hegemonic discourses are not likely to fit well with the circumstances of their daily life at all (Smith 1987, 1990). Even people's practices of resistance to oppression are not undistorted by the experience of oppression (Bar On 1993).

Standpoint epistemology points to the partiality of all knowledge. Researchers should seek to understand how each interpretation of experience is shaped and constrained by the interplay of specific location, material interests, access to interpretive frameworks, and ways of organizing the work of producing knowledge (Bar On 1993; Harding 1998). We can use the inconsistencies among hegemonic discourses, scholarly analyses, and the worldviews of everyday actors as an opportunity, a problem to solve through research and dialogue.

Maintain a Strategically Diverse Discourse

The biases and blind spots in the standpoint of researchers mean that critical scholars should consider how they might compensate. I have argued in this chapter that simply handing authority to some marginalized group is not a viable strategy, for pragmatic and epistemological reasons. While conventional epistemology represents the knower as an abstract individual, for standpoint epistemology the subject must be multiple, to generate the most valid knowledge.

The feminist movement knows this firsthand. Their racial and class privilege allowed white feminists to dominate the discourse on feminism. Feminists of color have struggled since the 1970s to demonstrate the theoretical and empirical salience of the racial and class diversity among women, and how social processes and policies had differential impacts. Over time this dialogue has become a central organizer of feminist discourse (Mascia-Lees et al. 1989). While often heated, it has been invaluable for the development of feminist knowledge on all sides, sharpening our thinking, broadening our scope, and increasing our rigor.

Wise researchers will construct and maintain dialogue with others occupying contrasting social locations. We can diversify our dialogue in several ways. First, social science researchers comprise women and men in varying social locations depending on their class, race, ethnicity, sexuality, disability, immigrant status, and so on, and can build dialogues across these differences. Second, researchers need to stay connected with the discourses of everyday actors, particularly those at the bottoms of social hierarchies. Popular culture forms like blues music, poetry, novels, folk wisdom, and graffiti are also venues through which people can reflect on their experience and share their analyses with others (Aptheker 1989; Collins 1991/2000). Researchers can maintain dialogue with members of groups that have coalesced to fight against their disadvantage. In the process of mobilizing, such groups develop analyses of their situation and alternative or even counter-hegemonic discourses.

Knowledge constructed from these multiple standpoints can, and in an unjust society will, sometimes be conflicting (Bar On 1993; Bhavnani 1993; Haraway 1988; Harding 1991). Whether and, more importantly, under what conditions the knowledges developed from contrasting standpoints are commensurable is an empirical question—an exciting and crucial question. Taking contrasting standpoints seriously and working to understand the sources of, and if possible to reconcile, differences among them is the heart of what critical scholarship can contribute to social understanding.

Create Knowledge That Empowers the Disadvantaged

Most feminists writing about power and research have focused on the actual process and products of research, and D. Wolf (1996) suggests that this is because these are easier to do something about than researchers' social power. However, the reason we have to be worried about systematic biases toward the worldview and interests of the privileged in the knowledge we produce is that we exist in an unequal society. The very need to ensure that research subjects have voice, are taken seriously as analysts of their lives, is the outcome of social power. People need to make claims that they can speak with authority only when they are silenced; part of being privileged is being able to assume that one has authority (Bar On 1993).

The inequality between the researcher and the subjects of research is usually grounded in the material—it is based in social structures organizing gender, class, race, nation, and so on (Patai 1991). Visweswaran argues that the key question is not whether a researcher can do a better job of representing people than they themselves can. Rather, it is "whether we can be accountable to people's own struggles for self-representation and self-determination" (Visweswaran 1988: 39) in the way we do our research. Self-representation requires self-determination. As long as we live in a social world that sorts men and women, whites and people of color, rich and poor, the West and the rest into such differing social locations, imposing a logic that creates conflicts in interest (so that for some to "win," others have to lose), that controls the flow of information and ideas to ensure the hegemony of the dominant, and that blocks so many from active legitimate participation in the production of knowledge, we cannot have a fully free and inclusive discourse about what is and what should be. The interests of critical researchers in valid knowledge coincide with their values for social justice.

Hartsock's analysis of differing conceptualizations of power casts light on how researchers might respond to the way social power coincides with authority in our society. Those who focus on ceding authority or control to people they study are thinking of power either as a commodity or as a relationship of domination between individual researchers and the researched. Recall, though, the third way of thinking of power, the conceptualization of power that, Hartsock argues, emerges from taking the standpoint of women: power as empowering, as making something possible.

What if researchers saw their power from the standpoint of caretakers, as making things possible? For example, what if we saw the role of producing knowledge as making cross-cultural understanding, true democracy, or social justice possible? We might agree with Wolf, who says "I think I would prefer to have my decisions grounded in a feminist politic rather than arising from a rhetorical need to 'decenter' the ethnographer and her authority" (Wolf 1992: 123). Creating knowledge that empowers the disadvantaged entails giving people an alternative to the hegemonic view, one that helps people see how many of the problems and irrationalities in their lives are understandable when linked to the domination by powerful social actors far removed from their daily awareness (Smith 1987).

Running through each of these guidelines—work from the standpoint of the disadvantaged, ground interpretations in interests and experience, maintain a strategically diverse discourse, and create knowledge that empowers the disadvantaged—is a general theme. From the perspective of standpoint epistemology, *truthfulness or validity is not the property of a particular research project or category of social actor, it is a characteristic of a social discourse.*

Standpoint epistemology implies a political stance as well as a methodological strategy. It poses political questions for each scholar: whose questions do we ask; from whose lives, needs, and interests do we begin; whose ordering of experience do we take seriously; to whom are we responsible to communicate; when has a question been adequately answered? In the next two chapters, I will review the work of feminists to transform both qualitative and quantitative methods to make their methodologies less vulnerable to the biases of privilege and more amenable to serving the cause of increasing social justice.

4

How Feminists Count: Critical Strategies for Quantitative Methods

Research generated through quantitative methods like surveys and experiments tends to be synonymous with social science in popular discourse. To many, quantitative research seems more trustworthy as a source of valid information because of its emphases on researcher control and standardization of procedures. These qualities make quantitative research reports more transparent, more open to critique of their methodology and interpretations. They also help make quantitative findings persuasive in public discourse. And, as I will show later in this chapter, feminist researchers have used these methods very effectively in order to demonstrate how inequality is created and sustained. Thus, critical social scientists should value them.

Yet these same emphases on control and standardization prompt the skepticism of many critical researchers about using quantitative methods to produce valid research, let alone to inform progressive social action. Many of the criticisms of quantitative methods are actually criticisms of how *positivists* do quantitative sociology. That is, the critics are sliding from a concern about a particular *methodology* to a wholesale rejection of a class of *methods*.

The logical error is understandable given the historical dominance of positivism in quantitative research methodology, yet it has left quantitative methodology underexamined by feminists. Because feminists and other critical researchers have tended to assume that quantitative methodology cannot respond to their concerns, there are relatively few analyses of specific procedures that are problematic in mainstream quantitative methodology and there is even less written on feminist ways of implementing experiments or surveys. First I will consider the kinds of critiques feminists have raised. Later I will turn to the primary source of ideas for alternative ways of using these methods: the strategies that are being developed in the trenches by feminist quantitative researchers.

PROBLEMS WITH STANDARD QUANTITATIVE METHODOLOGY

Quantitative methodology has emphasized the standardization of measurements and researcher control over the process of collecting and/or analyzing data because these are important for meeting the conditions for making a rational argument about causal processes. Making a persuasive causal argument requires being able to satisfy three criteria: (1) establishing that the "cause" and the "effect" covary; (2) showing that the "cause" precedes the "effect"; and (3) ruling out other reasonable explanations for why the "cause" and the "effect" would covary (cf. Cook and Campbell 1979).

The experimental method is designed specifically to test hypotheses about causal relationships by maximizing researcher control. If the researcher controls exposure to the hypothesized cause—who is exposed and when the exposure occurs—and the measurement of any outcome, the first two logical criteria can usually be met. Other experimental arrangements, most notably the use of control groups and the random assignment of subjects to either experimental or control groups, are designed to meet the third criterion. Researcher control is easiest to maximize in a laboratory setting, but some feminists question the degree to which we can generalize from lab studies to real-world situations. The argument here is that people's practices and beliefs are constructed and supported in a natural context, one that is saturated with power relations. Lab experiments "white-out" these ongoing power relations and create a "decontextualized" analysis that may be irrelevant to daily life (Fine and Gordon 1989; Sherif 1979). There is political substance in the critique that experiments maximize internal validity at the expense of external validity.

Occasionally, survey researchers conduct experiments—for example, testing the impact of various features of question design by exposing some respondents to alternative formats and comparing the outcomes across formats (e.g., Schuman and Presser 1981). But generally, survey researchers cannot control who is exposed to hypothesized causes or the conditions under which they are exposed. Rather, survey researchers exercise control through the processes of measurement and analysis. They choose measures, design samples, and use statistical techniques that control for plausible alternative causes in the process of data analysis.

For those who accept positivist assumptions about researcher objectivity, or critical realist assumptions that bias exists but does not systematically favor particular social positions, there is no downside to researcher control. If, as standpoint epistemologists argue, the subjectivity of researchers is systematically shaped by their specific social locations, then there is reason to worry about how the standpoint of researchers might be unintentionally introducing systematic bias into the processes of measurement, sampling, and the design of analyses.

Hidden Biases in Standardized Measures

The most common feminist criticism of quantitative methodology concerns the use of standardized measures. Standardized measures have some obvious advantages when doing large-scale research. They allow for direct comparisons and seem to remove variations in question wording as an explanation for variations in the distribution of responses. Closed-ended questions increase the likelihood that each person's responses will be made using the same frame of reference. Measures that have been used before have a track record on reliability and validity. Researchers know something about the kinds of data they can elicit, measurement errors to which they may be prone, and their relationships with other measures of the same construct and with measures of other constructs. Repeated use of measures also allows for direct comparisons between studies, including the study of changes over time. For example, because the General Social Survey has asked people in many samples over time whether they agree with the statement "A working mother can establish just as warm and secure a relationship with her children as a mother who does not work," researchers can find out that the number of respondents who agree or strongly agree with this statement rose from 48.9 percent in 1977 to 70.3 percent in 1994 (see data tables at www/icpsr.umich.edi/GSS/trend/fechld.htm). These characteristics of standard measures make them particularly important for those who want to generate data that can be used in public policy debates (Spalter-Roth and Hartmann 1991).

Every measurement approach creates a pattern of selective visibility: it taps some aspects of a phenomenon and hides others. Measures are always constructed within specific historical and political contexts that shape what is measured and how. Mainstream practices put researchers in control of what an idea means, how to word questions, and what will be on the menu of legitimate responses. Whether researchers write their own measures or use measures that have been used in other studies, the selection favors the standpoint of researchers, particularly the most prolific and/or prominent researchers and, as I noted in chapter 3, this tends to be a fairly homogeneous and privileged group.

The Case of the Census

The data set that most people are aware of is a crucial one for the knowledge base in our society: the U.S. Census. It is also a striking example of how historical context and researcher standpoint leave an imprint on the data. The census is a political project—the idea of doing the decennial census came out of a political necessity. Because one body of Congress, the House of Representatives, was to represent individuals proportionately, there was a need to count heads. James Madison, the designer of the Constitution and of the idea of doing a census, wanted to have some way of making sure the policies of the new government took into account the diverging interests of constituents. He believed that economic differences were a primary source of political conflict, but since he did not want to use the traditional categories (aristocrat, peasant, etc.) because they seemed inappropriate for a democracy, he decided to measure occupational groupings (Anderson 1994).

The most striking indicator of the standpoint informing the first census, in 1790, is in the very measure of people's existence: who is counted and how they are counted. The first census identified the name of the "head" of a family and then counted the number of individuals in these categories: free white males over 16 years, free white males under 16, free white females, all other free people, and slaves. Age distinctions were made among free white men because once over 16, they were seen as having an economic and military relevance that women and slaves did not have. The head of the family was a man and had a name; others just had a relationship to him. Slaves did not have a gender; they did not even have whole bodies—they were counted three-fifths as much as free whites. The U.S. Census, like those in Australia and Great

Britain, counted people using measures saturated with assumptions about gender, class, and race (Anderson 1994; Bose 1984; Deacon 1985).

Although they are more obvious in this first enumeration, gender, race, and class biases have continued for most of census history. For example, the gender of slaves was not recorded until 1820 (U.S. Census Bureau 2002). For most of its history, the U.S. Census has coded married women as dependents; in households composed of farmers and/or small business owners, the man is coded as self-employed and the woman as a dependent spouse. As recently as 1970, one respondent in the household was coded as its head, and other related individuals could be coded as wives, children, or other relatives of the head. Within the lifetime of many people living today, the only way for a woman to be the head of a household was if there were no adult man present (Anderson 1994).

The coding of women as dependents in households with family businesses or farms is not just an obvious message about the naturalness of male dominance; this strategy also led to serious measurement error. Christine Bose (1984) shows how identifying only the man in such households as self-employed resulted in systematically undercounting work done by women in these enterprises. From the domestic labor involved in supporting live-in farmhands, to field and animal work, to bookkeeping and other clerical work, women and children routinely made significant contributions to the work of family businesses and farms (Anderson 1994; Bose 1984).

Even women's paid work has been seriously undercounted. The coding schemes used to classify occupations have historically made finer distinctions for work typically done by upper- and upper-middle-class men—professional and managerial jobs—than for work historically dominated by women, like secretarial and service work. For example, Barbara Reskin and Catherine Ross (1992) argue that the standard census occupational classifications have a status-bias in the identification of decision-making power and supervisory responsibility. The census ignores the managerial quality of lower status jobs that involve the supervision of other employees and/or participation in organizational decision making, no matter what the workers or employers think about the nature of the job. Since women are concentrated in lower status jobs and in lower status units of the enterprise (e.g., clerical or human relations rather than production or engineering), they are less likely to be identified as managers, regardless of their responsibilities and decision-making power.

Classifying Work

The census's measurement scheme is not the only one to classify work from the standpoint of privileged men. The most common system that employers use for evaluating and compensating jobs, the Hay Guide Chart-Profile method, is also biased toward the experience of high-status men (Steinberg 1995). For example, as Ronnie Steinberg (1995) shows, it downplays client-oriented skills and the kind of autonomy involved in human service work, and ignores the kinds of knowledge associated with gendered expectations of women (e.g., language, psychology, human development, food preparation). These biases make it harder to detect race and gender differences in the degree to which skill and responsibility are rewarded with authority and income.

Measuring Domestic Violence

Another illustration of a measure constructed from the standpoint of men is a common measure of involvement in domestic violence, the Conflict Tactics Scale (CTS). The CTS asks respondents how they and their partner have responded to disagreements. The original form (1979, 1990) lists a series of violent acts (e.g., hit, slapped, shaken, scratched, kicked) and asks how often they have committed these against their partners in the past year. The initial scale has been widely used. The occasional study that shows that men are as likely to be victims of domestic violence as women is probably using the CTS (Flood 1999).

Michael Flood (1999) points to several methodological problems with this measurement approach. For one, it leaves out sexual assault, choking, suffocating, and stalking, and thus does not capture a representative sampling of the kinds of violence more commonly done to women than to men. As a self-report scale, the CTS cannot count the most extreme form of violence, marital murder. Since it asks about behavior between partners, this approach fails to capture violence that is committed after the couples separate, when as many as 75 percent of the attacks on women occur. Further, researchers typically interview only one partner while research, Flood (1999) says, shows that women are more likely to report their own violence than are men. Finally, the scale treats violent acts out of context, ignoring whether the acts were offensive or in self-defense, isolated or part of a pattern of violence, intended to hurt, or resulted in injury. The revised CTS (Straus et al. 1996) responds to some of these criticisms by adding measures of sexual coercion and of the extent of injuries resulting from violent acts. However, even these changes do not get at the most serious situations in which women find themselves: regimes of terror and subordination in the home, in which men dominate them through economic control, social isolation, and threats (Flood 1999; cf. Smith 1994).

Measuring Traits

Standardized measures of traits are premised on the assumptions that traits are stable and can be measured out of context. One illustration is a common measure in social psychology, the Twenty Statements Test, which asks respondents to give 20 responses to the question "who am I?" premised on an underlying conceptualization of the self as something that is unitary and consistent across situations, the predominant conceptualization in Western culture (Markus and Kitayama 1998). But this assumption is not always supported by the data. Hazel Markus and Shinobu Kitayama (1998) argue that in many Asian, African, and perhaps some Latin American cultures, the self is group-oriented and contextual. Many Asians, for example, understand their selves differently depending on whether they are with family or in work contexts (Markus and Kitayama 1991). For them, a self-description would need to specify the relationship and social context. This points to the possibility that the assumption of a unitary, trans-situational self is problematic for some peoples of the West as well, certainly those who have grown up in certain non-Western cultures.

Racial/ethnic identity can also be situational. Reynolds Farley (n.d.) observes that in the 2000 census, about 2.4 percent of the population identified multiple races; that number goes down to 1.6 percent when excluding those who indicated Spanish ethnicity as their second race. He suggests that people of mixed race in the United States have an interest in identifying their race strategically depending on the situation. For example, someone of Asian and white ancestries might identify as Asian when applying for a humanities program on the East Coast, but white if applying for engineering school in California. A business owner might identify as African American when applying for a federal contract, but white when applying for a loan. This raises the issue of contextual factors that might shape how multiracial persons would respond to a survey question.

Overall, these critics are pointing to ways that conventional quantitative methodology builds measures from the experiences of men, particularly racially and economically privileged men. They have the status of full adult/citizen, their work counts for more, and their experience of violence informs its operationalization. Ways of understanding identity that erase a context of rights, responsibilities, power, and privilege prevail. Using these measures can and often does generate "facts" that legitimate privilege and even help to reproduce inequality.

However, researchers cannot simply defer decisions about measurement to respondents. The Bem Sex Role Inventory (BSRI), now much maligned by feminist researchers, is a cautionary case. Sandra Bem (1983) was trying to develop a measure of masculinity and femininity. She asked hundreds of students to identify traits that were desirable in men and those that were desirable in women. She used those traits on which there was strong convergence to develop scales to measure how much individuals identified themselves as conforming to cultural conceptions of what was appropriate for their sex. However, subsequent analysis has shown that Bem's masculinity and femininity scales conflate multiple attributes that do not necessarily coexist in individuals. For example, the femininity scale combined measures of expressiveness with those of dependence, and the masculinity scale elided instrumentality with autonomy. Yet, for example, women can be expressive and attentive to the needs of others and still be independent (Gill, Stockard, Johnson, and Williams 1987). By building measures on the opinions of respondents, Bem was incorporating the dominant ideology as these respondents had internalized it.

Measurement is a process of creating categories, identifying distinctions, but in the empirical world, phenomena are much more likely to exist on a continuum. Where and how those distinctions are drawn is a matter of judgment, and that judgment is the product of one's social location, interests with regard to the matter, and access to discourses. The point is that measurement is never independent of a standpoint, and historically the dominant standpoint has been a privileged one.

Samples

The representativeness of research samples has been a weak spot for experimental research. Experimenters have also often sought homogeneous samples as a way of keeping characteristics of subjects they consider to be irrelevant from creating noise in their findings. What is normal and what is noise is, of course, dependent on standpoint, and over the history of experimental research the prevalent standpoint has been clear. From psychological experimenters' use of albino male rats to medical research's preference for all-male human samples, the "normal" subject has often been a white male (cf. Dresser 1992).

Even when researchers are not intentionally seeking homogeneity among those they study, uniformity can be the unintended consequence of other demands of experimental design. Experiments are premised on control over who gets exposed to some causal agent, and when and how much exposure occurs. While some experiments have been done in natural situations and, for a brief period, the United States was host to large-scale experimental tests of social policies (cf. Campbell 1969; Oakley 2000), most researchers have found it much easier to ensure adequate control in a laboratory situation.

Experimental researchers who work with human beings usually do not talk about samples or sampling frames; they talk about "subject pools." Because laboratories are, like experimenters, typically housed on college campuses, the groups of people who are available for experiments are very often undergraduate college students, for whom participating in an experiment is a class requirement or at least a way of improving a class grade. In a society that is seriously stratified and segregated by race and class as well as gender, unintended homogeneity is hard to avoid on a college campus, particularly in the more elite institutions that have the resources and personnel to generate the most research. In interpreting experimental outcomes, however, researchers rarely consider how findings might be specific to the particular social categories on whom they were generated. By default, the experiences and preferences of the privileged are normalized.

On the other hand, representativeness is a potential strength of survey methods. Surveys are open to use with heterogeneous samples: people living in varied locations, in different economic and racial/ethnic positions, in varying stages of their lives. Still, survey researchers also have to contend with obvious class biases built into survey sampling. For example, to be in a sample drawn through contacting people's residences, one must have a residence and be in it at the hours when contact is attempted. Households that can afford multiple telephone lines and/or a stay-at-home homemaker are well situated for survey sampling. Those with no telephone, with no regular address, working double shifts, or who are seldom "home" for other reasons are less likely to end up in residence-based survey samples. Self-administered surveys are dependent on literacy, which makes them inaccessible to those who by virtue of cognitive limitation or exclusion from education are not able to read.

The costs involved in reaching more diverse samples, obtaining data, and analyzing them may be beyond the resources available to all but the most privileged social researchers, who can secure external funding to support their work. Many survey researchers rely on the use of either a few major public data sets or data collected by government agencies. Many others make do by sampling those who are most easily accessible to them, again leading to fairly homogeneous samples. For example, the research literature on the sexual preferences and experiences of heterosexuals is heavily weighted toward samples of college students, not only fairly homogeneous in race and class background, but also, relatively speaking, close to the beginnings of their sexual lives (Sprague and Quadagno 1989).

Level of Analysis

Another theme in feminist critiques of quantitative research centers on the level of analysis. Conventional quantitative research relies on the individual level of analysis almost exclusively. Judith Stacey and Barrie Thorne (1985) identified the problem under the rubric of "gender as a variable" research, that is, analyses in which "gender is assumed to be a property of individuals and is conceptualized in terms of sex difference, rather than as a principle of social organization" (1985: 307). Barbara Reskin (2003) raises a similar critique in observing that sociologists studying gender and/or race inequality in unemployment focus on individual-level data.

The problem, Reskin argues, is that individual-level data can only generate individual-level explanations. If researchers only examine the relationship between workers' characteristics and their outcomes, they can only see the degree to which these figure into inequality, not how this process happens. In drawing conclusions about how inequality happens, these researchers are left to draw inferences about motives—workers' reasons for choosing devalued jobs or employers' biases in favor of certain groups—to explain the connection between who workers are and what their outcomes are. Researchers can ask employers about their motives for having promoted someone, Reskin says, but they cannot know whether the motive preceded the action or is a post hoc accounting of it. Further, motives are not necessarily the causes of people's outcomes; they could be the consequences.

Citing Elster (1989), Reskin asserts that "the best way to change people's minds may be to change their circumstances" (2003: 5). This point suggests the most serious limitation of the individual level of analysis for those who want to inform social change for increasing equality. Knowing what characteristics of an individual are associated with their outcomes gives us little guidance on what to do to make things fairer.

The Importance of Context

In order to guide social change, we need to understand the mechanisms that are creating the situation within which people identify their options and choose from among them. In the case of the relationship between gender and income inequality, for example, we need to understand how women get sorted into different kinds of jobs than men do, and what about the way work is evaluated results in the work women do being valued so much less than the kind men do. Researchers need to develop ways of taking context and mechanisms into account (Reskin 2003).

For example, Bose (1984) analyzed factors influencing increases and decreases in women's employment at a time when patterns were shifting. Using the 1900 census, Bose examined the influence of individual-level attributes like age, education, and marital status, but she also looked at contextual factors like household composition, urban/rural residence, and region of the country. Other investigators who look at contextual factors are finding that contemporary income gaps between men and women or among racial/ethnic groups are affected by the area's racial composition, level of unionization, and gender segregation of the local labor market, as well as characteristics of the work setting like its race and sex composition and whether it is government or private sector employment (Cohen and Huffman 2003; Reskin 2003).

The level of analysis also impacts measurement. The history of the Australian census, as Deacon (1985) describes it, shows how the level of analysis can impact such basic findings as who is counted as working. The first Australian census in 1851, like the British censuses on which it was modeled, considered domestic labor as productive work, part of what generates the nation's wealth. By 1880 the British had switched to classifying housewives in the "unoccupied class," and in 1890, Australian statisticians chose to define women as dependent unless explicitly stated otherwise. Underlying the change in coding was a shift in the level of analysis. The British census initially took the household as the primary unit of economic activity. If the household operated a farm, then the man, the woman, and the children above a minimum age were all engaged in farming; family members were similarly coded as being engaged in family businesses. Work sustaining the household was part of the economic activity of the household. By 1880 the level of analysis had shifted from the household to the individual. In Australia and most other countries today, the labor force is conceptualized as individuals who earn income or are actively seeking to earn an income, creating a dichotomy between "breadwinners" and "dependents".

The individual level of analysis is important. Some feminists have pointed to the danger of ignoring individual variation among group members, particularly in referring to households. One of the "seven sexist problems in research" identified by Margrit Eichler (1988) is taking the family as the smallest unit of analysis, thereby obscuring distinctions in the situations of men, women, and children and the existence of power relations among them. A case in point is the practice of using the economic class of the male "head of household" to indicate the class of all members in that household, a practice that obliterates very real differences in ownership and control over the disposition of family resources (Acker 1988). Rather, the level of analysis critique asserts that we cannot explain individual-level beliefs, practices, or outcomes without seeing how these are shaped, constrained, and strategically developed within social contexts. We need research at multiple levels of analysis.

Statistical Analysis

Statistics, the overwhelmingly most prevalent contemporary approach to analyzing data, developed within a specific historical context. As Donna Hughes (1995) tells the story, those who invented the first statistical methods were working in a general climate of "improving the race," meaning whites of European ancestry, and using statistics to look for racial differences, especially in intelligence. Francis Galton developed the first correlation and regression analyses to study the intergenerational transmission of traits. He is known as the founder of both biostatistics and eugenics. These two efforts were linked together as parts of his goal to improve the human race by increasing the reproduction of some groups and depressing the reproduction of others (Hughes 1995; Oakley 2000).

Karl Pearson, developer of the product-moment correlation, the chi-square statistic, and substantial parts of multiple correlation and regression, computed the correlation between male and female siblings on physical traits (eye and hair color, head length) and teachers' ratings of them on mental traits (assertiveness, introspection, intelligence). The correlations between siblings on mental traits were close to their correlations on physical traits, and Pearson argued that this showed that heredity, not environment, was causing both (Hughes 1995). Ronald A. Fischer refined tests of significance, including inventing the Analysis of Variance (ANOVA) and establishing the 5 percent-level criterion for hypothesis testing. He too was explicitly interested in the use of scientific methods to select for the production of the "best" humans.

Of course, the fact that the developers of commonly used statistical approaches had racist and sexist motivations does not mean that statistical analysis is inherently racist or sexist. However, this history should make researchers mindful of the emphasis on differences and dichotomous cutting points in hypothesis testing. Tests of statistical significance can prompt researchers to emphasize differences to such an extreme that underlying continuities disappear from view. Findings of *statistical* significance can erroneously morph into conclusions about *substantive* significance. This tendency to exaggerate minor distinctions is particularly common when these differences are between women and men and among people of different races/ethnicities (Eichler 1988; Williams 1991).

The Fetishization of Technique

While some scientists, mathematicians, and philosophers recognize that statistics, like other research techniques, are socially constructed, Donna Hughes (1995) says that in the daily practice of quantitative social science, this awareness is obliterated by a pervasive emphasis on technique. Technique often outshines substance, or at least makes substance hard to identify, in too many published reports of quantitative research, particularly in the most prestigious journals. By the 1990s some psychological researchers were complaining that their colleagues were relying too heavily on the model of research as hypothesis testing, and that the practice was hampering the development of knowledge (Shea 1996). The American Psychological Association became concerned enough to convene a Task Force on Statistical Inference in 1996.

The task force, composed of distinguished quantitative scholars and statistical experts, identified four problematic areas in quantitative research practices: (1) inadequate descriptive information about data; (2) the devaluing of exploratory research; (3) the use of increasingly complex analytic strategies when simpler approaches would be adequate; and (4) the reporting of statistical results in ways that reflect little understanding of what they mean, including to greater precision than the data warrant.

The common thread running through all four points is a fetishization of complex statistical analysis, facilitated by computer programs that can rapidly generate these analyses and provide statistics so that researchers do not necessarily need to think about what they are doing and whether it is justified. The task force argues that social science needs "theory-generating studies," by which they mean studies that are exploratory. They note that the biases of reviewers and editors work against such studies by pushing for research to be constructed to conform to hypothesis testing models. Further, the task force advises quantitative researchers to use "minimally sufficient designs and analytic strategies" (American Psychological Association 1996). Reviewers, the panel notes, push for "cutting-edge" or "state of the art" designs and analysis. Such techniques are occasionally the wise choice, but not routinely so. In fact, the task force argues, high-powered statistical techniques are usually *not* preferable on statistical grounds. Simpler approaches, they observe, usually require fewer and less restrictive assumptions, so analyses will not come into question because of the violation of assumptions. Simpler statistical approaches are also less error-prone, and any errors are easier to detect (American Psychological Association 1996).

Depending on the question and the data, technical complexity is sometimes required in a research project. But why would quantitative social scientists prefer highly technical statistics when simpler tools would be more responsible? One possible answer resonates with Bob Connell's (1995) identification of the varying forms of masculinity circulating in Western culture. One strand of competing models, the one associated with the urban middle class and the stratum that manages global capital, relies heavily on technical rationality and expertise to legitimate power. Men in this stratum prove their masculinity through technical mastery. Emphasizing an unnecessarily high level of technical complexity in evaluating research is similar to holding quantitative social scientists to the standard underwriting a specific form of masculinity.

The Form of the Model

Another way that the design of analysis can embed hegemonic worldviews is through the organization of the data into models. A common approach is to analyze data from all cases simultaneously. Fitting a model to all cases amounts to assuming that the same processes are at work to the same degree and in the same ways for all respondents. Yet there is ample evidence that that is not the case. Feminist sociologists have been demonstrating for some time now that social processes work in different ways for people living in different intersections of race, class, and gender (cf. Calasanti and Slevin 2001; Cancian and Oliker 1999; Espiritu 1997; Howard and Hollander 1997; Messner 1997).

The simplest statistical response to the recognition that social processes may not work uniformly across differences in social status is to convert categories of a measure of gender, race/ethnicity, or class into "dummy variables," coded 1 for those in the category and 0 for all others. For statistical reasons, one category must be left out and becomes the reference group. The significance, size, and direction of the estimated effect of a category signals differences from the excluded category. Single equations breaking up status groups into dummy variables give some sense of the bottom line of a benefit or disadvantage to social category membership. However, they have ideological and theoretical limitations.

Dummy variable analyses can have subtle ideological effects. Privilege is normalized in daily life through the way we differentially mark people. Gender seems to be about women, race seems to be about people of color, and economic inequality seems to be the property of the poor. This cultural pattern has often been expressed in researchers' selection of categories to flag, for example, women rather than men, African Americans and Hispanics rather than whites of European origin. When category membership has a significant effect, then, our attention is drawn to the problems of the lower status category and not to the privileges of those who are in relationships of dominance over them. Think what a causal model would look like if the reference group were single poor women of color caring for children, and if terms were incorporated to reflect the increments to being white, male, economically privileged, and/or childless.

Dummy variable models also have the analytic and theoretical limitations of the individual level of analysis. For example, a central tenet of much contemporary feminist theory is intersectionality—the impact of gender depends on a person's race and class, how race works depends on a person's gender and class, and so on. For example, in some contexts age may enhance men's outcomes but decrease women's. The dummy variable approach is not able to address the claim that causal forces may work differently—have different degrees of strength or even work in different directions—depending on group membership. This approach provides an aggregate picture of who ends up where in the distribution of variables, but not a sense of *how* they get there.

Another strategy is to incorporate interaction terms in the model. Interaction terms examine the difference in the impact of a variable on outcomes for members of a particular subgroup. Thus they begin to link group membership with specific kinds of effects, moving us in the direction of seeing exactly where it is that race and/or gender and/or class matter in determining people's outcomes. Interaction terms also derive their meaning by comparison with some "excluded" category or categories. For example, a model estimates the way being female changes the coefficient of a particular variable; the implicit message is that there is a normal, more direct set of processes that get distorted in certain cases. As long as researchers specify a single causal model, even though they incorporate multiple interaction terms, they are de facto defining some social category or process as normal.

A strategy that is more sensitive to potential dynamics of power relations in an unequal society is to fit separate models to distinct groups. This "separate models" approach allows investigators to see how the mix of causal factors might change in different intersections of race, gender, and class. It also facilitates a direct comparison of a model's overall explanatory power across these intersections. Of course, a separate models strategy has its own problems. It will often require larger samples and oversampling of less common groups. Further, the choice of which groups merit separate analysis is just as value-based as the choice to analyze only one group. The important point is that the organization of the analysis into specific models involves value-based choices.

To summarize, conventional quantitative methodologies tend to embody the standpoint of privileged groups. Measures emphasize the experiences and interests of men, particularly of privileged men. While samples are generally more representative than in qualitative research, what biases do exist tend to underrepresent the economically and culturally marginalized. The predominance of the individual level of analysis obscures contextual features contributing to observed outcomes, making it hard to see social solutions to social problems. Statistical analyses tend to emphasize technique over substance and to construct variations in position in social relations along the dichotomy that underlies all social relations of power: normal/other.

At the same time, the transparency of quantitative methodological practices has facilitated critiques of them. Scholars have been able to look, for example, at an approach to measurement and examine its adequacy. Still, feminist methodological discussions have tended to stay at the level of criticism of mainstream quantitative methodology, much less rarely discussing alternative strategies. There is, however, one vibrant body of literature that offers first clues on how to proceed: quantitative research done by feminists.

HOW FEMINISTS USE QUANTITATIVE METHODS

While discussions of quantitative methodology through a feminist lens are rare, feminists who use quantitative methods in their research are not. A good first step in exploring how to use quantitative methods in critical ways, then, is to go to those who are working in the intersection of feminist and quantitative social science discourses. In order to develop a sample of quantitative work by feminist scholars, I asked a group of prominent feminist sociologists who are doing quantitative research to name their favorite papers in that genre, including their own work. My strategy here was to tap their technical knowledge in combination with their feminist sensibilities in a kind of "gut response" index.

There are obviously biases in this sampling strategy. It is dependent on my own personal and professional networks.[1] In asking scholars with national prominence, I am selecting those who regularly make it through the gatekeepers of our top journals, a reasonable indication of their strong technical competence. It may be, though, that other equally competent scholars whose projects and standards differ more radically from the mainstream are excluded from this pool. Further, the articles I have identified are concentrated in a few substantive areas—stratification, work, family, politics, medical sociology, and social psychology. Although these have been crucial areas in the development of feminist sociology, there are obviously other important areas that are excluded here. Still, the researchers in this sample are highly skilled; their work is respected by their peers within and outside feminist discourse. It is worth seriously considering their approaches.

Feminist Exemplars

How do these feminists do quantitative research? Do their practices differ in any systematic way from those identified as problematic by the critics of quantitative sociology? If there are methodological adjustments, are these adjustments clues to how to address problems identified by the critics of quantitative sociology? I want to begin by sharing a little glimpse of what I found fascinating about this sample—the findings and interpretations—by describing five studies that illustrate some of the general patterns I found and will describe later.

Brines: How Couples Divide Housework

Julie Brines (1994) used data from the Panel Study of Income Dynamics, a national survey of members of families (oversampling poor families) that began in 1968 and has continued annually since then (http://psidonline.isr.umich .edu). Brines's goal was to find out why it is that even though many women are working for wages, unpaid housework still remains *women's* work. For many years social exchange theory has attempted to explain this "bad deal" for women in economic terms—women cannot strike a better bargain at home because they have lower incomes, their alternatives are more limited, and/or their contributions to the relationship are not as easily transferred to another relationship. By comparison, men's higher earning potential and social status are independent of any specific personal relationships, and thus much more transportable assets. From this perspective, the greater a woman's economic independence from the relationship, the less housework she should do.

Brines found that an economic imbalance between partners was not the only important determinant of who does more housework; reaffirming one's partner's and one's own gender identity was a major factor as well. For example, while men who had been unemployed for a *short* time *did* increase their work around the house, those who had been unemployed *for many months* (and thus had lots of time) did no more housework than men who were employed full-time. Similarly, while up to a point women's hours of housework decreased as their proportion of household earnings increased, those women who were sole providers or close to it actually did *more* housework than women whose proportionate contribution to household income was lower. When household economic circumstances might otherwise undercut men's ability to display masculinity and women's to display femininity in culturally defined ways, the couples compensate: men end up doing less housework, and women do more.

Glass and Camarigg: The "Flexibility" of Women's Jobs

Some economists argue that women are in lower paid, more marginal jobs out of *choice*, because those jobs are less demanding and more flexible, and thus fit better with their family responsibilities. Jennifer Glass and Valerie Camarigg (1992) looked at data from the 1977 Quality of Employment Survey, which asked a national sample about their working conditions, job satisfaction, and the degree to which work interferes with other dimensions of life (www.icpsr.umich.edu:8080/ICPSR-STUDY/07689.xml). They found that the people *most* likely to be in jobs that were compatible with parenting (flexible about scheduling and not highly strenuous mentally or physically) were actually *men without dependent children.* In fact, the best predictor of being in a job that was compatible with parenting responsibilities was gender—men were more likely to be in these jobs. The jobs that conflicted most with family responsibilities for women were blue-collar and professional jobs, though even here the gender pattern was opposite the stereotype. The jobs that *men* held in these occupational groupings were more compatible with parenting than were women's jobs. On average, job compatibility with family life was the worst for those women with dependent children, especially those who worked in firms of more than 100 employees.

LeClere, Rogers, and Peters: What's Killing Black Women

White and African American women have about the same incidence of heart disease, but African American women's death rates from it are more than twice as high. Since stress is a known factor exacerbating heart disease, Felicia LeClere, Richard Rogers, and Kimberley Peters (1998) asked how much of this difference could be explained by the way structural racism creates a correlation between race and the amount of stress in one's social context. Racial segregation creates neighborhoods in which there are concentrations of African American people who are poor and in single-parent families. Neighbors in poor communities, especially African American ones, tend to be tied in reciprocal relations of support. Racial and economic segregation means that African Americans are more likely to be living near relatives than are whites, increasing the likelihood of reciprocal relationships in their neighborhoods. While social ties can be important sources of support, these researchers reasoned, they can also be sources of stress. Social relationships entail sets of obligations that poor women, especially single parents, may not have the financial resources, time, and/or energy to meet.

LeClere, Rogers, and Peters (1998) used data from the National Health Interview Survey (www.cdc.gov/nchs/nhis.htm), which gave them information about individual attributes such as body mass index, preexisting medical conditions, per capita income, education, marital status, and employment status. They linked this information with death certificates in the National Death Index (www.cdc.gov/nchs/r&d/ndi/ndi.htm) and information about people's neighborhoods from the U.S. Census (www.census.gov/). Integrating these data allowed them to control for individual factors contributing to mortality as they looked at the impact of neighborhood factors. Measures of neighborhood context included the degree of racial segregation, median household income, concentration of people at extreme levels of poverty (at or below 75 percent of the poverty level), amount of unemployment, number receiving public assistance, and proportion of households that were single-parent and headed by women. LeClere, Rogers, and Peters found that these neighborhood conditions were all significant predictors of a woman's likelihood of dying from heart disease. Further, each of the other measures of social context was no longer significant once they entered a measure of neighborhood concentration of female headship into the model. These findings suggest that a direct consequence of race discrimination is "poor health and early death" (LeClere, Rogers, and Peters 1998: 104) for African American women.

Carli: Gendered Speech Patterns

Linda Carli (1990) used an experimental design to investigate a common perception of gender differences in speech patterns. We have heard a lot about how women speak more tentatively than men, using more hedges (e.g., "sort of") and disclaimers (e.g., "I'm no expert, but . . ."), more intensifiers (e.g., "awfully") and verbal reinforcers in support of another's speech (e.g., "yeh" and "uh-huh"). The typical conclusion is that in speaking tentatively, women communicate that they are not competent. In effect, if women are not being taken seriously, it is our own fault.

Carli (1990) argued that while hedges and disclaimers do communicate tentativeness, intensifiers and verbal reinforcers more accurately display expressiveness, a social connection with the speech partner. In one experiment Carli identified topics that were controversial on her campus but on which there appeared to be no sex difference in opinions (the drinking age and free day care). She randomly selected students to form mixed and same-sex pairs, each of which were to discuss topics on which the parties disagreed, videotaped the discussions, and had observers code speech patterns. After the discussions Carli asked subjects to indicate what their current feelings were on the issue they had just discussed, as well as to rate each other on competence and likeability.

What Carli found was that women's speech patterns varied with the gender composition of the group: they used more tentative speech with men and more expressive speech with other women. Men's speech patterns did not vary with the gender composition of the group. Carli also found that women who spoke more tentatively were more likely to persuade men, but those who used more assertive speech were more persuasive to other women. Men, regardless of their style of speaking and the gender composition of the group, exerted more influence than women did. Putting these two findings together, Carli argued that women seem to be using tentative speech strategically, to be persuasive to men. Since we interpret assertiveness in women as a sign of competence, Carli's findings imply that women have to choose between appearing competent to men and being able to persuade them.

Ridgeway: Gender and Influence in Groups

Cecilia Ridgeway (1982), also using experiments, gives another angle on the dynamics of influence in work groups. Previous work had shown that groups tend to be most influenced by members who seem to have the most to contribute to the successful completion of the task. In the absence of specific information, however, group members tend to fall back on the speakers' social status outside the group. We assume, for example, that men have competence in most areas, but that women do not. Thus men exercise more influence in groups overall.

Ridgeway was interested in figuring out what women could do to counter the handicap of their lower social status on their ability to influence work groups. She suspected that their influence might depend on whether the women appeared to be motivated by the desire to serve the group rather than their own self-interest. She ran an experiment in which groups of four, including one confederate, were given a task to accomplish—to decide on a meaning for nonsense syllables that were represented as words from a primitive language. Ridgeway wanted to know the conditions under which a confederate was able to convince other group members of a particular definition. Confederates gave cues to indicate that they were either self-oriented or group-oriented. Group-oriented confederates were friendly and supportive and said things about the group's getting it right being the most important thing. Self-oriented confederates were more detached and a little critical, and communicated that they were interested in earning points for themselves.

Ridgeway found that male confederates were more influential overall, and that their apparent motivation did not matter. However, women's apparent motivation for participating made a significant difference in how much influence they exercised. In speaking with men, women who conveyed that their primary interest was in the group and its success, rather than their own personal gain, had more influence. This strategy did not work when women were trying to persuade other women, though. Women did not *like* the self-oriented woman but were more willing to be *influenced* by her than by the group-oriented woman. (Note the parallels with Carli's findings.)

There are many more examples like these, research using quantitative methods that provides fascinating and important insights about social process and social structure. These are projects that reveal power and injustice where we might have missed it, and they help us think of what we might do to address problems. Does this mean that feminist and other critiques of mainstream quantitative methods are wrongheaded, or are these feminist researchers making substantive changes in how they use quantitative methods? I want to suggest the latter—that we are seeing the emergence of distinctive methodological patterns, specifically in the kinds of questions asked, the ways measures are developed, and the organization of the analysis.

What Kinds of Questions Are Feminist Exemplars Asking?

Perhaps the most striking feature of these research projects is the questions they ask. The papers in my sample tended to address issues that can be described as one or more of four categories of questions. Some focus on the idea of essentialism: are women really a different kind (other)? Others move to an analysis of how inequality gets created in social interaction. Another agenda examines the construction of inequality in more institutionalized but still changeable practices. A fourth category of research is directed toward providing the analysis needed for specific political struggles. In what follows, I will provide examples of each.

Are Women Really a Different Kind of Human Being?

Feminists have used quantitative methods to challenge the mainstream assumption that sex differences are innate. As I mentioned in chapter 1, mainstream science has been asking questions about the differences between men and women for at least a century, and the dominant tendency has been to construct women and men into an essential dichotomy, represented most explicitly in popular culture by notions like the one that "men are from Mars and women are from Venus." Feminist quantitative scholarship has often taken the form of respecifying questions, from essentialist ideas about the naturalness of gender differences in behaviors and outcomes to questions that ask how gendered patterns might be responses to imbalances in power.

For example, in the study described above, Carli responded to the essentialist approach to conceptualizing observed gender differences in speaking patterns by posing an explicitly political alternative: are women responding to situations strategically? As another example addressing communication differences, Peter Kollock, Philip Blumstein, and Pepper Schwartz (1985) asked whether it was sex that best explained domestic partners' participation in doing the work of and dominating the content of a conversation, or was it the person's relative power in the relationship? Denise Bielby and William Bielby (1988) asked if the data actually support the popular assumption that the reason men receive higher pay than women is that men have harder jobs and work harder on the job. I (Sprague 1991) examined how much gender differences in political attitudes could be explained by gender differences in power and responsibility, both in the home and in the workplace. At a different level of analysis, Ridgeway (1987) challenged the notion that social organization is inherently masculine, that is, built on macho dominance contests, by asking whether groups responded more to dominance and threat than to signs of competence.

How Does Inequality Get Created in Social Interaction?

A second set of studies moves our attention from challenging the idea of essentialism to asking whether and how we create or legitimate social inequality through the way we perceive and evaluate one another. Ridgeway's study described earlier is a good example of this category. She asks two key questions: how does social status get translated into handicaps in interacting in decision-making groups, and what can women or other low-status people do to combat the tendency of work groups to discount their contributions? In other work, Ridgeway (1988; Ridgeway et al. 1985) asks how people's awareness of their relatively lower social status in a decision-making group makes them less confident and leads them to behave in ways that are subsequently taken as evidence of their lack of competence.

Students of attribution processes have established the tendency in our culture to blame victims for their misfortunes, but Judith Howard (1984) asked whether we respond differently to male and female victims. She found that when people do blame victims for their victimization, they are more likely to blame women's characteristics (e.g., poor judgment, trusting nature, carelessness) and men's behaviors (e.g., did not fight back, looked scared, did not try to escape). That is, they explain women's victimization in terms of something that is harder to change. Further, people tend to see men who have been victimized in more feminine terms than men who have not, suggesting that the fact of victimization is a feminizing attribute in our culture.

Is Women's Lower Status Voluntary?

This is perhaps the kind of question most frequently asked by these feminists. Two examples of survey research I described earlier challenge the basis for the common assumption that women's lower social position is a matter of personal choice. Glass and Camarigg asked whether it made sense to conclude that the reason women are in low-status, low-paid jobs is that those jobs are more compatible with their domestic responsibilities. Brines asked whether it made sense to think that women do a disproportionate share of the housework because they are balancing their contribution at home with the higher value of their male partner's income and status contributions. Many feminist researchers have asked how social relationships in the home influence women's and men's relative attainment in the workplace. For example, Shelley Coverman (1983) asked about the impact of women's higher burden of domestic labor at home on their ability to earn an income comparable to men's at work. As another example, William Bielby and Denise Bielby (1992) noted that part of the gender gap in earnings could be the outcome of married women's greater reluctance to move for job reasons. This reluctance depresses women's earnings relative to men's in two ways: it decreases the pressure on employers to pay married women employees competitive salaries, and when couples move for the man's job, it usually increases the man's salary and decreases the woman's (Bielby and Bielby 1992). Neoclassical economics argues that women are reluctant to move for a job because of a family's rational calculation of whose career is important to invest in. Bielby and Bielby (1992) ask whether better predictors might be people's gender role ideologies and how their beliefs about the appropriate roles for men and women determine who in a household is more involved in caring for the children, and thus more sensitive to the impact of moving on children's lives.

Do Institutionalized Practices Create Inequality?

Many feminists have used quantitative methods to ask whether workplaces are treating men and women equally. Barbara Reskin and Catherine Ross (1992) asked whether organizations accord women managers the same amount of authority and pay as men with similar responsibilities and skills. Paula England and her colleagues (England et al. 1994) asked whether sex differences in pay are the consequence of differences in education, experience, and demands of the jobs men and women are in, or whether the kind of work women are typically assigned to, taking care of people, is being devalued.

Other quantitative feminists take an even broader view, asking how local and even national contexts can be organized in ways that either facilitate or inhibit gender equality. The study I described by LeClere and her colleagues asked how the imprint of racial segregation and economic discrimination on their neighborhoods explained African American women's higher mortality from heart disease. Kristen Harknett and her colleagues (2003) asked whether variations in public expenditures on children across the 50 states explain variations in the health and mortality, learning, and level of poverty of their children, and rates of dropping out of high school, pregnancy, and criminal arrest among their teenagers.

David Cotter and his colleagues (1997) asked whether a high level of occupational sex segregation in a metropolitan area can increase the pay of all men and decrease the pay of all women, regardless of what jobs they are in. Rachel Rosenfeld and Arne Kalleberg (1990) asked whether government involvement in employment policies can reduce gender inequality, specifically examining whether nations that are actively involved with employers and workers setting employment policy and that institute family-friendly policies have smaller gender gaps in earnings. Janet Gornick and Jerry Jacobs (1998) asked if public sector employment is a good avenue for increasing gender equality, increasing women's access to jobs, and increasing their income relative to men. Also, if women do earn more in public sector employment, they asked, is it because the public sector pays better across jobs, or because it has a higher proportion of the kind of jobs that are relatively high-paying, that is, managerial and professional jobs?

Serving Specific Struggles for Social Equality

Another cluster of papers provides the data and analyses needed to support specific struggles for gender and other forms of social equality. As part of the struggle for comparable worth, several of these feminist scholars are using quantitative methods to ask whether existing forms of salary determination are biased in favor of whites and of men. Ronnie Steinberg (1995; Steinberg and Haignere 1987), working in collaboration with labor unions in several states, asked whether the dominant technique for evaluating jobs to determine pay, the Hay system, was biased toward men, especially managers. The goal was to develop fairer systems for work evaluation so that employers could be encouraged, or legally forced, to adopt them.

Myra Marx Ferree and Julia McQuillan (1998) were asked to participate in a pay equity study at a state medical school and found that faculty and administration on the investigating committee were operating under different models of how inequity is produced. Administrators saw gender discrimination as the product of individual acts of discrimination, while the faculty saw institutional factors also at work: factors like gender bias in the evaluation of skills, the internal labor market, and reliance on market value in an external market that devalues women. Arguing that the usual methods for doing equity studies were geared to the individual model, Ferree and McQuillan posed the question of what statistical technique would help in detecting an institutional level of gender discrimination.

The political debate over the Family Medical Leave Act was initially organized around the issue of whether such legislation was too expensive for employers and for the economy. Employers were claiming that the cost of the leg-islation was the full cost of hiring and training replacements. When support-ers of the legislation came to them for research on the issue, Roberta Spalter-Roth and Heidi Hartmann (1991) countered with the argument that replacement costs also exist if the employee is fired for missing work. They maintained that the only additional cost of protecting those jobs was the cost of maintaining health insurance premiums while employees are taking care of infants or sick family members. Spalter-Roth and Hartmann turned the ques-tion on its head by also asking about the cost to business, and to taxpayers and society more broadly, of *failing* to protect the jobs of workers who had family responsibilities or medical needs.

To summarize, some of these feminist quantitative researchers are re-sponding to the specific needs of movements to increase equality. All of them are asking questions about the naturalness of gender differences, including challenging the notion that women are essentially different than men, explor-ing the situational features that lead women and men to make different choices, and identifying the structural features that produce gender differ-ences in outcomes.

What Measures Do They Use?

Many of these quantitative feminists use standard measures. Spalter-Roth and Hartmann (1991) give a sound practical reason for doing so: critical scholars have to use measures and methods that are widely accepted in order to have any legitimacy in political debates. Using alternative measures opens critical researchers up to charges that their findings are merely artifacts of their unusual methods. Still, there are many instances of feminists using in-novative approaches to measurement.

Unpacking Assumptions in Prevailing Measures

In many cases, feminist researchers uncover the narrowness and gender-blindness of standard approaches by unpacking assumptions embedded in them. For example, economists had long used the concepts of division of la-bor and labor markets in analyzing the organization of work. Feminists intro-duced ways of expanding these concepts by tapping how both labor markets and jobs are organized by gender. Looking at occupational segregation by sex by taking into account the percentage of workers in an occupation who are women, for example, has helped researchers examine the degree to which women's segregation into certain low-paying occupations explains the overall gender gap in pay (e.g., England et al. 1994, 1996; Reskin and Roos 1990; Tomaskovic-Devey 1993). Cotter and his colleagues (1997) brought the notion of occupational segregation by sex closer to a concrete social context by operationalizing it as a variable feature of the organization of the labor force in a metropolitan area, analogous to variations in the degree of residential segregation by race from one community to another.

Ferree and McQuillan (1998) expanded the idea of wage discrimination beyond specific cases of intentional discrimination to include biases in institutionalized standards for evaluating worth, like pegging the worth of academic jobs to those in the job market outside the academy, with its well-documented gender biases. In the same vein, England and her colleagues (1994) criticized the standard approach to measuring job skills in the research literature on how wages are determined in jobs, noting that standard practices take into account cognitive skills and physical skills but not social skills. To tap social skills, they developed measures of the nurturing component of jobs, including whether duties included significant face-to-face contact with clients or customers, and how much the work involved helping or supporting the development of people.

Sometimes these researchers ask whether a particular conceptualization glosses over distinctions that are important to retain. For example, Carli, in the experiment described earlier, unpacked the popular notion of "feminine speech" and found two distinct forms with contrasting functions—one to enact submissiveness and the other to express social connection. This allowed her to confront connotations of natural feminine difference with indicators that could tap strategic speech strategies. Similarly, in experiments on what behaviors produce leadership in groups, Ridgeway (1987) decomposed the construct of dominant behavior into two dimensions: cues that involve threat (staring, shouting, commanding) and cues that involve competence (quick response, confident tone).

Drawing on Everyday Discourse

Some of these researchers draw their measures from the language and issues of everyday life. Carli (1990) used a hot issue on her campus—whether or not students should have to start paying for riding campus buses—in the experiment in which confederates tested the effectiveness of contrasting persuasive approaches among men and women. Howard and Pike (1986) gave their subjects text taken from transcripts of actual parole board hearings to generate attributions about the causes and blameworthiness of a criminal's behavior.

Several researchers use self-reports to measure objective situations, in order to avoid the systematic gender bias of measures commonly used in the literature. Finding bias in job descriptions in the conventional standard, *The Dictionary of Occupational Titles*, Glass and Camarigg (1992), in the study described earlier, chose workers' own assessments as the more reliable estimate of the amount of stress and autonomy associated with their jobs. Similarly, Bielby and Bielby (1988) used employees' reports of the mental and physical demands of their jobs and how hard they worked at them to avoid the gender bias in conventional measures of work effort. Reskin and Ross (1992) rejected the biased census classification of occupations in favor of simply asking workers if they had supervisory responsibility. Bielby and Bielby (1992) asked survey respondents who indicated on a closed-ended scale that they were not very willing to move for a job an open-ended follow-up, "Why not?" in order to assess whether the reluctance was due to family responsibilities.

These researchers recognize that respondents are not immune to the biases in hegemonic ideology, biases that can shape their understandings of their lives. Each of them uses multiple indicators to maximize the reliability of their measures and statistical procedures to check for construct and/or criterion validity. For example, Glass and Camarigg examined the correlation between their index measuring the family compatibility of a job and a standard item in which respondents indicated the degree of conflict they experienced between work and family. Similarly, Bielby and Bielby checked to see if their measure of work effort varied in predicted ways with the age of the employee—highest among the young, moderate among the middle-aged, and lowest among the oldest.

As I argued in chapter 3, the discourses to which people have access are not necessarily constructed from their standpoints, and that can depress the reliability of self-reports in some contexts. Ronnie Steinberg and Lois Haignere faced such a situation when they wanted to develop unbiased measures of job content. Most pay systems are based on a detailed description of a job—skills, stresses, responsibilities—but existing systems often overlook "compensable aspects" of jobs that have historically been done by women or minority men.

However, Steinberg and Haignere could not just ask people to describe their job in an open-ended format, because research shows that women underdescribe and men overdescribe their jobs; self-reports would likely contribute both gender and class bias to the data. They also worried that open-ended reporting on this topic requires conceptual and verbal skills, and that those with less education would not be as effective in detailing their job components (1987: 166).

Steinberg and Haignere designed a multistage strategy that is an excellent illustration of how to balance respondents' perspectives with those available to researchers. First they developed a comprehensive list of possible job attributes, by talking with lots of different workers in a wide variety of jobs. Then they provided this list to employees, who rated their jobs on each attribute. Finally, they calculated average scores on attributes for each job and used factor analysis to identify dimensions of job content.

Some feminist quantitative researchers work to control for gender biases in composite measures by examining covariances among indicators separately by sex. Howard (1987) developed a measurement model for the structure of attributions made by subjects in an experiment by analyzing correlation matrices for men and women separately and choosing the model that best fit both. I (Sprague 1989) developed a measurement model for the structure of political attitudes on the pattern of covariance among responses by female respondents, then tested the adequacy of fit of the model on male respondents. Ridgeway (1987) used women as a generic case. She ran experiments on group dynamics on all female subjects and argued that the results were reasonably generalizable to men.

Building from Marginalized Standpoints

Many of these researchers are constructing new variables from the standpoint of women and devalued groups. This strategy is frequently more complex than simply relying on self-reports—it amounts to taking the situation of marginalized and devalued people as normal, and taking their knowledge, skills, and strategies seriously. Two of the studies I described at the outset illustrate this practice. Glass and Camarigg developed the notion of a job having more or less compatibility with family responsibilities, operationalizing the family compatibility of a job as a function of mental and physical strain on the one hand, and degree of flexibility of work rules and scheduling on the other. LeClere, Rogers, and Peters developed measures of the stressfulness of a person's neighborhood that are sensitive to the interaction between race, economic and residential discrimination, and demands on women for care work.

There are many more cases. For example, Annemette Sorensen and Sara McLanahan (1987) conceptualized a partner's economic dependency on his or her spouse as the proportion of pooled household income that the partner him- or herself contributes. Spalter-Roth and Hartmann (1991) introduced new variables into the debate over family/medical leave, all of which shift attention to interests previously excluded from the discussion, those of workers, taxpayers, and through them, the broader society. These researchers developed ways of estimating the costs to workers and taxpayers of not having employees' jobs protected. They measured costs to women workers by comparing wage rates, hours of work, and hours of housework in the years prior to and following the birth of a child or an extended illness. They used higher transfer payments, including food stamps, AFDC, and unemployment compensation, as indicators of costs to taxpayers.

In general, by unpacking the assumptions in prevailing measures, drawing on the discourses and challenges of everyday life, and building measures that center on the experiences and issues facing the marginalized, these feminist researchers are shifting from conventional approaches to measurement toward the standpoints of everyday people.

How Do They Organize Their Analyses?

The researchers in this sample employ a range of approaches to specifying statistical models. Some focus on direct comparisons of conventional models with models that include measures of gender and other dimensions of social inequality. Others estimate the effects of variables on socially distinct groups in separate equations.

Comparing Models with and without Controls for Gender

In some of these projects, the analysis adopts the strategy of showing how mainstream approaches are limited by their inattention to gender. Researchers build a model that includes all the conventional explanations that have been offered for why groups have different outcomes and estimate how well observed gender differences are explained by those factors. In a second stage, sex or some dimension of gender bias is added as an additional causal variable to see if it is still a significant predictor of inequality. If the effect of a gender measure is significant after controlling for an exhaustive list of other potential causes, its impact is interpreted as indicating some form of discrimination. For example, LeClere, Rogers, and Peters (1998) first used age and race, then added known health risk factors like hypertension, diabetes, and adiposity, and then individual social attributes like SES (socioeconomic status) and marital status to predict the relative risk of death from heart disease. At each stage the race difference decreased, but it actually reversed in the fourth step, when they added rates of female headship in the neighborhood to the model.

Similarly, England and her colleagues (1994, 1996) tested the limitations of conventional, gender-blind economic models explaining wage differences by specifying an equation that estimates the impact on wages of a wide array of occupational features (authority, cognitive and physical skills, discomfort or danger, economic sector, region of the country) and characteristics of the worker (education, experience). Then they added measures of gender discrimination to the equation, including the earnings impact of the proportion of women in an occupation and whether or not that occupation involves taking care of people. Bielby and Bielby (1992) first used the variables that neoclassical economists use to predict a worker's reluctance to relocate for a job. In a second step they added indicators of gendered considerations like information about the spouse's job and whether or not the worker subscribed to traditional gender ideology. Comparing the variance explained before and after including gender measures in the model provides clear evidence about the (in)adequacy of gender-blind explanations.

Many of these scholars look for interactions of causal factors with gender and other dimensions of social inequality. That is, they explore how discrimination is not an "add-on" to legitimate causes, but rather, whether the standards we are applying are not applied in the same ways to men and women, whites and others. Survey researchers sometimes include interaction terms within a single equation. For example, Reskin and Ross (1992) tested the significance of the interactions between sex of the manager and all of the other causal variables they used to predict wages, and kept those terms that were statistically significant in their final model.

Analyzing Groups Separately

Another approach is to do separate analyses on socially distinct groups of people. For example, Brines (1994) calculated the impact of economic dependency on hours of housework separately for men and for women. Similarly, Spalter-Roth and Hartmann (1991) separately explored the costs of birth for African American and white women employees, and the costs of major illness for white men, African American men, African American women, and white women. Rosenfeld and Kalleberg (1990) and Gornick and Jacobs (1998) looked at the determinants of men's and women's income separately in each of the countries they studied.

Feminist experimenters build gender interactions into their designs by creating distinct experimental conditions. Both Carli, in her study about the impact of assertive versus tentative speech on influence, and Ridgeway, looking at the impact of apparent motivation on interpersonal influence, had separate conditions for each combination of sex of confederate and sex of subject. Howard and Pike (1986) had subjects read transcripts of two interviews—one of a man under arrest, and the other of a man applying for unemployment benefits—in one of four conditions to cover each combination of race (Black, White) and class (working class, middle class).

The persuasive power of analyzing groups separately emerges in the way this strategy has been used in struggles for pay equity, as Ferree and McQuillan (1998) show in their analysis of pay determination at an academic workplace. The common view of administrators is to see gender pay inequity as the result of evaluations by individual "bad actors," so they look only for individual cases of discrimination. Typically, they compare men and women in a particular department or a set of related departments, and they tend to only consider the cases of those women at the bottom end of the income distribution. Such a strategy cannot detect systematic gender biases in standard evaluation practices throughout the institution, biases such as devaluing specialty areas with more women, devaluing indicators of women's success, and using outside offers—a career path that women are more reluctant to consider—to spur pay raises.

Ferree and McQuillan suggest that in order to capture institutional discrimination, equations should be estimated on the total male population at an institution to generate coefficients to fit to the total female workforce at that institution. The pattern of residuals, reflecting excluded variables that should impact income such as variations in productivity and skill, should be normally distributed with the same mean for both men and women. To the extent that the distribution for women departs from that for men, there is statistical evidence for institutionalized pay inequity.

There is one striking commonality across each of these studies: every one of the above examples added significantly to the power of the models being developed. New questions accounted for discrepancies in the literature. Changed measures demonstrated significant effects and greatly enhanced the amount of variation explained. Interaction terms were often significant. Separate statistical models revealed different strengths or patterns of relationships. By fairly conventional methodological criteria, counting like feminists seems to pay off in improving our understanding of social structures and social processes.

CONCLUSION

Admittedly this analysis is limited, but given this sample, it does seem that feminists laboring in the quantitative trenches are responding to the criticisms that critical scholars, particularly feminist ones, have made of social science. How far have these efforts taken quantitative methodology toward the standards implied by standpoint epistemology?

(1) Work from the Standpoint of the Disadvantaged   This guideline is particularly challenging for researchers employing quantitative methods that operate at fairly high levels of abstraction from lived experience and entail high levels of researcher control over the collection and interpretation of data. Yet all of these projects are challenging the naturalness of existing inequalities, and these are questions that are posed from the standpoint of those on the downside of social hierarchies. By interrogating conventional assumptions or traditional accounts for why the inequality exists, revealing the biases embedded in allegedly objective social processes or policies, challenging the notions of inherent differences between men and women by locating personal attributes and actions in social contexts, and reframing contemporary debates about the equity of social policy, these feminist quantitative researchers ask questions that problematize inequality and privilege.

Many of these researchers are drawing on the standpoints of women and other disadvantaged people in developing new measures. They develop variables that identify and make visible the processes through which gender inequality operates in everyday life. They organize data from a different perspective than has traditionally prevailed—the perspective of everyday social actors, particularly women. Further, the design of many of these analyses challenges the notion of a "normal" subject or respondent. At a minimum, investigators check for the possibility of interaction effects on major dimensions of social power and inequality like gender, class, and race. Often they build on the notion that social processes will work differently based on these power dimensions, through separate conditions in experiments and separate statistical analyses in surveys.

(2) Ground Interpretations in Interests and Experience These researchers are mindful of the ways standard measures may express the standpoint of privileged men. Many challenge conventional approaches to measurement in their literatures and develop alternative measures by centering on issues and experiences common in the daily lives of women and other disadvantaged people. They use the realities of those lives to specify the domain of content from which to sample to create more valid measures. As a result, they have constructed variables that identify and make visible the processes through which gender and other relations of inequality operate in everyday life. They put credence in the ability of regular social actors to provide accounts of their objective situations that may be more adequate than conventional measures. At the same time, they incorporate procedures to compensate for the ways dominant ideologies might shape these actors' perceptions. Thus they explicitly take privilege and power into account as they develop measures.

Another set of interpretations that could and should be grounded is the researchers' own. This practice is less common, though a couple of authors put their current project in a biographical context, for example, working on a federal commission or serving as a consultant in a dispute. Current publication standards, particularly in the "top" journals, make biographical considerations hard to incorporate, even if the author wanted to do so. But feminist standpoint epistemology implies that each of us should ask ourselves questions about the connection between our personal biographies and material interests and the questions we pursue and the arguments we find compelling throughout the lifetime of each project. And, as I argued in chapter 3, we should be particularly careful about jumping to conclusions that serve our own interests—for example, that gender doesn't matter if we are male, that class doesn't matter if we are economically comfortable, or that race is not interesting or important if we are white.

(3) Maintain a Strategically Diverse Discourse One indicator of the larger discourse in which that project is embedded is the literature review, an

indicator of whom researchers are "listening" to. A scholarly discourse can be homogeneous or diverse in many ways, including race, class, and gender, area of expertise, and methods used. Discussions of literature in most of the papers in this sample are actively integrating feminist critiques with standard mainstream scholarship. On the other hand, the literature reviews in these papers tend not to discuss qualitative work, evidence of the chasm between qualitative and quantitative research. Yet critical quantitative researchers can use qualitative findings to help compensate for the abstract character of their methods and gain more access to alternative standpoints.

Another indicator of the degree of diversity in the discourse is whom the researchers seem to be "talking" to by virtue of the language through which they speak. Feminist quantitative researchers have not, for the most part, developed writing strategies that allow any broader communication than the reports of more conventional quantitative research. Here is an illustrative clip:

> Both the linear and the cubic polynomial specifications are consistent with the premises of the dependency perspective, the latter attempting to model the consequences of cumulative advantage or disadvantage. The second-order model, on the other hand, reflects the functional form of the effect under the gender display perspective.

Certainly this text is interpretable, but it takes active translating, even for trained researchers. I often found myself struggling with dense jargon and a tendency to speak in equations as I read these papers, particularly those outside my areas of expertise. Jargon is a form of shorthand that saves communication time, and equations illustrate the logic of analytic procedures succinctly. However, assuming that readers have high levels of familiarity with specialized terminology and statistics is assuming that the readers are very much like the authors.

(4) Create Knowledge That Empowers the Disadvantaged A central goal of these research projects is to identify the contextual features that produce and reproduce systematic differences in outcomes of individuals, from the gender composition of the parties in interaction to the gendered organization of local neighborhoods, to gender segregation in local and national labor forces. Quantitative research by feminists, including many discussed in this chapter, has formed the basis for testimony by expert witnesses in legal pro-

ceedings or before legislators and other policy makers, striking evidence of the potential of these methods to help the disadvantaged.

These authors frequently directly address implications of findings for social change. They relate their findings to public debates on issues, particularly in terms of the interests of women, people of color, and/or people in more exploited positions in class relations. Some of these researchers suggest strategies that women and other disadvantaged readers could adopt in their own everyday lives, for example, to exercise more influence in decision-making groups or to shape pay-equity studies at their workplaces. On the other hand, sophisticated analyses and restrictive language limit the degree to which quantitative research findings will directly empower people other than experts.

Still, these feminist researchers have used some strategies to implement quantitative methods that provide the basis for critical researchers to continue the effort. They are helping us see how we might make social research really count for large numbers of people.

NOTE
1. These run through the Sex and Gender section of the American Sociological Association, Sociologists for Women in Society, and the *Gender Lens* book series.

5

Qualitative Shifts: Feminist Strategies in Field Research and Interviewing

Qualitative methods are a diverse lot, including in-depth interviewing, field observation, the analysis of historical documents, and the analysis of visual and verbal discourses. Each of these strategies could be employed quantitatively, too. What makes their use qualitative is *how* they are used—the way researchers collect and analyze the data. Qualitative approaches emphasize interpretation and nuance; researchers address interviews, texts, and observation with an intensive focus, seeking a detailed analysis of process and/or meanings—what Clifford Geertz (1973) described as "thick description."

For example, researchers use in-depth interviews to get people's "witness accounts of the social world," to encourage interviewees to reflect on their experiences or beliefs, or to provide segments of talk that researchers can analyze to learn about their inner worlds (Hammersley 2003: 120; cf. Weiss 1994). Researchers doing fieldwork spend time in the places where people live, work, play, and so on, to learn about and describe some aspect of a group's way of life, both its practices and their meanings for the members of the group (Agar 1986; Emerson 2001; Lofland and Lofland 1995). Researchers use historical records and analyze documents, diaries, and other remnants of material culture to piece together how things were in an earlier time (Blee 1991; Honey 1984). They analyze cultural artifacts like magazines, television shows, song lyrics, fashions, architecture, and toys, looking for patterns in the kinds of meanings these convey (see Griswold 2004; Rose 2001; Walters 1999).

Any particular research project may combine multiple qualitative methods. Ethnographers learn about group practices and beliefs in part through interviewing members and interpreting artifacts. Researchers doing intensive interviews often ask questions about a group's cultures and practices. Discourse analysts may examine the connections among cultural texts, who produces them, and the ways people use them in their lives (see Rose 2001; Walters 1999). Historical researchers often focus on questions about cultures and ways of life in a particular period, engage in textual analysis, and sometimes interview those who are still living who experienced the period they are studying firsthand.

Qualitative methods have great promise for those who want to avoid some of the pitfalls in conventional social science that I described in chapter 1. Researchers concerned about the kinds of questions social scientists have been asking can use qualitative methods to learn about the questions of the people they study. Those who are wary of conventional analytic frameworks can observe the ways the people they study organize and make sense of their experience. Talking with and observing human beings in their daily social contexts provides information that combats the tendency to see people as abstract individuals. Listening to people speak in their own words, and watching them make choices and take action, makes it much easier to recognize them as subjects. Listening to people who are members of groups that have been underrepresented in conventional research provides rich opportunities to discover what scholarly discourse may have obscured, and to see the limits of prevailing "truths."

The history of qualitative methodology runs rich with feminist contributions. For example, feminists were working on giving voice to those they were studying and decentering the perspective of the researcher for at least a decade before these emphases were "introduced" by nonfeminist postmodern methodologists, and in some cases much earlier than that (Gordon 1988; Mascia-Lees, Sharpe, and Cohen 1989). Most feminist social scientists who have been explicitly struggling with the implications of either postmodern or standpoint epistemologies for how they should do their research have worked with qualitative methods.

Yet the fact that feminists and others have had to alter conventional practices demonstrates that the connection between qualitative methods and critical social research is by no means automatic. The implementation of qualitative methods presents many of the same problems that characterize the use of quantitative methods, though usually in more subtle forms. Since interviewing and field research have been more prominent in feminist discussions of qualitative methodology, they are the primary focus of this chapter. Further, field research and qualitative interviewing present some challenges that would extend to the analysis of texts. First I will review warnings feminists have raised about the conventional methodologies in field research and interviewing. Later I will describe and evaluate strategies that feminists have developed to address some of these critiques. Finally, I will consider how these various approaches respond to the implications of standpoint epistemology I outlined at the end of chapter 3.

FEMINIST CRITIQUES OF QUALITATIVE METHODOLOGY
Feminists have raised four kinds of concerns related to traditional practices in interviewing and field research: (1) the increased salience of race/ethnicity, gender, and class in the research relationship; (2) the objectification of research subjects; (3) the influence of social power on who becomes a research subject; and (4) problematic assumptions in the conventional analytic approaches.

Research Relationships Heighten the Salience of Gender, Race, and Class
Qualitative research is grounded in particularly intensive relationships, usually involving face-to-face interactions, and often for extended periods of time. In both interviewing and field research, "the interaction is the method" (Cassell 1980: 36), and the investigator is the primary research instrument. Chapter 3 describes how all research operates through social relations organizing power and difference. The intensive relationships of qualitative research make differences in social position even more salient than in quantitative research.

In the case of field research, both the field and the way the researcher enters into and participates in that field are organized by gender, class, and race. Gender structures most social settings, assigning men and women to different spheres of responsibility and expertise and limiting entry to specific sites of social activity. In more complex sexual divisions of labor, systems of class and racial/ethnic inequality further stratify responsibility and expertise within each gender. Members of privileged groups may dominate the public roles and head up major social institutions, but they are often peripheral to the daily work and lives of the community and so cannot tell an ethnographer much about those (Wax 1979).

Gendered fields provide gendered opportunities. Bell (1993) found that having her children with her conferred the status of a "normal woman" in the aboriginal community she was studying, making the women more open to her and motivating them to teach her the kinds of things a mother in their culture should know. Abu-Lughod (1995) tells of how being a childless woman prompted the women she befriended in a Bedouin society to teach her their practices for enhancing fertility, including taking her to a specialist whose secret rituals could help her become fertile.

Gendered fields also create gendered obstacles. For example, those interested in studying athletes of another gender are barred from a key site of athletes' work lives and interactions: their locker rooms (Reinharz and Chase 2002). The sexism in the local culture can be enacted against the visiting researcher as, for example, Diane Bell (1993) learned doing fieldwork in an aboriginal community and Jennifer Pierce (1995) experienced doing participant observation in a U.S. law firm.

Privileged status vis-à-vis the field may keep researchers from being aware of what they are missing. It can keep men from realizing that they are observing gendered practices, particularly in sites where gender is not made salient by the presence of women (Morgan 1981). For example, Morgan (1981) describes Whyte's classic *Street Corner Society*, the field research most sociology students learn about, as a masculine text. The study was organized around a masculine site: women did not hang out on the street corner. Whyte was unreflective about the degree to which the practices of the men on the corner as well as his interactions with them were gendered. For example, he offered as evidence of his successful inclusion in the setting his being able to participate in a debate with the other men over the relative merits of the bodies of different "girls" who walked by (Morgan 1981). Similarly, whites studying other whites are typically unaware of the racial/ethnic character of the situation they are observing (cf. Frankenberg 1993).

Interviewing is a form of social interaction, and social psychological research has amply demonstrated that in social interactions we tailor our speech for the context within which we are speaking. In co-constructing an interaction, each participant takes into account the projected identities of the others involved and how these match or contrast with the identities they want to present. Prior experience shapes how both the interviewer and the interviewee respond to the situation (Laslett and Rapoport 1975). Interviewees can project beliefs and fears onto the investigator. Interviewers' personal experience shapes how they respond to what the respondent talks about, leading them to perhaps have a stronger emotional reaction to some stories, and thus to overestimate the importance of the story to the respondent (Laslett and Rapoport 1975).

Mainstream accounts of interviewing discuss the complexity of interpersonal dynamics but stay on a psychological level (Ribbens 1989). Yet the elements of an interaction are socially, as well as interpersonally, organized. Potential identities, projected identities, available cultural scripts for a situation, and prior experience are all powerfully shaped by gender in interaction with class, race/ethnicity, immigrant status, ability/disability, and so on. It is reasonable to expect that interviewees will speak differently with someone whom they see as "the same" than they do with someone they see as "the other" (DeVault 1999: 100–101). Yet Jane Ribbens (1989) asserts that while ethnographers have long recognized gender as a dimension of entry to the field, mainstream articulators of interviewing methodology have paid much less attention to how the dynamics of gender, race, and class shape their access to data. Feminist researchers often reflect on the gender, class, and racial/ethnic dynamics of their research relationships, as the "insider" researchers described in chapter 3 illustrate. However, there has been little systematic empirical examination of the impact of researcher social status relative to that of the researched. What little there is suggests that salient social differences do shape what parts of their stories interviewees share and how they frame them.

Christine Williams and Joel Heikes (1993) discovered that in independent studies in different regions of the United States, they had both interviewed male nurses. Since the interviewers were a man and a woman, their data constituted a quasi-experiment on the impact of interviewer gender. They found many similar themes across the two studies, suggesting that the data were comparable (evidence, they note, of the reliability of qualitative interviewing). Williams and Heikes compared interviews that made similar points but to different gendered interviewers. They found that the male nurses constructed their answers differently depending on whether they were talking with a man or a woman. For example, men were more likely to attribute things to biologically based sex differences in talking with another man, but referred to sex differences more in-directly and allowed that they might be socially based when talking with a woman interviewer. These respondents were also more critical of medical doc-tors with the woman interviewer and more explicit about their own heterosex-uality with the male interviewer, a pattern that suggests they anticipated that a different frame of reference guided the interests, expectations, and anxieties of men and women.

Yvonne Tixier y Vigil and Nan Elsasser (1978) conducted a rare experiment on the way ethnicity interacts with gender in interviewing. A Chicana and an Anglo, they separately interviewed 15 Latina women. A comparison of their transcripts revealed that the interviewees responded very differently depend-ing on the race/ethnicity of the interviewer. Latina interviewees spoke much more freely about sex, birth control, and abortion with the Anglo interviewer, while with the Chicana they observed "in-group" norms about not talking about sexual matters, using euphemisms and denying the use of birth control (cf. Phoenix 1994). The Latina women that Tixier y Vigil and Elsasser (1978) interviewed talked as much about discrimination with the Anglo interviewer as with the Chicana, but how they talked about it depended on the race/ethnicity of the interviewer. With the Anglo interviewer, the interviewees were more likely to restrict the terms they used to refer to discrimination, to talk about having Anglo friends and family members, and to volunteer that Ang-los are also subject to discrimination.

These findings, though slim, are consistent with a much larger body of re-search on interaction in social psychology (cf. Howard and Hollander 1997). It seems safest to assume that differences or similarities in gender, race, class, and other salient dimensions of social power and privilege have an impact on interactions within the context of research, and thus influence "*how* people talk to each other and *what* they say to each other" (Ribbens 1989: 579, em-phasis in original).

Objectification and Othering

As I described in chapter 1, feminist scholars in the West have long criti-cized the objectification of women in Western scholarly discourse. Although it is easier to see how standard quantitative methodology objectifies human subjects of research, traditional practices of qualitative methodology are also vulnerable to this criticism. The insights of postcolonial scholars, people whose experience bridges non-Western and Western social science discourse, are particularly enlightening in this regard.

Postcolonial scholars have criticized ethnography for the way it constructs the subjects of study as "others," that is, somehow not as fully human as the investigators, the presumed "normal" (see Aggarwal 2000; Minh-ha 1993). Certainly, the history of ethnography gives plenty of evidence. As Emerson (2001) traces that history, ethnography began in nineteenth-century Great Britain and the United States. Scholars at the height of the British Empire saw non-Western societies as "primitive" and "exotic" and believed that learning about them would enlighten us about the precursors of modern civilization. In those early days, the goal was to understand the process of "social evolution," that is, how the human race evolved from more lowly forms like "theirs" to the highly developed form that is "ours." The main question was to learn from "primitive" societies how civilization developed and why some "regressive" cultural remnants (e.g., religion) remained in modern civilization.

Of course, ethnographers today would not use terms like *primitive* or *regressive* to describe the groups they study. But this does not mean that the problem of othering them has disappeared. Ravina Aggarwal (2000) suggests that the very notion of "the field" that is basic to field research is a Western construction with an ideological impact. It emerges, she says, out of the way Western culture creates perceptions of social difference around a dichotomy: us versus them, the West versus the rest of the world. In this construction, the First World is defined as "home," the site of normal lifeways. The First World is also the place where intellectual work is centered. The social construction of otherness becomes clear as it is dismantled in this quote from Margaret Mead:

> When automobiles replace outrigger canoes, apples replace mangosteens and papayas, and boxes of chocolate are substituted for octopus pudding as a suitable gift to take on a date, the whole incidental paraphernalia of strangeness which I could use to convey the cultures of other peoples is gone. (1965, quoted in Martin 1992: 3)

Those ethnographers working from the standpoint of the West construct the Third World as the exotic distant, a place to visit to collect data and then to return home to make sense of it. Aggarwal argues that even describing a group's culture is an act of othering, the consequence of attributing "exotic, abstract essences and characteristics to places and then naturalizing them," construing people in those places as "natives" (2000: 20).

Though the imputed goal of anthropological fieldwork has been to learn about the nature of humanity, it has represented those it studies as "other," not as fully human as "we" are (Minh-ha 1993). Trinh Minh-ha asks why locals cannot speak with authority about their culture unless they have been trained in Western schools. She suggests the reason is that locals have to be taught to see their own people and lifeways through a different lens: they have to learn to objectify their own kind. This is because anthropological discourse has been "mainly a conversation of 'us' with 'us' about 'them'" (Minh-ha 1993: 125).

Constructing and exoticizing others is not the exclusive domain of those whose fieldwork is outside their home society. The notion of "the field" is not a location as much as it is a description of a researcher's orientation, "a form of motivated and stylized dislocation" (Gupta and Ferguson 1997: 36–37). Many Western field researchers are drawn to "the exotic, the bizarre, the violent" (Fine and Weiss 1996: 259) in their own societies, with the result that fieldwork becomes a form of voyeurism. Thorne says that fieldwork can be a form of "controlled adventure" (1983: 222). The observer can taste the excitement of deviance or rebellion, while using ideals of scientific detachment as an excuse for not taking real risks. Thorne illustrates this potential from her analysis of her own experience: doing research on the draft resistance movement during the Vietnam War allowed her to be involved with groups to which she felt politically committed, yet gave her an excuse for avoiding getting arrested.

Standard practices for interviewing also put interviewees into the position of being objects of the researcher's direction and manipulation. Interviewing projects are organized around topics selected and controlled by the researcher. Traditional interviewing practice involves posing questions, getting people to talk as much as possible, actively listening to support their continued talk, and moving them back to the researcher's agenda when they stray (McCracken 1998; Weiss 1994). Interviewees are relevant to the research as sources of data, not as analysts of their own experience (Riessman 1993).

In an early paper, Ann Oakley (1981) argued that mainstream interviewing practices are masculine in their emphasis on detachment and control. Conventional methodological advice is that the investigator should keep personal disclosure to a minimum. The investigator is to be "professional," which is to say, have some but not too much rapport with the interviewee. Guidelines differ on how to accomplish this goal. Some call for the investigator to act as a "mechanical" passive reporter, others as a psychoanalyst encouraging the respondent's free association. In either case, Oakley noted, the investigator controls the situation. The flow of questions and answers is strictly one-way: respondents are not to ask questions of the investigator, and if they do, the investigator is supposed to deflect them. The common practice of making only one contact with a particular interviewee, Oakley added, makes it easier to maintain investigator detachment.

Oakley (1981) called mainstream interviewing a "pseudo-conversation," and said that a comparable demeanor would be rude within any other social context. She pointed to accounts by interviewers describing their difficulty in maintaining detachment as exposing how unnatural a posture it is. The difficulty, Oakley said, is particularly obvious when women are interviewing women, because in talking about one woman's life, the interview participants are talking about struggles they both face. Their common stake in topics like women's access to health care or the experience of being a mother makes their shared personhood salient. In such circumstances the interviewer and interviewee will (and in her view, should) connect as women.

Others disagree with Oakley's analysis. For example, Ribbens (1989) maintains that research contexts are distinct social situations that, appropriately, have their own norms for interactional practice. Some degree, or at least some moments, of objectification are necessary to develop an analysis that is informed by a sociological or other social science perspective (Acker, Barry, and Esseveld 1983/1991). The point is that the assumption that qualitative research does not objectify its subjects seems naive.

The Influence of Social Power on Who Becomes a Research Subject

Systems of social power influence who becomes a participant in qualitative research projects. Interview researchers determine what type of interviewees they want to recruit based on preconceived conceptual categories, in a process variously called theoretical, purposive, or selective sampling. Standard practices for recruiting participants for interview studies include writing letters to groups, advertising in mass media, snowball sampling, and word of mouth. Most of them depend on people's volunteering to participate. But these standard recruitment strategies can produce systematic race and class biases in interview samples, as Lynn Cannon, Elizabeth Higginbotham, and Marianne Leung (1988) demonstrate.

Seeking to understand the experience of women in professional, managerial, or administrative jobs, Cannon, Higginbotham, and Leung (1988) sought to recruit equal numbers of white and African American incumbents. They encountered a marked race difference in responses to standard recruitment efforts. When they wrote letters to organizations and their members, 31 percent of the whites they needed responded, but only 13 percent of the African Americans. Announcements through both general and target-specific media generated another 23 percent of the whites, but only 4 percent of the African Americans. In order to recruit enough African American women to generate an equivalent subsample, they had to use group-specific strategies. Their most successful approaches included personal presentations to meetings of organizations who had significant numbers of African Americans among their members, snowball sampling, and word of mouth.

What explains the discrepancy in the effectiveness of sampling techniques? Cannon, Higginbotham, and Leung (1988) note several barriers to professional, middle-class African American women's volunteering to be in a qualitative research sample. African American women's histories and biographies are likely to raise their concerns about the possibility of being exploited. They also tend to have less free time than white women, both because of being in jobs that allow less autonomy, and because they are much more likely to be mothers. Further, African American women in upper-middle-class jobs are highly visible, and thus they would justifiably be concerned about their risk of being identifiable in research reports.

Participation in qualitative interviewing tends to be time- and energy-consuming. The less privilege people have, the less control they have over their time and the more demands they experience on their energy. For token women in powerful positions, their token status generates additional demands on their time, for example, they may have to exceed the productivity of their male peers in order to get equivalent credit, represent the whole category of women on various committees, and mentor a disproportionate load of junior colleagues or students (Reinharz and Chase 2002). And these heavily burdened tokens, if they are women, may still have to do more than their share of domestic work (Hochschild 1989; Shelton 1992). People who are poor also face extra burdens on their time and energy. For example, in interviewing poor women, Phoenix (1994) encountered much more than the usual difficulty with "no-shows" on interview appointments. She found that poor people may be interested in cooperating, but when the day comes for the interview, they may have more pressing things they need to do just to survive and meet basic needs, such as getting the utilities turned back on, finding a new place to live, or dealing with a crisis in child care (cf. Madriz 1998).

Social power and privilege also shape who is accessible to and who can hide from field researchers. People and institutions with power can use that power to shield themselves from view. Often they hire people specifically to deal with outsiders, to manage impressions, and to enculturate them to the preferred analysis (Nader 1969: 308). The affluent can buy the legal, medical, and psychological services that help keep them from entering official statistics. The powerful meet behind closed doors in exclusive clubs. Private institutions like private hospitals, schools, corporations, and privately owned shopping centers can more easily refuse entry to the field researcher than can public parks, streets, and school boards (cf. Warren and Staples 1989). Yet institutional review boards, which must approve of research projects involving human subjects, can take the position that it is a violation of subjects' privacy rights to use deception to conduct observation of private organizations or clubs.

On the other hand, poor people must rely on public institutions like schools, hospitals, and social services, and have no alternative but to conduct more of their activities in public places, for example, the corner bar instead of the country club. Because of their reliance on public spaces, they have a harder time avoiding becoming public statistics. Thus the powerful can more easily avoid surveillance, while the powerless are routinely subjected to it. In fact, Nader (1969) suggests that observational research in the life domains of the truly powerful may not be possible; researchers may need to rely instead on available documents and other sources of data.

Selection bias in qualitative samples is an important issue, because biased samples prompt distorted findings. To the extent that gender, race, and class influence the time and inclination to participate, interview samples are distorted often in the direction of the relatively privileged, even within a less privileged social location. Or, as Cannon, Higginbotham, and Leung (1988) demonstrate, the distortion may be even more subtle and difficult to discover. Because they went to great lengths, these researchers were able to get a class-diverse sample of African American women. If they had compared the backgrounds of the women they were studying only by race, the data would have supported the conclusion that African American families were less supportive of their daughters' achieving higher education than were white families. Their extra efforts to recruit enough African American women from middle-class backgrounds to make cross-class comparisons possible allowed them to discover that it was African American working-class families that failed to encourage a college education. What might have been interpreted as a "cultural deficit" among African Americans was actually an artifact of African American women being much more likely to come from poor and working-class families, for whom a college education and professional career might reasonably seem unrealistic. Such a serious discrepancy in apparent findings should raise warning flags on many qualitative samples.

Problematic Assumptions in Conventional Analytic Approaches

Traditionally researchers begin a project by analyzing the existing research literature. In the interest of sidestepping any biases in traditional conceptual frameworks for organizing their understanding of social phenomena, many qualitative researchers have adopted some form of grounded theory (Charmaz 2004; Glaser and Strauss 1967; Strauss and Corbin 1990). The goal of this approach to analysis is to be as faithful to the data as possible. Investigators begin by immersing themselves, without preconceptions, in the phenomena they are trying to understand. Field researchers enter and spend lots of time in the field; interviewers do some interviews and then closely read and reread transcriptions. After a period of intensive observation, patterns begin to emerge in the data. Researchers pursue the validity of these by going back to the empirical source, checking with informants, doing more interviews, rereading transcripts, and so on. In this way, proponents argue, theoretical frames are built on, that is, "grounded in," the data. Note the epistemological assumptions that underlie this approach: the focus is on the data and on finding the patterns that are in the data. Observers work to minimize their subjectivity, or at least the way that subjectivity is organized by some theory or scholarly framework, as a source of bias. The assumptions that underlie the grounded theory model bear a striking resemblance to the assumptions of positivism.

With the increasing popularity of postmodern epistemology, more and more qualitative researchers see the process of data collection as constructed:

investigators are not simply observing patterns in the data, they are interpreting phenomena (Geertz 1973). Every research interaction and the stories they generate are co-constructed by the researcher and the researched (cf. Charmaz 2004; Paget 1983; Warren 2002). Researchers are raised in a culture that schools us in the hegemonic worldview and have also been trained in a scholarly discipline. A wealth of feminist and other critical scholarship on the social construction of knowledge shows how power relations systematically shape what is interesting and important to us (cf. Sherman and Torton Beck 1979; Tokarczyk and Fay 1993). Chapter 1 describes how the hegemonic worldview shapes the framing and content of sociology.

Simply refusing to read prior research on a particular topic does not protect the researcher from the organizing frames and values of these discourses. They are so embedded in the ways we learn to see, that even the most well-intentioned and critical observers can miss the dynamics that surreptitiously reconstitute privilege in the process of choosing topics, observing, responding emotionally, and interpreting data.

Few have systematically explored the question of whether and how systematic social frames organize how qualitative researchers see and listen. Thorne (2001) provides a cogent case study of how status differences in the field can resonate with the researcher's own experiences of negotiating positions within status hierarchies, shaping observation and analysis. She uses her ethnographic research on children to show how hegemonic culture organizes even the most perceptive and thoughtful researcher's reactions in the field. She describes how her observations in a school setting resonated with her own experiences as a student. She found herself fascinated with the most popular girl, avoiding the overly needy girl, and repulsed by the poor girl, just as she had when she was their age.

Tellingly, Thorne (2001) reports, the same thing did not happen in her reactions to the boys she was observing. She did not return to the emotional response of her own childhood, but rather to a later one: if she made a personal connection with the boys she observed, it was maternal. This she also connects with her own biography. Her relationship history with her own son provided psychoemotional resources for constructing her relationship to these boys. At the same time, she reports being able to see what the boys were doing more clearly, and to analyze it. Thorne suspects this ease was the product of the way dominant analytic categories tend to come out of, and thus better express, masculine experience. It may also be that it is easier to use analytic frameworks to make sense of someone whom we see as an "other," a person of a different kind than oneself.[1]

Just as Thorne found that cultural biases shaped her priorities of making observations in the field, Finch and Mason (1990) found similar biases in their responses to interviewees. Their research design involved doing initial interviews with a large sample in order to identify a smaller number of theoretically interesting cases, which they would then pursue in greater depth in follow-up interviews. However, after identifying many subjects this way, they became aware of a pattern in the cases they selected as interesting and worth pursuing further. They were drawn to interviewees who were more articulate.

Researchers are understandably attracted to subjects who are articulate. However, here as elsewhere, the practices of privileged groups are hegemonic. Linguistic patterns vary systematically with class background (Bernstein 1971; Mueller 1973). The linguistic patterns favored in the academy are not those of people from the working class (Tokarczyk and Fay 1993) or the African American ghetto (Ferguson 2000). In such circumstances, judgments of articulateness become evaluations of people's facility with upper-middle-class linguistic patterns. Similarly, social psychological research shows how status shapes beliefs about performance quality that become self-fulfilling prophecies. For example, in many situations women are more likely than men to anticipate that their speech will be devalued and, under the increased social pressure, they falter (Ridgeway 1993). To the extent that researchers use articulateness as an indicator of a good informant or interviewee, they are employing race, class, and gender biases.

Hegemonic biases also infiltrate our judgments of what are the interesting aspects of people's lives. Fine and Weiss (1996) describe how they found themselves avoiding sections of their interview transcripts that seemed boring, and that these were the ones that detailed the mundane aspects of their interviewees' lives. This selection pattern seems to characterize the work of many researchers, as Fine and Weiss (1996) observe, since ethnographies of poverty rarely report on poor people's daily lives and struggles. Daily life involves the work of meeting basic needs, of maintaining life. It is important work, work that can be the site of creativity and drama (Aptheker 1989; DeVault 1991; Luxton 1980). However, it is also work that is devalued by virtue of who does it: women and poor people, and disproportionately people of color (cf. Ehrenreich 2001; England et al. 1996; Glenn 1992).

The bottom line is that analytic strategies that try to minimize bias by avoiding scholarly discourse and simply immersing oneself in the data are not clearly more effective than those that explicitly build on prior scholarship. Investigators taking this approach may actually be imposing even more serious distortions on their observations, by virtue of their being implicit rather than explicit, and so less open to critique.

In summary, qualitative methods can increase the likelihood that race/ ethnicity, gender, and class will shape the process of data collection, objectify research subjects, and operate in ways that interact with social power to create systematic biases in who becomes a research subject, and may uncritically employ analytic approaches that are vulnerable to the working of hegemonic ideologies.

Some of the problems feminists have identified in ethnographic and interview research seem endemic to these methods. As long as gender, race/ ethnicity, and class are central dimensions of social organization, they will be salient in most social interactions, including those that happen within the context of research (Ridgeway 1987). The best that individual investigators can do is to acknowledge the differences and take them into account throughout the process. As long as there are significant differences in social power, these will shape who has the time and trust to participate in intensive social research and who has the power and resources to evade the scrutiny of field researchers and interviewers.

However, the treatment of research subjects and the analytic approaches employed are amenable to adjustment, and I will turn next to describing the kinds of strategies that feminists have used to respond to the criticisms of mainstream practices. Some of these feminist experiments have been more well-intentioned than they have been carefully examined in light of their underlying epistemological assumptions. However, many are creative and promising responses to the implications of critical epistemologies. In what follows, I will organize feminist approaches in terms of one of three overlapping strategic emphases: (1) building on the connections between the investigator and the investigated; (2) decentering the researcher's perspective; and (3) drawing on the power of strategic collaborations.

INCREASING THE RESEARCHER/RESEARCHED CONNECTION

The key practice in objectifying a person or a group is constructing a dichotomy between the self and the other—the way that we "know" that "we" are distinctive is through "understanding" that we are "not-them" (Fine 1994). Instead of working to maintain a sharp dichotomy between the researcher and the researched, feminist qualitative researchers have built on the enhanced insights that come from emphasizing the connections between them. Researchers working in this vein have developed three kinds of strategies: they have tried to make the relationship with research subjects more reciprocal, they have used their emotions as analytic guides, and they have drawn on their own biographies to increase empathy and understanding.

Making Relationships More Reciprocal

Oakley (1981) was an early advocate of this approach, going so far as to call for the formation of "sisterly bonds" between the researcher and the researched as a standard for feminist research, and arguing that such a connection enhances subjects' trust and researchers' empathy, producing better research. She presented an interviewing strategy founded on developing a close, mutual relationship based on women's shared personal and social interests. For a study of women during pregnancy and new motherhood, she interviewed 55 women four times over a period of a year, in order to provide time for a relationship of trust to develop. Oakley approached each interview as a meeting of peers, encouraging the respondent to introduce themes for their conversation. When respondents asked her questions, she was forthcoming in answering them. If, during the course of an interview, demands for domestic work cropped up, she would help the interviewee do the job.

Oakley's model of interviewing was innovative, and her article has been widely cited. The strategy of doing multiple interviews over a period of time, also advocated by Laslett and Rapoport (1975), enhances a research project in several ways—building trust and comfort, allowing time for reflection between interviews, and enhancing the view of lives and situations as historical, contextual, and changing. The idea of investigators' disclosing personal information, especially parallel to the information they are requesting from others, has been popular with some researchers and may in some cases put the subjects of research at ease (Naples 1996/1997; cf. Reinharz and Chase 2002). On the other hand, Jane Ribbens (1989) notes that research subjects may not even want to know personal information about the interviewer. Ribbens points to the data that Oakley herself provides. The vast majority, 76 percent, of the questions Oakley's interviewees asked her were for general information; only 15 percent were personal questions (1981: 42).

Shulamit Reinharz and Susan Chase (2002) argue that investigator self-disclosure seems a risky practice for exactly the reasons mainstream methodologists advise against it. In talking about themselves, researchers constrain the opportunities for respondents to talk. In fact, in talking about themselves, investigators can communicate the wrong message altogether—that they are not really interested in what the interviewee has to say. Research subjects could interpret this as a violation of the deal they thought they were making with the investigator—the investigator listens while the interviewee talks. Further, Reinharz and Chase (2002) observe, investigator self-disclosure can increase social desirability bias. The more the respondent knows about the beliefs, values, and feelings of the investigator, the more he or she can take these into account in constructing a response that would please that investigator.

In sum, self-disclosure is a practice that should not be entered into without carefully considering the consequences. Investigators talking personally about themselves may do more to ease the discomfort of the investigators or to create *the illusion of equality* than it does to produce more valid data or to empower those under study.

Using Emotions as Analytic Guides

Some feminist researchers use their own emotional response to the field as a source of insight and direction for how to proceed, what to pursue, when to ask questions, and how to interpret observations (e.g., Anderson and Jack 1991; Bell 1993; DeVault 1991; Ellis 1991; Krieger 1985). Carolyn Ellis argues that emotions are not purely private experiences. "Emotions result from applying personal interpretations of collectively-created rules to the situations in which we find ourselves" (1991: 26). Thus emotions are the personal links to the social, and researcher introspection is a strategy for social research. When one is studying a community in which one has played a role, interactions with other members are not just occasions of collecting information (Krieger 1987). Rather, these interactions are instances of that community's practices, shaped by its values. Thus the researcher's feelings about those interactions are primary data about the community.

Susan Krieger developed an analytic strategy that explicitly used her emotions as interpretive tools. She acted as participant-observer in the lesbian community of a midwestern university town during a yearlong stint as a visiting professor in the late 1970s (Krieger 1983). She collected community newsletters, kept journals, wrote stories about her experiences, and conducted 78 interviews with nearly all the members of the community. However, once she had amassed this rich set of data, she struggled for years in trying to analyze it, even though she was able to produce other pieces of scholarship during that time. What finally made it possible for her to find her feet in analyzing the data, Krieger claims, was confronting her emotional response to her interviewees and asking what her response might reveal about community expectations and practices.

Krieger (1987) developed a three-step strategy to draw on her emotional response, writing up separate memos for each interview at each step. First she considered how she felt about the circumstances leading up to that interview—how she met the interviewee, how she arranged for the interview, and how she felt as the time for that interview drew near. Then she thought about how she felt during each interview. She examined these memos, looking for underlying patterns or themes. Then she used these themes as a lens for analyzing the transcript of that interview.

In other words, Krieger used her own feelings about members of the community as indicators of community norms, expectations, and frustrations. Once she focused on these feelings as information, she says, they became a way into the data, providing analytic categories for understanding it. For example, thinking through how she responded to various interactions prompted her to ask whether and how interactions in the community were socially constructed as intimate occasions in which the legitimacy of people's identities as lesbians was on the line.

Researchers' attending to their own emotions as data and/or analytic guides is innovative and intriguing. Part of the critique of positivism is based on its assumption that the subjectivity of the investigator can be minimized in the process of research. Emotions are an expression of the nature of a relationship—to a community and/or to an individual member of that community—and thus valuable data about that relationship. Investigators cannot help but respond emotionally to what—and whom—they are studying, and these emotions are bound to influence emphases and interpretations (cf. Laslett and Rapoport

1975). Being explicitly aware of this dynamic, as Ellis and Krieger are, is much better than letting it steer research implicitly.

The danger is that investigators might fail to be adequately reflective about the biographic and social bases for their emotional response, or might even privilege their own emotional response over other data. For example, Janet Holland and Caroline Ramazanoglu (1994) give several examples of investigators giving undue attention to a topic, like an experience with rape or the death of a loved one, because it resonated with their own personal experience. Recall Thorne's reflections on how her emotional responses to children in a classroom incorporate hegemonic biases. An uncritical reliance on the investigator's emotions would be the inverse of the error that positivism makes—instead of ignoring researcher subjectivity, letting it dominate. This is particularly problematic because of the class, and often race and gender, homogeneity of those who tend to conduct research.

In summary, researchers' emotions are a part of their analytic apparatus, important to attend to, and they can be a source of important observations and insights. However, they are also expressions of a standpoint and should be subjected to the same critical interrogation as more strictly cognitive approaches.

Researcher's Biography as a Resource

Another strategy based on enhancing the connections between the researcher and the researched is through researchers drawing on their own biographies for sources of insight. Ann Ferguson (2000: 183–85) demonstrates these techniques in her fieldwork in a low-income, racially diverse elementary school. In her interviews with boys in the school, Ferguson noticed that fighting seemed an important part of their experience. They were much more interested in talking about fights, and their accounts were much more vivid and rich than their descriptions of more normative school activities. Ferguson had no recollection of fights being significant in her own childhood and started asking other adults in the school about their memories. She found that men remembered fighting as an important aspect of their early lives, but that women could not remember being involved in fights. Then she spoke with her own brother, who reminded her that early on she had been a ruthless fighter. This led her to realize that somehow she had learned to repress her own early physicality (and perhaps so had many of the women she asked about this). She had become "ladylike" and had even turned into a person who was afraid of violence.

Ferguson's identification and pursuit of the role of fighting in children's experience shows how gendered selves and biographies can be gateways to insight and enhanced understanding. Being in a gender-marked social position (woman) helped her to be sensitive to gendered patterns in the adults' recollections. Her gendered biography helped her uncover something of the social construction of aggressive and passive bodies, and made it possible to pose the question of how this occurs in the boys she was observing.

The principle of *grounding interpretations in experiences and interests* requires that researchers analyze the basis of their feelings of closeness and self-comparison. Differences in power influence how sensitive we can be to how our own experience might differ from that of those we are studying (cf. Luff 1999). Confidence that we understand where another is coming from can be a sign of our relative privilege, a mark of which is the freedom to define ourselves and our experience as "normal" and impose assumptions based on our own situation. At the very least, working hard to identify with the subjects of research can lead researchers to gloss over real differences in social status and experience (Ribbens 1989). In the process, researchers' attention to their own feelings and experiences "can slide into narcissism, self-indulgence, and a tiresome confessional mode" (Thorne 1994: 139).

Those who do not share researchers' privilege are likely to see the arrogance in such assumptions (cf. Dill 1983). Rather than assuming a sisterly connection with someone in a relatively disadvantaged racial/ethnic location, Rosalind Edwards (1990) argues, the best way for a white researcher to build trust is to openly acknowledge racial/ethnic differences, their implications for social power, and how that could impede the researcher's ability to understand. Similar advice could apply in studying people who are in more oppressed class locations, or those who are more disadvantaged by gender, nation, or disability.

Strategies that build on the connection between researcher and researched extend the standard practice in qualitative research of using empathy as a gateway to understanding by trying to reconstitute the nature of the research relationship. Emphasis on personalizing the research relationship presumes that researchers share core values with those they are studying. This presumption is tacit because so many feminists have focused their attention on describing the lives and the stories of those who are disadvantaged and with whom they can empathize. However, that is not always the case, nor should it be if we are going to organize research to problematize the powerful or the hateful. Expectations that interviewers and fieldworkers should foster closeness and draw on commonality place a special burden on researchers studying people with whom they disagree on core values, for example, people who are racist (cf. Phoenix 1994) or homophobic (cf. Luff 1999). How are investigators to respond when research subjects voice beliefs that are abhorrent to them—should they be honest, a criterion of establishing closeness that would surely influence further data collection, or should they remain quiet, which implies support for such positions?

Even when researchers and the researched are social peers who share basic values, closeness is, at best, a double-edged research tool. Shirley Harkess and Carol Warren (1993) challenge the common assumption that the more rapport an investigator has with the investigated, the more valid the data will be. Rather, they argue, the relationship is curvilinear—both too little and too much closeness can distort our understanding. Being too close to the group could lead the researcher, like those he or she is studying, to miss noting what is being taken for granted (Ribbens 1989). It also raises the stakes on some kinds of disclosures; subjects might be wary of revealing embarrassing information to people they know. Friendship with those we study can actually lead individuals to abandon the role of investigator and become full participants, talk too much, thereby suppressing the other's storytelling, and even seek self-validation (Harkess and Warren 1993).

Worse, building close relationships with those we study can make them more vulnerable to our exploitation, more willing to share secrets that they would not consider reporting to a more detached observer, and more invested in a long-term relationship than the researcher, who inevitably will leave (Acker et al. 1983/1991; Stacey 1988). Judith Stacey (1988) powerfully demonstrated from her own field experience that the greater the intimacy and feelings of connectedness in research relationships, the more vulnerable the researched is to exploitation. Trust and intimacy led a woman who was married and a fundamentalist Christian to disclose her lesbian affair to Stacey. Later the woman wanted Stacey to keep that information secret, putting Stacey in an ethical dilemma over the conflicting obligations generated by her personal relationship with this woman and her professional relationship with the community of scholars. The intimacy of the research relationship led the woman to confide a secret but did nothing to counter the fact that it was the researcher who ultimately had the power to decide whether or not to disclose the information to broader publics (Stacey 1988; cf. Acker, Barry, and Esseveld 1983/1991).

Ribbens (1989) wonders if the feminist attraction to more intimacy in re-search relationships is itself gendered, an expression of the way women in Western culture learn to elide the work of listening with an obligation to nur-ture. Reinharz and Chase (2002) argue that what is needed is an adequate level of rapport, not a long-term relationship, and the best way to build rapport is to be a good listener who is sensitive to the dynamics of power and privilege.

In summary, the nature of the relationships between the researcher and the researched are important to consider and to incorporate into the analysis, but not to idealize. These relationships are both a resource and an obstacle. Em-pathy and emotional responses to others can provide insight, and ignoring emotional responses can be deadening. On the other hand, being too close to those we study can limit respondents' willingness to disclose unfavorable in-formation, influence our reading of the data, lead to loyalty issues, gloss over real differences in social position and experience, and call for hypocritical en-dorsement of violations of one's core values.

COMPENSATING FOR THE RESEARCHER'S STANDPOINT

Feminist researchers have attempted a range of strategies to compensate for the limitations of their own standpoint. Some have focused on the perspective of the researched, either taking the identification of their priorities and con-ceptual organization as the primary goal of analysis or, in rare cases, actually involving them in the analysis of data. Others look for partial analyses from the standpoint of the researched, as these are communicated in discourses that are usually not considered authoritative. And Dorothy Smith and her col-leagues have developed an approach called institutional ethnography that builds on the argument that the researcher and the researched have different kinds of authority emerging from their distinct standpoints.

Emphasizing the Perspective of the Researched

Beginning in the 1970s, in an effort to counter the objectification of their research subjects and the imposition of hegemonic frameworks on the data, some feminists began to redefine the roles of the researcher and the subject of research. For these investigators, the subject is not just a source of information, but rather a person who is constructing meaning for the researcher. The goal is not about developing a causal explanation of social phenomena; it is more one of "illuminating human experience: the complexity, opaqueness, and mystery of an essentially subjective species" (Paget 1983: 88). The agenda is no longer set by the interviewer, but by the interviewee. The interview becomes a process of interaction directed toward "the dynamic unfolding of the subject's viewpoint" (Anderson and Jack 1991).

The most fully developed approach is narrative analysis (Riessman 1993), in which the basic premise is that we are all—interviewers and interviewees—making sense and creating order through telling stories and constructing texts. In narrative analysis, Catherine Riessman explains, both the content and the form of the story are the data. Just as with written stories, people's oral stories have structural elements. For example, Riessman (1993) notes, a common structure organizing people's accounts of their lives includes (1) a summary of the substance of the story; (2) orienting information; (3) complicating action; (4) an evaluation of the meaning of the action; (5) a resolution; and (6) returning to the present. Together, the story content and form tell us something about the identity the narrator is constructing. They also tell us about the narrator's cultural framework: "culture 'speaks itself' through an individual's story" (Riessman 1993: 5).

As in more conventional methodology, the interviewer begins the conversation with very open-ended questions. For example, Riessman develops an interview schedule with five to seven open-ended questions and some probes. However, the questions have a different function—the goal is to generate stories, and interviewers focus on the subjects' logic and storytelling strategies. Interviewers, Anderson and Jack (1991) say, should pay attention to how the interviewee interprets the question—what question does he or she actually choose to answer? Whose question is that? How does he or she seem to feel about what he or she is describing? What seems to be his or her interpretation, analysis? What is he or she not talking about? Interviewers should resist the temptation to cut off the narrator, because that breaks the flow of the story he or she is constructing, making it hard to see the logic by which he or she is ordering experience (Riessman 1993).

Riessman approaches analysis in a two-way flow between transcribing and analyzing the interview. In the first rough draft, she transcribes all the spoken words, plus the major paralinguistic features, like laughing or crying, and numbers the lines of the text. Then she reads several drafts over and over, looking for linguistic markers of the beginning and end of narrative segments (e.g., "I'm going to tell you . . . And that was an example of what I mean"). She does a more detailed transcription of selected sections for close analysis, marking more detailed components of expression (e.g., audible exhalations, points of emphasis, occurrence and length of pauses). She also marks elements of the story's structure. Putting together observations of what is said with how it is said gives her a sense of the logic the narrator is using to make sense of experience.

Narrative analysis has great potential for identifying the perceptual frames circulating in a given culture and how they shape group members' sense of their own experience. However, it also has some serious limitations, many of which Riessman (1993) recognizes. For one thing, it emphasizes the making of meaning at the individual level to such an extent that it can make it hard to do studies of a culture. The intensive analytic strategy is impractical with any but very small samples, but small samples make it very hard to distinguish a cultural pattern from an idiosyncratic approach. Presumably this is a problem that can be addressed by increasing the labor involved, either extending the number of interviews over time or increasing the number of investigators (see chapter 7).

Riessman (1993) discovered a more difficult problem during a study on marital dissolution. A white, middle-class interviewer was trying to support a working-class Puerto Rican interviewee in telling the story of her marriage and its failure. The interviewer struggled through what felt like a difficult interview. What the interviewer was trying to do was apply the organizing conventions of Anglo culture as she tried to establish a time sequence and ground events geographically. Her efforts succeeded only in disrupting the narrator's own organizing logic. That narrator was using a set of episodes to illustrate general principles about her marriage being a problematic relationship between two different kinds of families. This was not an easy error to identify. Riessman reports that she figured it out only after repeatedly reading the transcript and listening to the tape of the interview.

Because narrative structure is a cultural product, researchers are likely to assume their own culture's framing devices as rational and mistake other cultures' organizing strategies for inarticulateness. As Riessman's account of the interview with the Puerto Rican woman shows, even subcultures within a complex society give rise to distinctive narrative structures. Similarly, Gwendolyn Etter-Lewis (1991) found three different narrative styles in her interviews with African American women. How much more difficult is it to detect narrative structures cross-nationally?

A limitation of interviewee-dominated interviewing more generally is that not all people are anxious or even willing to be so actively involved in determining the course of the conversation. For example, Acker, Barry, and Esseveld (1983/1991) found that some of the middle-aged women they interviewed over the years that they were moving from unpaid domestic labor into the labor force did not want to guide the agenda for the conversation—they preferred that the investigators ask questions. There may be systematic social biases in who is and who is not willing to take the lead in an interview.

For example, prior experience with self-disclosure influences whether or not an interviewee is comfortable taking control of the conversation. Birch and Miller (2000) independently conducted research projects using interviewee-guided agendas with first-time mothers and therapy group members. They report that interviewing new first-time mothers typically required a great deal of investigator participation to draw out their stories. On the other hand, interviewing people in therapy groups took very little questioning or encouragement.

Interviewee-dominated research projects aim to respond to the principle of *working from the standpoint of the marginalized,* but the strategy limits achievement of that goal. These techniques require intensive analytic effort on the part of the researcher, and verbal skill and confidence on the part of the researched. Researchers who aim to uncover the logic of people's thinking are vulnerable to the biases of their own cultural assumptions. Thus these strategies are likely to work better with the educated and relatively privileged than with members of groups who have been silenced in one way or another in their lives. Letting the respondents determine the agenda may be an egalitarian strategy in search of peers with whom to use it, that is, people who are accustomed to Western professional middle-class interactional styles.

Involving Research Subjects in the Analysis

Feminist researchers often talk about the desirability of involving the researched in the analysis of data. The approach that Carolyn Ellis, Christine

Kiesinger, and Lisa Tillmann-Healy (1997) call interactive interviewing involves research subjects so completely as to blur the line between the investigator and the investigated. They describe interactive interviewing as "the sharing of personal and social experiences of both respondents and researchers, who tell (and sometimes write) their stories in the context of a developing relationship" (Ellis, Kiesinger, and Tillmann-Healy 1997: 121). These researchers offer no specific rules for implementing their methodology, but they do say that an important part of the process is paying attention to each person's thoughts and feelings and how these are influenced by the relationship.

Ellis, an ethnographer who had been experimenting with interactive approaches to interviewing, had Kiesinger and Tillmann-Healy as students in a class she was teaching on the sociology of emotions. For course assignments, the two students wrote of their life with bulimia, and the teacher and students eventually decided to collaborate on a study of the experience of bulimia. The three interviewed one another in different combinations of two-person interviews over a period of time. Because they found that some things were easier for them to write about than to risk losing control during an interview, they generated additional data through a great deal of self-reflection via journaling, including recording their thoughts before, during, and after interviews. In addition to the formal interviews, they had regular project meetings at Ellis's home, and she kept notes on those conversations. The three also spent informal time together, for example, going out to eat, and wrote field notes on those interactions as well.

Ellis, Kiesinger, and Tillmann-Healy maintain that their approach was fruitful in learning about what it feels like to be bulimic, and argue that interactive interviewing is promising for those who want to "understand emotional and bodily practices" and even work to overcome them personally or culturally (1997: 145). Their use of journaling, asking respondents to write about their feelings and experiences, is an innovative way to deal with topics that generate such strong feelings as to make subjects unwilling to discuss them face-to-face with a researcher. However, interactive interviewing as a whole has serious limitations for critical research.

For one, these researchers acknowledged that their relationship was an obstacle to, as well as a source of, talk. They report a conflict between wanting to know more about the experience of bulimia and wanting to protect themselves and the others from exposing too much. At times they postponed asking about something because the timing didn't seem right, because it might hurt the others' feelings, and because they might not have enough time to deal with the likely emotional reactions.

This process has some other limitations as well. It requires a huge investment of time on the part of all participants and tends to build on local relationships, both of which would lead to small, fairly homogeneous samples of those who have adequate resources and few caretaking responsibilities. Also, these researchers' own experience shows that the degree of closeness developed in these face-to-face relationships raises the costs of, and thus becomes a barrier to, embarrassing self-disclosure. Personal loyalties can conflict with scholarly openness. For example, Ellis reports that she asked the others' permission to talk about her horror at their behavior. These are problems that raise serious concerns, given the implications of standpoint epistemology. In addition to the serious interpersonal restrictions, the reliance on a fairly privileged subject pool brings interactive interviewing conflict with the principle of working from the standpoint of the disadvantaged.

Sharing Drafts with Research Subjects

A more modest, yet still problematic, strategy for involving research subjects in the analysis is sharing drafts of early analyses with them and soliciting their feedback. The difficulties involved in this strategy may explain why it is rare. First, actively involving those under study in the analysis of data entails serious logistical problems. It takes more time and effort on the part of both the investigator and the investigated (Mauther and Doucet 1998). Time demands fall heaviest on those who have the least control over their time—the poor, the overworked, the unhoused. Asking them to even read research reports assumes that they are interested, and may be more of an imposition than a form of empowerment (Patai 1991). The basic mechanics of sharing drafts of the analysis are particularly a problem when those under study do not read, or do not read in the language of the investigator; live at a great distance from the investigator; and/or are at risk if others learn about their participation in the research (M. Wolf 1996).

Second, in most projects it would be very difficult to involve every research subject in the analysis, so researchers must choose among them. Yet research subjects are not a monolithic lot, so what are the criteria for selecting among them? Acker, Barry, and Esseveld (1983/1991) found themselves reluctant to share their analysis with research subjects whose views would be contradicted by the analysis, because they were understandably uncomfortable with challenging the legitimacy of others' opinions. But if researchers choose those whose opinions they believe will not diverge too far from the analyses in the text, what is the point of the exercise?

Michelle Fine and Lois Weiss (1996) offer a particularly striking example of this problem from their research on working-class people. They report that they have found many white working-class women living in situations that the researchers would identify as physically abusive do not label their experience as abuse and rarely criticize the men who do it. Fine and Weiss suspect that these women are working hard to sustain a notion of domestic life because it creates a "safe space" for them emotionally. Their example underscores the ethical implications of inviting those we study into the process of data analysis. Do researchers have the right to undermine people's tenuous emotional grounding by naming their situation as abuse (Fine and Weiss 1996)? Will researchers sharing drafts of their analysis avoid involving vulnerable research subjects, or will they censor their own analyses?

A third issue is the question of what researchers are to do when they share drafts with research subjects and encounter significant areas of disagreement. Katherine Borland (1991) describes such a situation emerging in the course of an oral history with her grandmother. Her grandmother tells the story of going with her own father to the horse races during the 1930s and getting into a disagreement with him about the horse on which she had chosen to bet. The grandmother holds her ground, even though the disagreement and her assertiveness intensify over the three heats of the race, each of which her horse wins. At the end she triumphantly chastises her father loudly enough to be clearly audible to those in the stands around them. Borland interprets the story as a kind of feminist struggle for autonomy and authority within the context of traditional patriarchy. Her grandmother's response to reading Borland's analysis was that she had distorted the story so much as to have totally changed it.

Borland (1991) and her grandmother resolved their disagreement by incorporating the grandmother's response into Borland's text. In the future, Borland says, she'll arrange for a second visit with those she interviews, at which she will have him or her discuss the transcript of the first interview and what it meant. Her point is not that consensus must be reached, but rather that the "narrator" should have some "textual authority." Borland argues that extending the conversation to include early stages of interpretation might enrich understanding on each side.

Sharing drafts of initial interviews or observations is an interesting way to elicit further and more directed talk from the subjects of study. However, increasing the depth of one's understanding of a research subject's viewpoint is not the same thing as giving that viewpoint final authority. This situation demonstrates some of the problems with giving analytic authority to the subjects of study I discussed in chapter 3. On the one hand, Borland's grandmother seems to have been drawing on discourses about gender that predated modern feminist analysis, and that is a limit of her perspective that her researcher granddaughter does not share.[2] On the other hand, the grandmother was well educated and assertive. Many feminists study people who are neither, and thus who might feel less free to challenge a researcher's analysis.

Beyond the logistical challenges, those whom researchers study may feel that analysis is the investigators' job, not theirs. In fact, this is what Acker and her colleagues (1983/1991) found: those respondents who read early, highly descriptive drafts of the analysis wanted more than to see their experiences described. These women wanted sociological analysis; they pushed the investigators to make sense of that experience for them. It is quite reasonable for research subjects to be unwilling to do the work of helping with the analysis. Further, people in less powerful social positions are more likely to be deprived of the tools to guide them in developing a satisfactory analysis of their experience, one that would justify confidence in advancing an analysis, or especially in debating with an expert. Nancy Naples's observations during her fieldwork in rural Iowa of group discussions among people in diverse economic situations suggest that this is the case. She reports that in contrast with the others, people with lower incomes "rarely spoke openly about their perceptions and experiences" (Naples 1996/1997: 86).

In general, then, involving the researched in the analysis has limited usefulness. It depends on research subjects having time, access, and a fairly developed alternative analysis. It is likely to include a bias toward those whose analysis is unlikely to undermine that of the researchers, and when significant disagreement occurs, there can be ethical issues in undermining the worldview of the subjects of study. These problems explain why even though there is a great deal of discussion of involving subjects in the analysis of data, investigators rarely do it (Olesen 1994). Researchers favoring this approach seem to be relying on the subjectivist reading of standpoint epistemology, equating a standpoint with the subjectivity of individuals. As I argued in chapter 3, that is a misreading of the arguments of standpoint theorists, and as the above examples illustrate, not very pragmatic empirically.

Drawing on Alternative Discourses

Marginalized groups are often restricted in their ability to develop a standpoint through formal institutions of knowledge like the academy and organized religion, but many members of these groups have found other channels to communicate their perspectives on their values and lives. Some qualitative scholars have found it useful to listen to what members of these groups are saying about their lives in venues outside usual social science discourse, and take these statements into account as they develop their analyses.

One source of alternative worldviews is literature written by group members—including fiction, essays, and poetry. For example, Virginia Woolf's novels offer insightful commentary on the gendered options, expectations, and constraints within which some women struggled in the nineteenth century. Marjorie DeVault (1991) draws on Woolf's writing about women's work in the home. Social science researchers have usually analyzed this work by collecting data on who does tasks such as cooking, cleaning, ironing, taking care of the children, and so on, and on how much time people spend doing each. DeVault (1991) uses a scene from Virginia Woolf's novel *To the Lighthouse*, which reveals the inadequacy of the usual social science approach.

In this scene Mrs. Ramsay, an upper-middle-class housewife, is hosting a dinner party. Woolf shows Mrs. Ramsay working to make sure that the party flows smoothly, that the food is served promptly and appropriately, and that people are coming together as a group. Even while she is engaging in conversation, Mrs. Ramsay is also constantly monitoring sounds that might alert her to signals of something that needs her attention. When she notices that down the table another guest, Lily Briscoe, seems unwilling to fulfill her feminine obligation by appearing to be interested in the conversation of a dull male guest, Mrs. Ramsay casts her a glance that reminds Briscoe of her duty and threatens repercussions should she ignore it. In this scene Woolf reveals what social science usually misses: "the planning and coordination involved in household work as well as the constant juggling and strategizing behind the physical tasks" (DeVault 1991: 56).

DeVault's passage conveys the heart of her analysis of the complexity of contemporary women's work in "doing family," for which she interviewed diverse women about their work in contemporary U.S. middle- and working-class families. In her research she found that the mental labor of figuring out how to have enough time to do family work and how to do it better fills many "free" moments of a person's day, often while doing other things. DeVault also learned how criteria and standards, and thus the nature of the work, vary in different intersections of gender with race/ethnicity and class. For example, while professional middle-class people prefer innovative and exotic menus for special occasions, working-class people tend to look for traditionally prepared meals.

Ann Ferguson (2000) developed ways to conduct her ethnographic research on the social organization of discipline in an underresourced urban elementary school from the standpoint of the African American boys who were overwhelmingly the targets of disciplinary practices. Her fieldwork was "by the book" in many ways. She spent three and a half years observing at the school, spending time in the major sites of student and/or staff interaction: the hallways, student cafeteria, teachers' lounge, and playground. She attended classes, spent time in the library, and also served as tutor to a boy named Horace as part of the program. In the second year she chose to focus on Horace's sixth-grade class, and selected 20 African American fifth- and sixth-grade boys, ten of whom school personnel thought of as "troublemakers," and another ten who seemed to be on the opposite track and whom she called "school boys." Ferguson interviewed each of the boys and spent time hanging around with and getting to know a smaller subset of them. She interviewed all the school personnel who were involved with the boys and also interviewed the boys' parents, over time forming close relationships with some families.

Ferguson's interviews with the boys followed a fairly standard format, except that at the end of the interview she offered to reverse roles and let the boys interview her. Many of them accepted the invitation, and she noticed that they asked her the standard sociological questions. Taking on the standpoint of an interviewee led her to reflect on how the interview situation limited what she could learn from her subjects. As a reward for participating in interviews, Ferguson took the boys out for pizza and then for some kind of entertainment—a video arcade or a sightseeing trip. She quickly found that she learned much more about the boys' lives and worldviews from the informal conversations during these post-interview activities than she did from the interviews.

Ferguson's primary informant was perhaps the most troublesome troublemaker, a boy she calls Horace, the student assigned to her by the tutoring program. Analyzing the struggles in their relationship from his point of view taught Ferguson how she had been objectifying him, and all of the children, when they were agents actively negotiating the terms of their situations. She began to see Horace as someone who could teach her, and eventually invited him to be her research assistant. Horace advised her on topics to cover in her interviews with the other boys and critiqued her interview questions.

Perhaps his most important suggestion, Ferguson says, was that he insisted she learn about the children through listening to the rap music they liked. She began listening to their favorite radio station, the song lyrics, the DJs, the call-ins, and the commercials. She found that the rap lyrics, while sometimes offensive and typically misogynistic, were also witty and insightful, "often sharpened by a measure of social criticism and political commentary," even bringing up some of the same themes that she was finding in her own analysis (2000: 16). Note that Ferguson gives credibility to some aspects of the music while disagreeing with other aspects. Similarly, she takes what her informants have to tell her as valuable information, but does not adopt their worldviews uncritically. She retains final authority in interpretation.

There are many other good examples. Aptheker (1989) uses the words of Latina and Asian American women poets as sources of analyses of the experiences of their groups. Collins (1991/2000) uses blues songs as sources of insight about the lives and worldviews of African American women. Cheryl Gilkes (2003) reads religious songs written by African American women as expressions of their own accounts of their struggles and conceptions of faith. In each case the scholar is taking marginalized discourses seriously, considering the analyses they offer while grounding people's interpretations in the specifics of their experience and interests.

Listening for Alternative Standpoints

The language we use in daily life, like the mainstream scholarly discourse I described in chapter 1, is organized from a particular standpoint, uses categories and metaphors that make sense from that perspective, and thus is riddled with blind spots and inadequacies (Lakoff and Johnson 1980; Zerubavel 1991). For example, the word "work" typically connotes work done for pay, and overlooks domestic, emotional, and volunteer work—all work commonly done by women (Aptheker 1989; Collins 1991/2000; Daniels 1987; DeVault 1999; Hochschild 1983). Similarly, talk about government policy in public discourse tends to be organized through the metaphor of a controlling father family, emphasizing discipline and punishment and the rights of the dominant rather than nurturance and support and the needs of the vulnerable (Lakoff 1995; Sprague 1996).

Researchers and research subjects must rely on everyday language for communication. This increases the difficulty of adequately describing daily life and sensibility for people in marginalized groups: women, the poor, people of color, people from non-Western nations. The words we use can misrepresent or even hide important parts of marginalized experiences.

For example, neither "housework" nor "feeding" is adequate to describe the complex intersection of physical, mental, and emotional work that women do for their families (Yeatman 1984). When DeVault (1991) wanted to get at this usually invisible work in her interviews, she had to ask women about "all the housework that has to do with food." In listening to women's talk about what they took into account in planning and providing food for their families, DeVault could identify principles that the women themselves might not be able to articulate. This allowed her to learn, for example, how women took into account individual tastes, family traditions, and class-specific expectations about the right kind of meal in their planning.

Traditionally, qualitative interviewers have dismissed people's hesitations, their stumbling over words, their comments about searching for the right words, and their seeking the interviewer's support for a statement as indications of inarticulateness and insecurity. In transcribing such speech, researchers have often corrected it to make it more fluent. DeVault (1990) suggests that what appears to be inarticulateness may be among the most revealing data. Struggling to find the right word may point to a problem with the words that are available. Adding "do you know what I mean?" to the end of an account can signal that the interviewee is struggling to describe an experience that is not adequately captured by mainstream discourse.

Listening carefully for "inarticulateness" during an interview can lead to more fruitful lines of inquiry. DeVault observed that sometimes the women she interviewed were talking "in shorthand," not fully expressing an aspect of a task. By paying attention to these instances and following through with further questions, she often learned important things about the social division of responsibility in the household (1999: 72). In talking about how they constructed grocery lists, she noticed that some women used "gallons" as shorthand for "gallons of milk." She pursued this idea in her questioning and learned that people who used shorthand tended to be people who were not used to talking about this work because they did not share it with anyone else and it was their sole responsibility.

What DeVault teaches us is not to be too quick to dismiss an expression as merely a sign of inarticulateness. Ease in articulating an experience is created by a language that captures the salient aspects of that experience. Verbal struggles can be indications of a lack of fit between one's knowledge of daily practices and struggles and the hegemonic worldview. Researchers should identify these struggles as potential critiques of the limits of our language, as new avenues to pursue in exploring the social world.

Investigators fail to listen carefully because they assume they already know what the respondent is talking about. Kathryn Anderson and Dana Jack (1991) say this assumption is a clue that an interviewer is simply applying mainstream conceptual categories. Those categories will fit to some extent, because growing up in a culture requires learning to fit within it, internalizing the "right" beliefs and emotional responses (Anderson and Jack 1991). However, to the extent that culture is constructed from a contrasting standpoint to one's own, there will be inconsistencies between the official version and one's sense of his or her experience. Under such circumstances it can be hard for people to figure out what they really think and feel, and this divergence can emerge in their talk about their lives. Their speech will express multiple voices.

Anderson and Jack (1991) use the metaphor of "listening in stereo" to suggest how interviewers deal with this challenge. They suggest that investigators watch for references to "the choices, the pain, the stories that lie beyond the 'constraints of acceptable discussion'" (1991: 11), because such references can point to a conflict between hegemonic and personal views of experience. Anderson and Jack offer three new listening strategies to avoid being trapped in mainstream categories of thought. First, they suggest, investigators should listen to the *moral language* people are using. People's moral language, their expressions of "shoulds" or "oughts," will call attention to where and how they experience a conflict between their own needs and desires and dominant cultural expectations and rules.

Second, researchers should watch for respondents' *meta-statements*. Sometimes respondents will make statements assessing themselves from the perspective of the dominant culture, noting how they fail to meet those expectations. A statement like "I guess I'm not a very good . . ." points to both social norms and social constraints, making those norms difficult for some to attain. Third, the analyst should pay attention to the *logic of the narrative*. The logic of their narratives may also reveal the way social structure creates a conflict between hegemonic expectations and many oppressed people's lives. For example, women may describe frustration or unhappiness about their subordination in a personal relationship as being better than being alone. The construction of the choice signals a structural situation in a sexist society: the chances of being able to negotiate an egalitarian relationship are slim (Anderson and Jack 1991).

Researchers like DeVault and Anderson and Jack are, in effect, grounding people's speech in their standpoints, taking into account their position in social relations and the kinds of discourses they have to draw on to organize their experience. By listening carefully, these researchers are able to detect signals of social power organizing that experience. The potential of this strategy for developing structural analyses through qualitative methodology becomes clear in institutional ethnography.

Institutional Ethnography

Institutional ethnography is an approach introduced by Dorothy Smith and her students to consciously build on the implications of standpoint epistemology (cf. Campbell and Manicom 1995; Smith 2005). Researchers doing institutional ethnography use the same kinds of data that other ethnographers use: interviews, observations, documents. However, the way they see the relationship between the data and their research goals is radically different. In traditional ethnography, these data are themselves the "object of analysis," while institutional ethnographers see the data as the means of "'entry' into the social relations of the setting" (Campbell 1998: 57). For example, traditional ethnographers study a site—a workplace, a street corner, a playground, or a household. Institutional ethnographers are interested in learning how that site is organized, "held together," by other institutions, for example, how people organize their households given the demands of work, educational institutions, the presence of child care, and so on (DeVault 1999).

Institutional ethnographers go into the field to see "how it works" (Campbell 1998: 60), to learn how people's everyday experience is socially organized. Individuals may not be able to describe that social organization, but they are the best authorities on their actual practices. The constraints they have to struggle with and the resources they can draw on are the basic indicators of social organization. Focusing on how people describe their daily (and nightly) lives is a way to counter the biases built into mainstream analytic categories. People's accounts of their practices are a form of access to what is actually going on (Campbell 1998). Because part of how power works in the modern world is through texts and how they organize our activities, institutional ethnographers say that it is important to pay particular attention to texts relevant to the activity under study.

Dorothy Smith and Allison Griffith's institutional ethnography of the relationship between families and schools provides an illustration (Griffith 1995; Smith 1987). A mother as well as a sociologist, Griffith (1995) was struck by how teachers talked to her about her children, and what that communicated about the vision of her children from the school's point of view. This drew her attention to three interrelated discourses: the educational discourse on "child-centered education," the professional discourse on child development, and the discourse on mothering. Together, over the course of the twentieth century, these discourses have transformed the work of mothering from primarily meeting physiological and medical needs to also providing culturally appropriate social, emotional, and cognitive care.

Griffith and Smith began their study of the educational institution by seeing what it looks like from the standpoint of the frontline actors in elementary education: the mothers of schoolchildren. They were interested in finding out the actual conditions under which mothering is done. Taking advantage of the way class organizes residential patterns, and thus school populations, Griffith and Smith began by selecting local schools in class-differentiated neighborhoods. First, they interviewed the mothers of children in those schools, asking them to describe their daily practices and noting those that were connected to the work of educating their children. Next, they used those descriptions and the social relations to which they pointed to develop research questions for interviews with the schools' personnel, beginning with the classroom teachers. At each subsequent stage they moved to a level further up the hierarchy of institutional power, and further away from the daily practices of mothers and children: school social workers and psychologists, principals, and administrators of school districts.

Interviews with mothers revealed that middle-class women are more likely than are working-class women to participate heavily in the child-development/ mothering discourses and to have the time and resources to conduct the tasks these discourses assign to mothers. Interviews with kindergarten and primary school teachers and administrators in a working-class school revealed that the educators attributed students' failures to parents, rather than to the educational system. They described those parents as not having "the right attitude" toward school. Their discussion of the problem made it clear to the interviewers that their concern was more than a matter of attitude—parents were not doing the right work. Among the tasks that working-class parents were failing to perform, in the view of the professionals, were stimulating children with creative play, teaching them the school's standards of work and order, and teaching them a set of skills that the organization of schools presumes they know how to do.

What Smith and Griffith have been able to uncover in this approach is how something that on the face of it appears to be an unquestionable, good, child-centered education helps reproduce class inequality without the actors wanting this or even being aware of the role their practices and expectations play in the process. Because schools depend on mothers doing a specific kind of labor, one that working-class mothers are not aware of and/or cannot do, working-class children do not do well in school. Some families don't have the resources (time, money, education, language facility, etc.) to do the work that the contemporary social construction of an ideal family/school relationship requires.

Institutional ethnography is an approach that addresses many of the feminist critiques of conventional practices without some of the pitfalls of other critical strategies. The technique was developed to meet the goal Smith sets for sociology: to make sense of what seems to be irrational in everyday life by showing how it is the product of power relations that are not immediately visible to social actors. Rather than either usurping authority, as conventional social science researchers have, or surrendering authority to the subjects under study, as some critical researchers suggest we should do, institutional ethnographers divide it. People have authority over accounts of their daily practices; they know better than researchers how their lives get played out. Researchers have authority over how to knit the accounts of multiple actors in distinct social structural locations together into an analysis of the institutionalization of social power. Rather than representing people at or near the bottom of hierarchies as marginalized others, institutional ethnographers see them as frontline actors who can provide essential information. Rather than developing a case study that allows "us" to look at "them," institutional ethnographers turn the camera to the social relations that connect us all (DeVault 1995).

There are also some limitations to this strategy. To really study the organization of a major institution from the everyday/everynight practices of all the actors involved would, as Smith (1987) admits, take the cooperation of many researchers. Also, there are some important questions that are not embedded in the practices of everyday life, notably questions about how things are distributed across populations. For example, institutional ethnography would not be the best way to develop information on distributions of educational resources and outcomes. But, then, it seems unlikely that any single method can adequately address all the pieces of any important social science question, a theme to which I will return in the final chapter.

CONSTRUCTING COLLABORATIONS

Thus far, I have described and evaluated some strategies that feminists have tried in order to achieve two key goals: increasing the connections between researchers and the researched, and compensating for the limitations in researchers' standpoints. A meta-strategy that can address both of these is to redefine the research project from an individual to a collaborative undertaking (cf. Sprague and Zimmerman 1993). First I will outline ways that feminist researchers have developed collaborative teams to compensate for limitations of the investigator's standpoint. Then I will describe a less common technique, building on the connections among research subjects in group interviews.

Researcher Teams

Researchers can collaborate with one another in diverse ways. The approach of Barbara Laslett and Rhona Rapoport (1975), "collaborative interviewing," shows a highly coordinated version. Interested in family dynamics, they sampled family units, selecting multiple members and doing a series of interviews with each. In an effort to make sure that each family member's story received equal consideration, different investigators interviewed each, using interview guides designed with that family member's position in mind. After an interview, the interviewer debriefed with another interviewer not involved with that family, working together to develop insights and minimize the distorting effect of the interviewer's personal cognitive and emotional response to the experience. The interviewer then wrote up an account of the interview, and eventually of the series of interviews with the same family member. Finally, the team interviewing members of the same family worked together to develop an account of that family.

Acker, Barry, and Esseveld (1983/1991) collaborated in interviewing 65 women, following 30 of them over the course of four to five years. As interviewers, they worked to establish "close and sympathetic involvement" with the women they interviewed. However, they also worked to develop their analysis collaboratively, meeting regularly to discuss their interviews. They found that their discussions as a research team facilitated "moments" of objectification that, like the moments of sympathetic identification with those they were interviewing, were a valuable stage in the research process.

Finch and Mason (1990), a university professor and a full-time employee of a survey and qualitative interviewing research project, made all decisions collaboratively through regular meetings, keeping a collective research diary in which they recorded all discussions and decisions. They shared all their individual notes and rotated serving as note taker in the meetings. When they found that they could not resolve an issue in the discussion, they wrote individual memos to each other, one raising the issue, the other responding, until some consensus emerged.

In an illustration of a collaborative approach to fieldwork, Naples (1996/1997) worked with four research assistants, diverse in gender, race/ethnicity, and age, in her study of the construction of "outsider" in two small towns in Iowa. Each member of the team stayed in the home of different community members, giving them multiple perspectives on the site. At the end of each trip, they discussed their experiences and discovered striking differences in their perceptions. Taking each perspective seriously and discussing the factors generating the diversity allowed them to develop a more complex picture.

Sometimes field researchers are interested in fleeting events in which it would be impossible for one researcher to capture more than a small part of what is going on. Steven Mazie and Patricia Woods (2003), a woman and a man trained in two different disciplines, accidentally discovered that they were both doing field research on women praying at the Western Wall in Jerusalem, a traditionally male-only privilege that generates strong emotional responses on all sides. By collaborating in their analyses, they argue, they were able to capture a more complex and nuanced glimpse of diverse crowd reactions to the incident.

Researchers can benefit from collaborating with scholars in different disciplines working on unrelated research projects, as Anderson and Jack (1991) have shown. A historian and a psychologist, they shared interview transcripts with each other in an effort to improve their listening skills by virtue of an outside critique. What they found was that their contrasting disciplinary outlooks enriched the analyses. The historian pressed the psychologist to look for the social context in their interviewees' stories, and the psychologist prompted the historian to ask what a sequence of events meant to the person.

Each of these teams reports that their collaboration was useful in compensating for some of the limitations of their standpoints. Collaboration among investigators in data gathering can increase the variety of their sources of information. When incorporated into the analysis, collaboration can make researchers more mindful of their personal biases, and can even be used to compensate for disciplinary blinders. Standpoint epistemology implies that these collaborations would benefit most if strategically organized across key social divisions of experience and interest like gender, race/ethnicity, and class background.

Group Interviews

The group interview, commonly called the focus group, is "a research technique that collects data through group interaction on a topic determined by the researcher" (Morgan 1996: 130). Group interviews are tainted in many researchers' minds by their association with commercial and political marketing efforts (Montell 1999). Frances Montell (1999) observes that a group interview combines the strengths of in-depth interviewing with those of participant observation for the collection of rich data. They can be a means to preserve the subjectivity of participants, decenter the researcher's perspective, and provide valuable comparative data.

In a successful group interview, the bulk of the interaction is among participants, and the leader merely prompts and helps focus the discussion. One advantage of the group interview is that group members can and do ask questions of one another, and may challenge as well as support one another's statements, insisting on a fuller or less self-serving telling than an interviewer could (Montell 1999). For example, Robin Jarrett (1993) shows how the poor African American women in a group interview pressed one speaker on whether she actually informed her boyfriend that she had stopped using birth-control pills. The speaker was initially vague, and another group member asked the question more directly. The speaker continued to evade, yet the other group members returned to the question until the speaker responded. It seems unlikely that a professional interviewer could have been so assertive in questioning without threatening the rest of the interview.

The process of dialogue and negotiation in a group interview provides information about the degree of consensus in a group that would be hard to get in any other method (Montell 1999; Morgan 1996). For example, Montell (1999) describes how members of a group uncovered and discussed quite different interpretations of the meaning of "good sex." Similarly, Gwen Richtermeyer (2001) found that professional women whom she interviewed individually were more interested in talking about their achievements than about barriers they confronted, while the statements of women in group interviews who failed to acknowledge obstacles were quickly amended and filled in by their peers.

Interview groups should be homogeneous on attributes that might be relevant to the research topic. To study how class background shaped experience in professional managerial jobs, Richtermeyer (2001) recruited African American, Latina, and white women who had achieved great professional success, some of whom had been born into affluent families and others who had been born into working-class or even poorer families. She constructed separate focus groups for each intersection of race/ethnicity and class origins, for example, some groups were composed solely of white women from the working class. Homogeneous groups have the added advantage of building a comparative element into the research design, allowing researchers to observe how intersecting social dynamics like gender, race, class, and sexuality work. Richtermeyer found systematic differences by race/ethnicity and class background in the kinds of obstacles women identified and the sources of support on which they relied.

For those who are silenced or isolated in everyday life, just participating in a discussion group on a topic can be empowering. Esther Madriz (1998) conducted group interviews with Latina and reports that these women who have been silenced in their local cultures used their discussion to create a group testimony about their struggles living in dangerous neighborhoods.

Focus groups, like any groups, are shaped by interpersonal dynamics. Members are in front of an audience, and to some extent are performing for one another, though Jarrett (1993) says that a certain amount of bombast or outrageousness can be an important means to build group rapport. She observes that participants use verbal markers (e.g., "I'm serious," "that's the truth," "but, really") to signal moments when they are making special efforts at being honest and sincere. Group interviews can also be disproportionately influenced by one or more overly assertive participants, one reason that a design should include multiple groups of the same type. Groups that are homogeneous in terms of factors related to the topic of research, for example, gender, class, race, and/or sexual orientation, facilitate freer conversation (Morgan 1996). Even then, researchers might consider administering a post-interview questionnaire or asking participants to write journals to get their current feelings on the topic and reports of how freely they felt they could participate (Montell 1999; Morgan 1996).

Group interviews present special logistical challenges. Scheduling a significant block of time (one to two hours) for six to ten participants to create a homogeneous group multiplies the usual scheduling problems associated with interviewing. In order to account for the idiosyncrasies of any particular group, a study should include four to six groups, sharply increasing the complexity of scheduling. Group interviews require a location, one that is both comfortable for and accessible to interviewees. This means that arrangements for transportation and child care may be necessary (Madriz 1998).

It seems likely that group interviews will collect different kinds of data than individual interviews, that people will say something different in individual versus group interviews (Morgan 1996). Some raise the concern that participants may be reluctant to discuss sensitive topics in public, but there is no systematic research on this (Morgan 1996). On the other hand, Montell (1999) proposes that some sensitive topics might be easier to discuss in a group of peers than in a one-on-one interaction with an interviewer. She argues convincingly that this is the case for discussions of sexuality.

The group interview could be an effective strategy for facilitating group members in developing their own standpoint on their experiences. As part of facilitating group discussion, the researcher can ask participants to compare their experiences, perhaps a more workable way than others of involving research subjects in the analysis (Morgan 1996). Organizing dialogues among the subjects of research may empower them to discover and interpret patterns that crosscut their experiences, following in the path of the consciousness-raising groups that propelled the development of a feminist analysis at the beginning of the second wave of the women's movement (cf. Montell 1999). Even though people in the United States are not accustomed to viewing their experiences in social structural terms, Richtermeyer (2001) found that women in her focus groups were able to collectively build a cross-workplace analysis of obstacles to their success, including identifying practices for distributing information and other resources that systematically disadvantaged those who were not male, white, and/or born to privilege.

The experience of those who have attempted group interviews does suggest that it might be fruitful to systematically study whether and under what conditions the methods that bring people together with their peers enhance their ability to develop their own critical analyses of their experiences. By bringing together people who share a social location to talk about their experiences in a facilitated conversation, a collective interview can provide the infrastructure for generating an alternative sphere of discourse.

Collaborative approaches hold promise for enriching both data gathering and interpretation. They increase the complexity of the research process, for example, the logistics of getting it done and the additional challenge of disagreements among all the parties to the process. However, they also increase the potential for gathering more complete information and the number of perspectives brought to bear in interpreting it.

CONCLUSION

Feminist researchers have attempted to address problems of objectification of research subjects through building on their connections with those they research: being more personal than professional, and drawing on their own emotional reactions and biographies as resources for interpreting data. They

have tried to compensate for the biases in the standpoint of scholars by focusing on the worldviews of those they study, from examining the logic underlying people's accounts to looking at the themes in their favorite elements
of popular culture. Researchers have adopted strategies for listening to people's accounts that are sensitive to not just what people say, but how they say
it, seeing hesitations, meta-statements, and the like as cues to the working of
power in their lives. Researchers have used collaborative strategies to encourage reflexivity about their own standpoint and to facilitate research subjects in
constructing theirs. How do these various efforts measure up to the guidelines
for critical research methodology developed out of a sociological reading of
standpoint epistemology?

(1) Work from the Standpoint of the Disadvantaged   Many of the strategies described in this chapter are working toward this goal. Examining the
narrative structure of research subjects' accounts gives voice to perspectives
and access to discourses that constitute an alternative to the researchers' but
do not go far enough in identifying their standpoint. Some of the more successful strategies in trying to work from the standpoint of the disadvantaged
seek to learn from subjects about the practices and constraints in their daily
lives, making visible what dominant discourses may hide: devalued and invisible labor, systematic disadvantages, structures of discrimination, and the social contexts giving rise to nonnormative behavior. However, completely
shifting the interpretive authority to research subjects simply replaces the current set of biases in social research with another set, failing to satisfy the next
guideline.

(2) Ground Interpretations in Interests and Experience   The methodologies of "listening for alternative standpoints" developed by DeVault and by
Anderson and Jack are strong on this point. These approaches analyze patterns in speech for the workings of social power and powerlessness—the conflicts between mainstream discourse and people's sense of their own interests
and experience. Smith's Institutional Ethnography, illustrated by Griffith,
provides another model in the way it divides authority based on social position and access to discourses. Researchers also have interests and experience,
and the work of Ferguson, Krieger, Riessman, and Thorne shows how researchers' reflecting on their own location, interests, discourses, and position
in the production of knowledge generates powerful insights about how their
standpoint shapes their research.

(3) Maintain a Strategically Diverse Discourse   Feminist qualitative researchers have provided several tactics for enriching our discourse. Taking marginalized voices seriously is a pivotal first step toward countering the hegemonic filters in academic discourse, as long as researchers remain critical of the workings of power in shaping which marginalized voices get distributed (hooks 1990). On the other hand, engaging subjects in the analysis of data is not a particularly promising tactic, given its logistical problems and ethical dilemmas. Another key contribution is the use of collaboration. Collaborative research teams can decenter the researcher's own assumptions and point of view, particularly if they are organized democratically and strategically (e.g., across major social divisions and disciplinary divides).

(4) Create Knowledge That Empowers the Disadvantaged   Which of these approaches to qualitative research helps us to support people's struggles for self-determination, to make cross-cultural understanding, social justice, and true democracy possible? Having people interested in what you have to say, in your own way of saying it, can be psychologically empowering to those who are not used to people being interested in their opinions. Ferguson's analysis of the creation of bad boys in elementary school, and Griffith's analysis of the way discourses construct good education and good parenting so as to disadvantage working-class families, show that field research can reveal the mechanisms by which social inequality is created in people's daily lives. Making these mechanisms explicit is the necessary precursor to disabling them. Collaborative interviews can support subjects' working together to develop their own analysis.

Feminists have exposed and enlarged the potential of qualitative methods to serve the cause of social justice. In the final analysis, whether or not social science knowledge empowers members of disadvantaged groups depends on the questions being asked and how and to whom researchers communicate their findings. These crucial issues—how to ask questions and provide answers that best serve the interests of sound scholarship and social justice—are the topics of chapter 6.

NOTES

1. Thanks to Judy Howard for pointing out this alternative explanation.

2. Thanks to Judy Howard for another sterling insight.

6

Whose Questions?
Whose Answers?

Mainstream discussions of how to do social science research focus on how best to implement a method, that is, on issues of technique. The previous two chapters do just that. Critical evaluations of techniques are important. With careful reflection on the underlying epistemological assumptions, they can produce useful innovations in methodology. However, in the production of knowledge, technique is a means to an end, and the ends, as well as the means, should be open to critique.

Most books about methodology devote some attention to the ethical requirements entailed by researchers' relationships with those they study. Before undertaking research with human subjects, researchers must convince institutional review boards (IRBs) that their research is not likely to harm those subjects, including denying them their individual rights to privacy and to free and informed participation. However, the relationship between the researcher and the research subject is only one of a set of research relationships.

Researchers also exist in definite social relationships with other scholars in our areas of study and broader discipline, and with taxpayers and others who provide the material support for our work. Further, the obligations to do no harm or to not expose subjects to unnecessary risk apply not just to the particular individuals with whom researchers have direct contact; they extend to *the whole social category of people* that these individuals represent. Yet textbook discussions of ethics and the considerations of institutional review boards tend to give much less scrutiny to the ethical implications of these other relationships that research impacts.

The ethical obligation to the individual can conflict with the ethical obligation to the individual's social category. For example, the obligation to protect the privacy of women CEOs of Fortune 500 companies, who are very rare, conflicts with the importance of understanding the gendered dynamics of how they got there, the obstacles they confront, the strategies they employ, and the consequences for their firms (cf. Ginorio 2004). The conflict between the individual's right to informed consent and the categories' right to information about how social power gets reproduced is a particular challenge for field researchers. Consider a hypothetical researcher who would like to observe classroom practices for possible gender or racial/ethnic biases. Knowing that they are being observed would prompt teachers to monitor their behavior with an eye to social norms about equality. Yet practices that create gendered or racialized consequences for students are probably unreflective and unintentional. Thus an emphasis on an individual teacher's informed consent to being the subject of research conflicts with the need for research on everyday practices of power.

Equally important ethical obligations of researchers, I believe, are that we produce knowledge that is as unbiased as possible and that somehow makes a contribution to the common good. As I pointed out in chapter 1, some systematic problems with the kinds of questions that sociologists tend to pose make it more likely than not that we will produce knowledge that serves elites better than it serves the vast majority of people. And the way we publish our answers limits readership. Constraining the audience for a research report to a narrow band of like-minded researchers limits the scope of scholarly access to the work, not to mention its potential to inform social action.

In this chapter I will explore some strategies that feminists have used to make our questions and answers more responsive to our obligations to the various communities with which we have social relationships. Since there has been much more work on alternative forms of publishing our findings, I will begin with these. Later I will describe some general strategies for developing research questions that maximize the likelihood that the research will be useful to creating a more just society.

ALTERNATIVE FORMATS FOR REPORTING FINDINGS

Conventional practices for providing answers to research questions deflect criticism, limit the size and scope of audiences, hide the workings of power, and deaden potential emotional responses to findings about the status quo (see chapter 1). In these ways, traditional standards of academic discourse serve the interests of the powerful. How might researchers do things differently? In the face of concerns about the politics of representation, some qualitative feminist researchers have responded by experimenting with alternative ways to present their research findings. Feminist researchers have experimented with approaches to writing that make the researchers' standpoint and limits thereof obvious in the text, that avoid objectifying the subjects of study, that have the potential to communicate to a broader audience, and that actively involve the audience in the topic, not just intellectually but emotionally (Hertz 1997; Stanley 1990). Although these strategies have been developed by qualitative researchers, some suggest alternatives that quantitative researchers might consider as well.

Making the Researcher Visible in the Text

Simple changes in the use of language begin to make the researcher visible in the text. A minimal way to call attention to the researcher as a person with a specific subjectivity is through using personal pronouns ("I saw," "my field notes"). Another is to use active rather than passive voice ("I believe," rather than "it seems").[1] The author of the text is rarely the only researcher whose personhood is hidden. Citations to the work of other scholars usually refer to authors only by their last names and, if these scholars worked in teams, they appear as the last name of one of them "et al." Both representations tend to depersonalize the sources of the information and represent it more as fact than as the work product of specific individuals (DeVault 1999: 41). Marjorie DeVault suggests that identifying authors by their full names is more likely to call their personhood, their specificity and fallibility, to the reader's attention.

A further step in making the researcher visible in the text is for the authors to describe why they are attracted to the topic and their own stake in the research question, and to consider the advantages and the blind spots created by their social position and biography (Hertz 1997). Sociological research amply demonstrates that gender, race/ethnicity, and class, among other social identities, determine people's stake in many social issues and shape interactional practices. Researchers who describe themselves in these terms provide important cues about their own standpoint. They also give information relevant to how research subjects are likely to respond to them, which is particularly important within face-to-face research contexts (Reinharz 1997; Riessman 1993).

Investigators who describe their reasons for being interested in a research question reveal more of their own agendas and biases. That is, researchers can see their own standpoint as data and include that in their reports (D. Wolf 1996: 34–35). For example, I am a white heterosexual academic woman who grew up in the working class, and that no doubt motivates my interest in how class and gender organize evaluation in professional discourses and makes me less sensitive than I should be to how race and sexuality enter these processes. Authors could, as I just did, explicitly reflect on their personal stakes in the research. This practice is more common in qualitative than in quantitative reports, though some of the authors I discussed in chapter 4 put their current project in a biographical context, for example, working on a federal commission or serving as a consultant in a dispute.

Kathy Charmaz and Richard Mitchell (1997) suggest that researchers present their observations in a narrative format, offering the reader a sense of how things actually went in the research process and calling the reader to relive the experience as the researcher did. If the text is true to the typical research experience, they note, the author will describe his or her experience of initial ignorance and confusion, making false starts and showing the fallibility and choices made. Authors may find research subjects more or less likeable, more or less trustworthy, and more sensitive about some topics than others, and revealing these perceptions gives readers important cues for interpreting subjects' contributions. Making the author's voice clear shows "the researcher's involvement with the phenomena" (Charmaz and Mitchell 1997: 210); the researcher's voice is a resource in the research report, something that readers can draw on in constructing their understanding of what is happening (1997: 208).

Calling attention to researchers' social location and active role in decisions and choices in the conduct of the research project has some benefits. For one, it counters what Haraway calls "the God trick." It provides readers with critical information about the role of the researcher's standpoint in shaping the research. Both qualitative and quantitative authors can easily incorporate information about who they are and why they are interested in the topic and be open about false starts and failed hypotheses.

There are dangers, too. A step-by-step account of the researcher's trials and errors could become unwieldy in length and incur costs in loss of focus. Talking about one's own privilege can draw the reader's attention to the author more than to the subjects of the research (Hertz 1997). The author's "assertive confessions" can end up taking so much literal and intellectual space that more marginalized voices are shut out (DeVault 1999: 216). Researchers who feel this information is essential to evaluating their research might be better advised to put it in an appendix. Daphne Patai (1991) warns of an even more subtle danger in researchers' indulging in apologies about their privilege: it can lead them to believe that this is all they need to do. That is, confessionals can end up substituting for contributing to actually changing the reality of social inequality.

Emphasizing Personhood of Research Subjects

Several authors reporting qualitative research have experimented with ways to represent their findings without objectifying the people they have studied. They have found alternative ways to report demographic data and to compare cultures. Many have emphasized retaining the voices of the researched in the text.

The classic example of depersonalizing research subjects is transforming human beings into numbers in a table. In her interview project on the work of feeding a family, DeVault (1991: 27) summarizes the relationships among the demographics of the 30 households she studied by using literal, rather than numerical, figures. Icons of humans signify the gender of the person they represent by whether they wear pants or skirts, their race/ethnicity by how lightly or darkly they are shaded, and their age by relative size and posture (infants are crawling). A dollar sign below a figure signifies employment for wages. Icons appear in family/household clusters and are vertically arranged along a line segmented into household income categories. In a glance readers can see how gender, race/ethnicity, and household composition interact with income in a format that reminds them that the data describe real people.

Many feminist qualitative researchers emphasize giving women voice in their texts, including using more of the actual words of research subjects. They

may include longer sections of interview transcripts, showing both interviewer and interviewee's words, to allow the reader to see more of research
subjects' line of thinking and the interactional context in which they are
speaking (see Paget 1983; Riessman 1993). Another approach is to reject the
idea of the researcher's voice organizing the text and seek to construct it as
multi-voiced, reproducing segments of the actual dialogue between the researcher and the researched (see Behar 1995; Riessman 1993; Shostak 1981).
Krieger (1985) takes this a step further, reporting her findings solely through
the voices of the research subjects.

As I noted in chapter 5, Krieger (1985) analyzed life in a lesbian community in a midwestern university town. Her voice as an author brackets the actual research report, appearing in an eight-page introduction to the text in
which she describes the setting and lays out the key points of her analysis, and
again in a three-page postscript to the text. In each, Krieger sketches her key
argument: that the social context of the community makes group identification so salient that feeling valued for one's unique identity is a struggle.
Krieger warns the reader in her introduction that the book is unconvention-
ally written, and that it is organized to help the reader see how the processes
she has identified get played out in women's lives.

In the body of the text, Krieger's voice is hidden. In fact, scholarship is hidden—the book contains no review of the relevant scholarly literature, although the reader is directed to one published in a journal article. Rather, in
the topically organized chapters (e.g., "A Sense of History," "Couples," or "The
Outside World I: Work"), Krieger weaves together the perspectives of those
she interviewed, not as direct quotes, but as a series of statements reporting
the substance of what each said on a topic, with an attribution to the speaker
(e.g., "Meg said"). Krieger has organized the statements so that each one
seems to follow from or comment on the ones before, including disagreement
and contradictions. The threads build to a highly textured tapestry of lives in
the community. The book gives the sense of a community speaking, a series of
overheard conversations mixed with a peek into some personal diaries, or, in
Krieger's words, a "multiple-person stream of consciousness."

Krieger's text communicates on an emotional level as much as on an intellectual one. It is an engaging read. However, her approach has some costs. The
voices in Krieger's text are ironically disembodied. Except for one chapter that
expresses the experience of a single individual (the author?) who recently

came into the community, and a few extended paraphrases in the other chapters, the reader gets little sense of the people expressing these words, of their individual lives and social locations. And aside from the broad issues of connecting and staying separate that clearly organize the text, the reader is given little other interpretive guidance.

The goal of retaining the personhood of the subjects of study in the text is an important one. However, pursuing it unreflectively can lead well-meaning researchers into conflict with other equally important goals. Texts that decentralize the researcher or even remove the researcher altogether do not offer what the researcher's standpoint can provide: guideposts for how to interpret the data. As feminist critics of conventional reporting point out, readers need information about social and interpersonal context and paralinguistic elements of speech (DeVault 1990; Oakley 1981; Riessman 1993). If readers are to put people's words and actions into the context of their interests, they need to know how those people fit into social structures of power and opportunity.

Researchers' commitment to honor the voices of the subjects of research in the text can come into conflict with a commitment to providing a critical lens on the social world. And what of those voices with whom researchers and their colleagues adamantly disagree? For example, some everyday social actors use racial labels as though these distinctions were biologically based and obvious (Fine and Weiss 1996). Race is a form of categorization that is ingrained in Western culture. Yet contemporary sociologists know that biological, comparative, and historical evidence all demonstrate that race is not biologically based, but rather is socially constructed (see Omi and Winant 1986). Thus researchers have to choose between the lived experience of their research subjects and their own best judgment as scholars.

It is difficult to publish without criticism statements that one believes to be false and possibly even hurtful. For example, Fine and Weiss acknowledge that in their own work they tend to let the voices of those who have historically been silenced stand without much theoretical analysis, but when white men speak in ways that blame African American men for their problems, they "theorize generously, contextualize wildly, rudely interrupting them to reframe them" (1996: 266). Letting research subjects speak for themselves can be reduced to letting those speak with whom the researcher agrees.

Giving those we study more voice also entails some other ethical challenges. The more the reader can see of the individuality of the speaker, the harder it is to protect that speaker's anonymity. Further, people's stories inevitably involve the other people in their lives. Does the researcher have an obligation to these others? Do researchers have the right to report on their lives without their permission (Fine and Weiss 1996)?

Finally, the more the text is taken up with "the data," the words of the subjects of research and/or the notes describing events, the less the reader is reminded of the presence of the researcher, the person who is choosing which quotes and/or selections from field notes to represent (Sprague and Zimmerman 1989). At the extreme, it becomes hard to distinguish this presentation of data without interpretation from the positivist notion that "the facts speak for themselves," guiding many traditional research reports (Charmaz and Mitchell 1997; Gusfield 1976).

These strategies for representing research subjects as persons vary in their applicability to quantitative methods. An iconic approach to representing the demographics of the sample could be adapted by researchers using larger samples, for example, by letting each figure stand for multiples of respondents. However, finding and analyzing patterns in large samples requires statistical analysis—quantitative researchers need to use and report numbers. Still, quantitative researchers can take some ideas from these qualitative experiments with retaining the personhood of research subjects. For example, they can describe samples as clusters of people with similar biographies or in similar situations. One day, as a graduate student bored with writing up a dissertation analysis based on a national sample survey, I started playing with other ways of writing about the standard demographics. Here are the opening lines.

> The group of people who provided the information that I analyze in this project are roughly evenly divided by sex—803 men and 802 women. They range in age from 18 to 90 years, with half aged 34 or under. Sixty-one percent are married or living with someone as a partner in a committed relationship and 48% live with at least one child . . . Comparing white women with women of color, we see that white women are more likely to be self-employed and women of color to be employees; white women are housewives, women of color unemployed and looking for work . . .

Writing this way changed my feelings about what I was doing—I was no longer crunching numbers, I was trying to understand people's lives. Reading it still makes me see real people.

Quantitative researchers can avoid reifying their variables by translating back to the real world of people as agents in social interaction in their discussions and conclusions. Many of the feminist quantitative papers I described in chapter 4 organize their discussions to allow the reader to see at least a glimpse of real people, for example, making strategic choices (Carli 1990), struggling to manage work obligations while meeting caretaking responsibilities (Glass and Camarigg 1992), and trying to cope with gendered expectations (Brines 1994; LeClere, Rogers, and Peters 1998). Several of these papers provide a glimpse of institutions not as reified abstractions, but as the consequences of powerful actors enacting systematic, institutionalized discrimination. For example, they talk about managers devaluing work if women do it (England et al. 1996; Reskin and Ross 1992) or granting the most autonomy to those who are least likely to use it (Glass and Camarigg 1992).

Many of these authors also address the readers of their reports as active subjects, discussing the implications of their findings for actions that readers can take in their own interpersonal interactions (Ridgeway 1982) and workplaces (Ferree and McQuillan 1998; Steinberg 1995), or policies for which they can advocate (Gornick and Jacobs 1998; Spalter-Roth and Hartmann 1991). Quantitative researchers might need to develop their own tactics to do it, but researchers, regardless of their method, can work against objectification by finding ways to represent the people we study as people.

Integrating Other Standpoints in the Researcher's Text

Another form of textual innovation is a kind of hybrid; the author's scholarly voice drives the text, but there are elements that retain some of the standpoint of the subjects of study. For example, Abu-Lughod (1995) provides an example of a tactic for avoiding othering: representing one's own culture as being on an equivalent plane with another. In reporting about her field research among the Bedouin, she interweaves experiences of women struggling with infertility in Bedouin and U.S. cultures. While she was in the field, an informant who had become a friend became pregnant, allowing Abu-Lughod insights into the experience of Bedouin women during pregnancy and after birth. When the local women learned of her childlessness, they tried to help her, including taking her to a shaman who had special remedies for the problem.

Abu-Lughod begins her report by describing her time among the Bedouin, learning about their beliefs and practices regarding fertility. Then she tells of her own experiences on returning to the United States, in the medical institutions as a patient for in vitro fertilization, of her feelings of apprehension about labor during her pregnancy, and about postpartum depression. Encountering these two stories literally side by side calls the reader's attention to the parallels between them as well as the contrasts between "Them" and "Us." The contrasts between the lavish social support Bedouin women give to a new mother stand out in sharp relief to the isolation that Abu-Lughod observes among new mothers in the U.S. professional class. On the other hand, what might in other contexts seem to be the superstitions of a Bedouin Other—believing in things one cannot see and placing trust in a specialist who has arcane knowledge—bear a striking resemblance to how patients in the U.S. organization of health care respond to infertility.

In her ethnography centering on the disciplinary treatment of African American boys in an urban elementary school, Ferguson (2000) organizes her book to give some voice to the standpoints of those she is studying. A chapter on how teachers and other school personnel see the boys is preceded by quotes of self-descriptions from Ferguson's interviews with the boys, quotes that undermine the objectifying stereotypes to follow. Learning from her mentee, Horace, about the key discourses in her subjects' lives, Ferguson uses rap lyrics as epigraphs to several chapters, offering an analysis of what is to come. For example, the first chapter, introducing the key argument of the book, begins with this quote from Public Enemy's "Don't Believe the Hype":

> The minute they see me, fear me
> I'm the epitome—a public enemy
> Used, abused, without clues
> I refused to blow a fuse
> They even had it on the news
> Don't believe the hype
> Don't believe the hype.

The structure of Ferguson's (2000) text also calls attention to its own constructedness and her role as the constructor by including selections from her primary data prior to the chapters to which they connect most strongly. The reader's first encounter with "the data" is a field note preceding the first substantive chapter. This field note describes Ferguson and Horace's trip to the movies one afternoon, where they are exposed to depictions of a kaleidoscope of masculinities, all of them dangerous. The notes display Ferguson's mental journey, under the leadership of Horace, from the perspective of responsible adult to the perspective of childhood, where one ignores linearity and order, is exuberant without worrying about what others will think, and lives in the moment instead of being ruled by deadlines.

These two strategies of representation—giving voice to other standpoints and providing data—come together powerfully in Ferguson's inclusion of a very long (nearly 25 pages) transcription of a mother's story about how the police arrested her for spanking her son after he had left home without permission and went to a forbidden area of town. Ferguson has organized the mother's words into thematic sections and presented them in the form of poetry, with stanzas, indentations, and other prompts to recognize the logic and the rich implications of the mother's account. She urges the reader to read these words aloud; doing so enhances their power as well as the power of the reader's identification with the speaker.

These texts by Abu-Lughod and Ferguson retain the sociological voice, and a critical one at that, while respecting and taking into account the standpoint of those they are studying. In the process these texts represent scholarly understanding as a material process, not a transcendent one, and thus open themselves up to critique (Stanley 1990). This seems a promising strategy for meeting the somewhat conflicting goals of retaining the subjectivity of those we study, calling attention to the interpretive work of the author, offering the standpoint of a critical social science, and engaging the reader intellectually and emotionally.

Adapting Fictional Formats

Feminists have been adopting and adapting fictional forms to report social science findings at least since Zora Neale Hurston wrote about her ethnographic research on African American folklore and cultural practices in *Their Eyes Were Watching God* (1937). And the (eventual) success of Hurston's book demonstrates the power of fictional forms to reach broad audiences.

Erika Friedl (1989) provides a more contemporary model of using fictional forms to present data. In addition to more conventional publications on her fieldwork in an Iranian village, Friedl (1989) wrote a set of short stories from the point of view of women she met. One story tells of a woman who has had more children than she wants and by local standards is too old to be continuing sexual relations with her husband, and finds herself pregnant again. Another tells of an ambitious and smart woman who never had children and how she struggles to retain her independence and control over her life once she becomes a widow. Since this is a small community, relatives and neighbors, they appear in one another's stories, and in one woman's story Friedl herself appears. Reading these stories, it was easy for me to gather information about the local social organization of roles, spaces, and power, and how these create constraints on all community members' lives, particularly those of women.

Some researchers have explored dramaturgy as a means of conveying research findings, publishing standard articles in scholarly journals and producing plays to communicate them to a broader audience. For example, Ross Gray and Christina Sinding (2002) had transcripts from focus groups with women living with metastatic breast cancer and interviews with oncologists. To convert the transcripts into a dramatic presentation, they brought together a team that included theater professionals, social science researchers, women living with metastatic breast cancer, and community activists. The team worked collaboratively over a period of several months, drawing on the words of the research subjects and their own experiences to construct two scripts, one for health care professionals and another for broader community audiences. They performed these plays almost 200 times in less than a two-year period, mostly in Canada. A video of the performance of one version of the resulting play, *Handle with Care?* is distributed along with their book describing their approach and experiences.

The videotaped production uses very simple costumes and set. It powerfully communicates the social and emotional realities of women fighting for their lives. The message is not universalizing—the players depict a variety of experiences and responses to them. Gray and Sinding (2002) report many instances of audience members, cancer patients, their family members, and medical providers, affirming the validity of the representations and/or reporting enhanced insights—"a-ha" moments.

Fictional forms provide the reader with a richer experience of the data and also widen the audience for research. Because these texts take the form of a narrative, they tend to be more engaging to read. They make the reader want to know what happens next, and create puzzles that the reader may decipher. They invite the reader's active involvement with the information. The reader is called on to identify with and even care about the subjects of the research.

Dramatic presentation, in particular, helps scholars publish research findings among those who do not read, cannot read, or do not have access to printed texts. Researchers working with women in underdeveloped (and overexploited) nations have used performances to communicate research findings with members of groups involved in their studies.[2]

Fictional forms also raise some questions about what the audience can learn from the text and how readers are to evaluate the persuasiveness of the arguments they conveyed. Krieger (1985) argues that the audience can learn more in fictional than in traditional formats, because conventions of fiction writing are more open to revealing the complexity of the real world than would be possible by the more conventional social science approach of organizing the data through abstractions framed in by a theory. Yet the work of Margery Wolf (1992) suggests otherwise.

Wolf uses three different formats to present an account of a series of events she observed over the period of a month while doing fieldwork in a village in northern Taiwan: a story, a lightly edited transcription of her field notes covering the days during which these events took place, and an article she published in a scholarly journal. Following each presentation, Wolf offers a commentary on it. The fictional format is well written and engaging; it is interesting to read, and the text stimulates the reader to want to see a resolution, to know what happened at the end. On the other hand, the reader is not called upon to challenge the storyteller's version; the form provides no basis for critiquing it.

The field notes validate Laurel Richardson's position that "the unanalyzed transcript is not worth reading" (1988: 205). The text comprises snippets of an experience and calls on the reader to figure out a sense-making scheme, an interpretive order, but the effort is frustrating. Wolf (1992) says this is because the notes provide no context, and context is an important source for sense-making resources. She tells of a researcher who read an earlier fieldworker's notes before going into the field, and then again after spending some time in the field. The second reading was much more informative, because the fieldworker had gained crucial knowledge of the context, knowledge that most readers do not have.

The scholarly publication is well written in accessible language (and thus not necessarily representative of scholarly publications). Still, reading it feels more like work; one must follow an intellectual argument that includes references to other research and theoretical arguments. However, I gained from it an analysis that I did not and could not have developed reading the story or the field notes. It provides contextual information and organizes that information in a particular framework, discussing how local notions of gender, family, and community belonging worked against the woman being accepted as a shaman.

Fictional forms usually give no guidance on how to interpret the stories sociologically. Each reader comes to a text with a finite set of interpretive frameworks on which to draw. A sociologist trained in the analysis of gender, social structure, and power can find the markers of those systems of social relations operating in Krieger's or Friedl's texts, or in the video by Gray and Sinding. But what about readers who do not have access to critical discourses? Will those reading individuals' stories be looking for evidence of social structures or processes? Will they, for example, see gender, class, and race dynamics in play? In the absence of cues to the contrary, many, if not most, readers and audience members are likely to fall back on hegemonic discourses.

The second issue is how open fictional forms are to their own critique. Krieger (1985) argues that social science accounts should be held to the same standard that seems important in evaluating fictional ones: do they seem true to life? But how will the reader make this judgment? Most readers are likely to draw on their own personal experiences and their preferred discourses among those available to them to interpret it. Will they draw discourses that are critical or those that are hegemonic? Richardson says that literary forms call attention to their own constructedness, and thus "demand analysis of themselves as cultural products" (1994: 521). This is not so clear to me. The traditional social scientific text format—present an argument and the evidence that tests it—seems to evoke more critique than narrative forms that pull the reader into the story and give the feeling of unmediated social experience. In fact, cultural conventions are that when something is "just a story," it can evade standards of truthfulness or accuracy.[3] The strength of these fictionlike formats is the emotional and experiential power of their vivid communication. This also makes them less inviting of critique.

In summary, fictional forms expand the audience and actively engage the reader, both intellectually and emotionally, in the research findings. However, they do not guide the reader in the interpretation of these findings, nor do they present information in a way that encourages or even enables critical evaluations of the argument. Thus, those who adapt fictional forms to report research findings also need to publish more conventional research reports to meet the obligations of their relationships with communities of scholars.

Some quantitative feminist researchers have adopted a different strategy for reaching a wider audience: they post research findings on websites directed at community members, activists, and/or policy makers. For example, the Council on Contemporary Families, a nonprofit organization of national noted family researchers, mental health and social work practitioners, and clinicians, hosts a website (www.contemporaryfamilies.org) that includes pages with information about families from census data, fact sheets reporting research findings on a range of family-related issues, discussion papers, and suggestions for further reading. The Center for Research on Child Wellbeing at Princeton University is composed of economists, sociologists, demographers, psychologists, and political scientists who conduct research on children's health, education, income, and family structure (http://crcw.princeton.edu/index.asp). They post downloadable research briefs that summarize recent research and make policy recommendations. Sociologists for Women in Society posts on its website (http://newmedia.colorado.edu/~socwomen/) downloadable pdf files of fact sheets that summarize research on social and political issues of particular importance to women. Of course, researchers who are actively engaged in social movement organizations can also publish results through organizational networks, newsletters, demonstrations, and press releases (Glucksmann 1994). However, each of these more public-oriented forms of research reporting, like the fictional forms used by qualitative researchers, is less likely to invite rigorous critique of its methodology and reasoning.

In summary, reporting innovations by qualitative researchers, including explicitly making the researcher visible in the text, emphasizing the personhood of research subjects, integrating other standpoints in the researcher's text, and adapting fictional formats, each address serious limitations with traditional research reports. Researchers should consider how they might incorporate some of these insights in their own publication practices, keeping an eye to the reality that simply changing the format used to report evidence does not guarantee enhanced understanding. In fact, if done poorly it can lead to "products that are more self-conscious than evocative" (Charmaz and Mitchell 1997: 195).

From a standpoint perspective, the best choice is two-pronged. Researchers should write scholarly texts that integrate other standpoints while maintaining the researcher's voice as the primary organizer. However, they should also find ways to publish findings through venues that reach broader audiences. Critical sociological researchers want to expose the mechanics of social inequality in order to discover ways of undermining them. "If our writings are not easily accessible to those who share our goals, we have failed" (Wolf 1992: 119).

But answers, no matter how researchers provide them, depend on the questions that researchers are asking. Before figuring out how they can best publish their findings, researchers need to determine what questions they should pursue. How do critical social researchers ask questions that serve the interest of social justice, or at the least do not serve the reproduction of inequality?

ASKING CRITICAL QUESTIONS

The research questions that have traditionally earned the most respect in academic social science are more likely to come out of prior research literature than out of the everyday struggles of groups working for social change, to focus on the areas of concern to privileged white men rather than those typically expressed by women, and to ask what is wrong with those who are at the bottom of social hierarchies rather than those who are at the top. These are not questions that are likely to challenge existing power arrangements.

The development of knowledge is a collective enterprise, built through dialogue, so it makes sense for those who want to participate in the conversation to carefully consider what has been said so far through a careful reading of the research literature. Following a sequence of research efforts leads the reader to deduce the logical next steps to pursue. Yet chapter 1 illustrated ways that the parameters of that conversation—the paradigms, conceptual frameworks, and approaches to measurement and analysis in the existing research literature—are shaped by the standpoint of the privileged. To the degree that this is the case, it is tricky to develop questions out of the literature without falling into a hegemonic worldview.

A strategy that has appealed to many feminists is to choose topics about which they have strong personal feelings or values (Reinharz and Chase 2002). However, every question is located in a standpoint. A major lesson of feminist methodological discussions is that critical scholars' questions are, like those of other scholars, linked to their own situations and lives. The intent to be critical is no protection against the limitations of personal experience and access to standpoints.

It is perhaps easiest to see the challenge in the case of gender privilege. Decades ago David Morgan observed that men "have to work against the grain," that is, resist their natural proclivities, to keep their work from unintentionally reproducing sexism (1981: 95). Critical researchers may have a harder time seeing the influence of class privilege on their research interests, something that became clear to me in the fall of 1998, when I participated in an international conference on "Gendering the Millennium" in Dundee, Scotland.

The conference covered a wide range of topics and drew more than 100 scholars from Europe, the United States, the Middle East, and Africa. Nevertheless, the diversity in the program and among its participants turned into a striking homogeneity in the actual sessions I attended. Participants and audience in the sessions on identity, sexuality, and theory were almost all white and Western; those sessions addressing issues like literacy and education, family planning, and equal economic participation attracted predominantly scholars of color, from countries of the Southern Hemisphere. All the people at this conference were committed to feminist social change, but their position of privilege or disadvantage in the global economy created stark divergences in their agendas.

Others have made similar observations. Ong argues that feminism has been blind to the way its own project is "tied to First World privileges and declining Western hegemony" (1995: 367). Mandle expresses concern that the priorities among many U.S. feminists parallel those of the students in the elite liberal arts college at which she teaches: "personal issues of identity development, lifestyle, and cultural expression" (1999: 102). In her history of feminist anthropology, Aggarwal finds that white middle-class researchers have "preoccupations with sexual freedom and consciousness-raising," while African American feminists focus more on "racism, slavery, and consolidation of family networks" (2000: 18).

What seems interesting to researchers may not be what best serves the needs and priorities of the groups those researchers hope to serve. How can scholars who are relatively privileged be aware of and perhaps counteract the impact of that privilege on what seems interesting and important to them? What follows are three tactics worth trying.

Get Engaged in a Community Group

One direct source of questions is ongoing social movements—movements engaged in struggle generate a need for knowledge (Glucksmann 1994: 163–64). Much of the research of feminist social scientists, including many of the projects I described in earlier chapters, is responding to issues the women's movement has been raising, including reducing and ending workplace discrimination and violence against women and increasing educational equity and support for the work of parenting and caretaking. A theoretical claim that has generated a great deal of interesting and important research, that discrimination is not just personal, but institutional and social structural, came out of the U.S. African American civil rights movement (Feagin 2000: 17–18).

Some feminist researchers look to the needs of local groups in developing research agendas. Engaged research takes many forms, including Participatory Action Research (PAR), research in which community members choose the research questions, participate in decisions about and sometimes implement the methodology, help shape interpretations and conclusions, and use the resulting knowledge in some form of social action to increase equality (Cancian 1996).

One illustration is the "El Barrio Project," in which Rina Benmayor (1991) and other researchers at Hunter College, part of the City University of New York, integrated research with a literacy project in the Puerto Rican neighborhood near the campus. Researchers taught community women to read and write through developing and sharing oral histories on their lives as women immigrants. The goal of the project, which lasted for 32 weeks a year, was more than functional literacy, it was critical literacy—developing skills through developing a sociopolitical analysis of their lives. Participants benefited by acquiring literacy skills; but even more than that, Benmayor (1991) says, reflecting and telling about their lives transformed them. Doing it in a collective setting helped foster a community based on common struggle. Further, participants' analyses of their lives taught the researchers more about those lives than they had learned in previous oral history projects (Benmayor 1991).

Another example is the Chagas project in Brazil, an effort to study poor women's experiences with sexuality (Barroso and Bruschini 1991). Working with a Mother's Club (a common offshoot of Catholic Church organizations), Barroso and Bruschini organized discussion groups to learn about women's issues and information needs. They used what they learned to put together books about male and female bodies, birth control, accepting children's sexuality, and self-exams of breasts and genitals, in a discourse that put sexual pleasure within the context of the whole array of life's pleasures. Barroso and Bruschini have since created or advised the creation of many more groups, some within the state service sector, and their booklets have even been distributed by the Ministry of Health. They connect their project with other strands that have fed the growth of a reproductive rights movement in Brazil since 1985.

Another implementation of engaged research is community-based research (CBR), a form of service-learning in which students do research requested by nonprofit organizations in the community (Strand 2000). Doing research for a community client helps students develop their methodological skills (Strand 2000). Through the research experience students observe actual communities, often quite different than the ones in which they have grown up, giving them a better perspective on the material they learn in sociology classes. Thus CBR both serves community needs and is a valuable form of pedagogy (Strand 2000).

Campuses themselves are communities in which larger social struggles get played out, and to which campus researchers can respond. For example, Peggy Sanday (1992) learned that a student's absence from her class had been precipitated by the student's being raped by a gang of fraternity members at a party. Sanday responded by organizing an ethnographic study of the culture of rape on her campus, engaging students in the data collection, analysis, and reporting of findings to interested parties.

Research that is engaged in and with local communities has several advantages. It connects scholars with activists "on the ground," who are likely to have access to local knowledge about needs and problems and a different standpoint on how to make sense of the situation. Local community activists can tell prospective researchers what kind of information will help them in their efforts (Fine and Weiss 1996). Leaders of organized groups, educators, policy makers, and church leaders can provide useful advice on how to construct the topic and organize data collection (Fine and Weiss 1996). Appropriately designed, Participatory Action Research provides a laboratory to explore the validity of claims about social organization and social practices (Cancian 1992).

As with any research protocol, there are also limitations. To the degree that client-driven research is particular to those who are involved in it, its generalizability and usefulness to other contexts may be limited (Wolf 1992). Further, the goals of scholarly research and political effectiveness can conflict, creating complicated working conditions and perhaps difficult decisions for researchers (Fine and Weiss 1996). Engaged research works against the grain of standards for evaluation of scholarly work in the academy. These standards devalue applied research in general, and distrust the validity of research that does not appear to be "value-free." Finally, community-based research tends to take more time, slowing the rate at which researchers can publish; thus the researcher is likely to be evaluated as "less productive" than other researchers, given prevalent norms for scholarly evaluation.

Interrogate Public Discourse

Researchers can take their direction from public policy debates. Embedded in political debates about the need for particular social policies are contending explanations for the existence of particular social problems, and conflicting predictions about the likely consequences of particular social policy options. Further, partisans in policy debates often use contrasting frames to organize their sense making (Lakoff 1995). These contending frames and claims are a wellspring of questions for researchers to explore and assertions for researchers to test.

As an illustration, conservatives have long circulated a discourse about social welfare benefits creating dependency among recipients, including claims that welfare was a way of life passed down from parents to children and that people on it were lazy. A prime icon in this discourse is the "welfare queen," an African American woman living an easy life off too-generous benefits. A competing discourse framed recipients as people like everyone else, who had run into hard luck and needed some assistance to get back on their feet, or who were dealing with significant obstacles that merited extra social support. The debate over welfare has prompted diverse research projects, all of which make important contributions.

For example, Nancy Fraser and Linda Gordon (1994) conducted a historical analysis of texts related to discourses on dependency in Great Britain and the United States since preindustrial times. They found a dramatic shift in the meaning, use, and value placed on the idea of dependency. Earlier notions of dependency construed it as a normal social relationship, in which most people are in the role of dependents. Current talk about dependency represents it not as a social relationship, but as a personality attribute, one that carries stigma. The political ramifications of this shift in constructions of the meaning of dependency become clear as Fraser and Gordon trace a parallel transformation in the understanding of women's domestic and child-rearing labor from the earlier recognition of this work as an important part of economic and political activity to the current trends rendering it invisible and of no value.

Roberta Spalter-Roth and Heidi Hartmann (1996/1999) of the Institute for Women's Policy Research addressed this debate using quantitative analysis of contemporary data from the U.S. Census Bureau. Spalter-Roth and Hartmann tested the claims about welfare recipients contained in the dependency discourse and found them to be myths. For example, they found that most women receiving welfare benefits also worked for income. Welfare recipients who did not earn wages had disabilities and/or lived in communities with high rates of unemployment and/or had more children, significantly raising the cost of child care. Further, Spalter-Roth and Hartmann found, welfare recipients were not from any particular race or marital history.

Using qualitative interviews, Kathryn Edin and Laura Lein (1996) examined life on welfare from the perspective of those living it. Specifically, they explored how poor mothers managed their finances, and how the strategies that were available to them shaped the degree to which they could reasonably move from welfare to work. They found that those who enjoyed strong personal networks could more easily enter the official labor force without risking financial instability. This was not the case for those who had to rely on charity and unreported work to make ends meet. In order for official work to be a reasonable survival strategy for these women, Edin and Lein concluded, several public policies needed to be changed. To protect their children, these women needed continued access to child care and health coverage as well as eligibility for unemployment insurance. Further, because the minimum wage is not adequate to enable a full-time worker to provide a basic standard of living for a small family, governments need to ensure to potential workers that there will be additional resources to fill in the gap.

These projects show how a social issue can generate a wide array of research questions, each of which contributes an important piece to social understanding. Many other important debates are circulating in public discourses, at every level of social life. Each includes its own contending accounts of causes, assumptions about the effectiveness of different options for action, and overarching interpretive frames. Each is open for social researchers to interrogate, explore, and test.

Study Up

As far back as 1969, Laura Nader argued that researchers should be putting more effort into "studying up," studying the powerful, including "the agencies which regulate them, the institutions that undergird [them] . . . such as legislative bodies, the universities and professional organizations, and such descriptions would be from the point of view of the *users* as well as the managers" (292; emphasis in original). Studying up amounts to transposing many questions common in both scholarly and popular discourse (Nader 1969: 289). For example, instead of asking why some are poor, researchers could ask why some are so rich, or why the affluent hoard so many resources. Instead of asking why the common people are resistant to change, we could ask why the auto industry resists innovation, or why major institutions are not more organizationally creative. Instead of asking why women do not advance to more powerful positions, studying up would entail asking why men do.

Nader identified several reasons for studying up that should still appeal to critical researchers. First, she says, studying how powerful institutions work provides information that generates feelings of indignation, and this is energizing. Second, because studying up amounts to expanding our view of the social system vertically, it exposes more of "the social field"; thus it creates better science. Third, studying up has "democratic relevance." Citizens need to understand how powerful institutions work in order to more effectively operate within them, not to mention change them. A further reason for studying up is ideological—it shifts the way we see who is "the problem" from those who are the victims of power to those who wield it disproportionately.

Studying up can make important contributions to our understanding of how power works. For example, through case studies of a committee searching for a high-level university administrator, and of the experiences and practices of managers in scientific research labs, Patricia Yancy Martin (1996) was able to learn how male advantage is reproduced through gendered criteria for evaluation of performance and promise and through gendered interactional practices between superiors and subordinates. Similarly, Cynthia Enloe's (1990) examination of the practices of multinational corporations, the U.S. military, and U.S. foreign policy showed the degree to which these revolve around concerns about masculinity and entail a dependence on certain forms of femininity.

Pay Attention to What Is Missing

Michelle Fine and Susan Gordon (1989) call for "studies of what is not." Feminist research often takes the form of "excavation," "pay[ing] attention to what is missing" (DeVault 1999: 208). Researchers can pose questions about what is not on many levels.

They can identify and address *the question that is not asked*. Researchers can ask what is not being measured in a debate, for example, the cost of not having a social program, or the hidden costs of a social policy. Or they can ask whether the deeply held assumptions of a line of thinking actually hold up. Feminists have often developed useful research questions through employing a strategy of immanent critique, that is, testing the logic of the conventional argument. For example, work that exhaustively controls for the variables conventionally used to explain the determination of wages and then shows that even after taking all these variables into account, gendered variables such as sex, occupational sex-density, or the gendered character of the work still explain a significant part of the variation, illustrates the power of immanent critique.

Another question that is often not asked is what is the context or set of practices that produce and reproduce taken-for-granted social categories. Mainstream researchers often treat a finding of significant differences in social outcomes across social categories like gender, race, and class as the answer to a research question. Critical researchers should take such findings as the beginning, the phenomena that require explaining. It is not good enough to show that women, poor people, people of color, or immigrants are in a bad situation; critical researchers should make it a goal to identify the processes and aspects of the social context that are systematically reproducing difference (Acker et al. 1983/1991; Reskin 2003).

For example, Ann Ferguson (2000) got into her field research by participating in a team evaluating a new program for serving "at risk" children in urban, underresourced schools. Program designers and the educators they worked with knew that most of the children who were at risk of failure in their school and/or of becoming involved in criminal activities were African American boys. Ferguson turned that "fact" into a question. She asked what social factors might be creating this difference and found an important part of the answer in the perhaps unwitting and clearly changeable practices of those educators and social service providers.

Another set of research questions is about the *social categories that are not marked*. Part of the way privilege works in the construction of knowledge is through identifying some categories as "normal" and marking those who deviate from that category. Critical researchers work against hegemony when they ask how men's gender, whites' race, economically comfortable people's class, and/or heterosexuals' sexual preference shape their opportunities and constraints, their choices and outcomes. For example, David Morgan (1981) asked how the organization of sociology as a discipline reflects masculine interests, preferences, and social situations. Similarly, Ruth Frankenberg (1993) asked how white privilege is reproduced through norms and practices in everyday life.

Researchers can ask what is not seen in the study of social life. In a world where gender, race, class, sexuality, and national origin organize so many social situations, all social researchers encounter roles, problems, privileges, values, and experiences that are somehow specific and particular. We can ask who is not there, how including people from excluded categories might make a difference in the analysis, and how homogeneity is an important aspect of the setting (DeVault 1999). And in a society with so much inequality, researchers can ask about what is not protested against, for example, why people do not file sexual harassment complaints (Fine and Gordon 1989).

There are many ways to ask questions that challenge the naturalness of existing inequalities or the inevitability of social problems. Some do it by interrogating conventional assumptions or traditional accounts for why the inequality exists. Others do it by revealing the biases embedded in allegedly neutral social practices. Still others challenge notions of inherent differences between categories that create major divisions by locating personal attributes and actions within social contexts, particularly relationships of unequal power. And some ask questions that challenge the terms of contemporary debates about the equity of a specific social policy. They all ask questions that problematize some aspect of the status quo.

Questioning Our Questions

Smith warns that "to begin with the categories is to begin in discourse," that is, to begin within the frames that help to hide and/or legitimate social inequality (1992). Rather than starting with a concept such as gender (or race, class, disability, or sexuality), Smith suggests, we should start where women are, where their bodies are. Women of color, lesbians, poor and working-class women, women immigrants, women in postcolonial countries all are at the bottoms of social hierarchies. *So are many men.* Listening to their stories and to what these stories tell us about the circumstances and struggles of their daily lives will help to decenter hegemonic ways of making sense of social processes (cf. Ong 1995).

Researchers operate from a standpoint, and thus we should ask ourselves questions about the connection between our personal biographies and material interests and the questions we pursue and the arguments we find compelling throughout the lifetime of each project. Researchers should be particularly careful about jumping to conclusions that serve our own interests. Warning sirens should go off in the minds of men who think that questions about gender are not relevant in their area of interest, people from or in economically comfortable positions who are ignoring class as an explanatory variable, and whites who think that race is not interesting or important to ask questions about.

Questions involve ethical considerations. The classic questions of political analysis, "Who benefits? Who pays?" are as appropriate in evaluating research agendas as they are in critiquing social policy. There is a distinction between putting one's sociological imagination into serving a cause and using research about social issues or problems to generate publications that are unlikely to help the cause and may even hurt it by making information about activists available to elites (Thorne 1983). Studying socially vulnerable groups entails extra ethical considerations (Holland and Ramazanoglu 1994). Vulnerable people may reveal damaging information. Their coping strategies may invite increased surveillance. The psychological and emotional scars of their oppression may easily feed into dominant stereotypes. All of these can raise issues of what the appropriate ethical response should be. Critical researchers should think carefully and specifically about how a particular possible research project might help progressive social change (DeVault 1999).

Mascia-Lees and her colleagues summarize the feminist admonition: "Do work that 'others' want and need . . . [be] clear for whom [you] are writing . . ." and be "suspicious of relationships with 'others' that do not include a close and honest scrutiny of the motivations for research" (1989: 33). Perhaps it has already become clear that the ability of social researchers to ask useful questions and provide useful answers is shaped and constrained by the organization of social research as a discipline. How we might build bridges where there now are barriers is the topic of the next, and final, chapter.

NOTES

1. Judith Howard, the editor of this project, described in her written comments how she reacted to words like "I" and "we" as she read through an earlier version of this manuscript, crossing out those pronouns and suggesting alternative formulations in the third person. "It sounds better this way [to me]," she said. And she points to the subtle enforcement mechanism: "I know full well that 'sounds better' is a sign of norms at work." Howard points out that the editor is also hidden in the text.

2. Thanks to Esther Chow for telling me about this.

3. Another perceptive observation contributed by Judy Howard.

7

Changing Sociology/ Changing the World

Sociology has contributed a great deal to our understanding of social structures and social processes, but sociology can do a much better job. Too often we have been asking the questions from the perspective of the powerful. We have tended to rely on analytic categories, like logical dichotomies and abstract individuation, that naturalize social difference. The way we ask and answer questions has tended to, however unintentionally, construct the disadvantaged as the Other; in doing so, we help make their position seem acceptable. We report about research in forms that sharply restrict the scope of our audience, limit critique of our research, underplay the role of dominant groups, and emotionally distance readers from the substance of what we have to say.

These shortcomings are, in part, consequences of our failing to take epistemology seriously in framing our methodology. Sociologists cannot be satisfied with positivism, because the sociological perspective logically leads us to accept that knowledge is a social product. The facts do not speak for themselves, but neither is systematic knowledge of the world an illusion or an impossible dream, as the most radical social constructionists assert. Knowledge is the product of the relationship between the knower and the known, and that relationship is not merely individual, it is socially structured. The biases in mainstream sociology are, in large part, the result of the predominance of one standpoint in its production. Sociology has constructed a worldview largely drawing on the physical location, social and political interests, common interpretive frameworks, and position in the social organization of the knowledge production of economically and racially privileged men.

While the ranks of official knowledge producers have diversified, thanks largely to the efforts of social movements like feminism and racial/ethnic movements for civil rights, relatively privileged groups still dominate the process and product of social research. Some argue that the safest response to this coincidence between social power and social authority is to transfer authority to the subjects of research, by privileging either insider researchers or the research subjects themselves. But, from a standpoint perspective, this is not a viable solution. It fails to take into account how class and education can create material differences between insider researchers and those they may study. It overlooks the value of the perspective of outsiders, whose access to different discourses can sensitize them to things insiders might take for granted. It disregards situations in which research subjects have more social power than the researcher.

Even more importantly, there is a serious epistemological error underlying the argument that we should simply transfer authority to members of a specific group, occupants of a specific social location. That position is premised on equating a standpoint with the subjectivity of a group, which is a mistaken reading of standpoint theory. The major standpoint theorists are making a social, not a subjectivist, argument. No single location is privileged. Each group's standpoint is facilitated *and limited* by its locatedness, its stake in the situation, the discourses circulating among its members, and its position vis-à-vis the social organization of knowledge production. Social researchers bring different constellations of these resources to bear on a phenomenon than do those they study and, by virtue of their own diverse positions in social relations, researchers vary in what they bring. Methodologies that are sensitive to this complexity will generate less biased knowledge.

Quantitative research seems objective and unbiased to many, but feminists have identified several forms of bias. Conventional measures tend to be based on the experiences of men and/or express the assumptions of dominant discourses. Samples for experiments are heavily drawn from college students, a fairly homogeneous and relatively privileged group. Survey samples are stronger than any other method on representativeness, but even here there are biases that lead to undersampling those at the bottom of social hierarchies. Quantitative researchers have traditionally favored the individual level of analysis and have underexamined social contexts as shapers of behavior and outcomes. Statistical methods of analysis tend to dominate the discourse, the more highly technical the better, prompting many analyses to focus on difference per se, eliding statistical differences with substantive ones. Researchers often construct models in ways that affirm the normality of the dominant group and obscure the possibility that differences among social categories could be expressing differences in social context.

Feminists working with quantitative methods have found ways to put them into the service of social justice. They ask questions that challenge the naturalness of gender, race, and class differences in behaviors and outcomes by challenging dominant stereotypes or identifying the mechanisms that perpetuate discrimination. Sometimes they do the research needed by specific groups in their efforts to increase equality. They develop new measures to unpack the gendered assumptions in conventional approaches and to tap the workings of power. In designing new measurement approaches, they begin from the standpoint of everyday social actors. They give credibility to self-reports when conventional measures are biased, incorporating procedures to verify their reliability. They have developed approaches to analysis that are sensitive to discrimination, for example, by showing the residual power of sex and/or gendered positions to explain variation or by looking for evidence of excluded variables that signal discriminatory treatment.

Qualitative methods have great promise for developing understandings that are less subject to the hegemonic bias of mainstream research, but qualitative research has its own vulnerabilities. Some of these are endemic to the method. For example, gender, class, and race are salient in face-to-face interactions, organize access to many parts of the social field, and thus are likely to influence the data collected. Qualitative samples have selection biases that can impact the findings. Interviewing, for example, requires more of the participants in time and verbal skills, making it harder for less-privileged people to participate. Powerful people are much more able to escape surveillance, including the observations of field researchers, than are the powerless. Other problems with conventional qualitative methods can be ameliorated. Assumptions that any theory is totally data-driven are no more tenable in grounded theory than in positivism, but qualitative researchers can strive to be true to the data while self-reflective about the ways gender, class, race, and personal biography shape what seems interesting and important to them.

Feminist qualitative researchers have developed alternative strategies for constructing their relationships with research subjects and decentering their own perspective in the analysis of data. Building on connections with the subjects of research through using emotional responses and our own biographies as resources can enhance understanding. Paying attention to discourses in which group members communicate about their lives can help researchers develop a sense of their standpoint. Interviewers who respond to inarticulateness, inconsistent speech, moral language, and self-reflective statements as possible indicators of the inadequacy of the dominant discourse to address people's experience and interests are putting standpoint epistemology to work. So are those doing institutional ethnography, that is, learning from subjects what they can best tell us—their daily practices, struggles, and strategies—and using these as indicators of the way social power mediated through discourses creates constraints and irrationality in their lives.

Collaborations among researchers in data collecting and analysis, if organized with standpoint epistemology in mind, can compensate for the limitations of personal bias, physical location, and even disciplinary blinders. If care is taken in their construction, group interviews can produce more complete and valid data on some topics. People occupying similar social locations can press one another more than an investigator could, for more authentic reports. Members of culturally silenced groups can empower one another to speak and even support one another in developing a standpoint on their common experiences.

Feminists have developed strategies for publishing research that make the researcher's own participation and stake in its construction visible, including using first names and first-person pronouns and explicitly discussing their motivation for the project. They have worked to retain the personhood and subjectivity of research subjects in the text, for example, by using extended quotes and samples from popular discourses. Some have adapted more popular formats for communicating to a broader audience about research findings, like narrative and drama or briefs on web pages. Because these forums tend to suppress critical readings, they should be supplementary to more scholarly publications that are explicitly organized around argument and evidence.

Feminists have worked to find ways to pose questions that go beyond the privileged standpoints shaping the contours of the research literature and researchers. Getting involved with a local community puts researchers in contact with members' felt needs and constraints. Social movements in general generate alternative discourses that have been rich sources of new insights and frameworks. Public discourse is rife with claims and debates about what is, what should be, and what can be; this discourse in itself constitutes a full agenda of research hypotheses. Finally, since the organization of knowledge production has prompted social scientists to ask questions from a fairly homogeneous standpoint, critical scholars can fill the gaps by doing studies of what is missing: questions that have not been asked, groups that have not been problematized, social settings in which some categories of people are not present, and resistance that does not occur.

Recall that the logic of standpoint epistemology calls researchers to:

- Work from the standpoint of the disadvantaged
- Ground interpretations in interests and experience
- Maintain a strategically diverse discourse
- Create knowledge that empowers the disadvantaged

The critiques and strategies developed by those seeking to follow one or more of these principles point to how we need to do more than change how we implement the methods we employ in particular projects.

CHANGING RESEARCH

The privileged standpoint has informed not just the content of our knowledge; it has also informed the way we organize our research. We construct a dichotomy between quantitative and qualitative methods. We construe research as an individuated phenomenon, abstracted from any social context, including the human lives of those who create it and communities who might contribute to and benefit from it. We create arbitrary barriers among scholarly, teaching, and service work (Sprague 1998). Each of these constitutes a barrier to implementing research that is informed by standpoint epistemology. If we are to achieve the methodological goals that standpoint epistemology sets for us, we need to reconsider some taken-for-granted aspects of the way we organize our research.

First, we need to break down the barriers we have constructed between quantitative and qualitative methods, both of which have weaknesses as well as strengths. There is much more overlap between the two families of strategies than is usually recognized in the heat of debates about which is better. Further, the strengths of one compensate for many of the weaknesses of the other, which is why *all researchers need a multi-method sensibility.* We need to bring many kinds of methods to bear on the questions we are pursuing. Because considerable expertise is involved in any method, it makes sense to *construct research* not as a series of individual projects, but *as a collaborative agenda* that integrates people who specialize in diverse methods. At a minimum, we need to read one another's work, across the divides of method. In order to do that, researchers need to write so that non-specialists can read, and read critically.

Collaborations between quantitative and qualitative researchers will not just produce better knowledge; the integration of findings from both better empowers everyday social actors. Quantitative analyses can provide convincing arguments about the existence of inequality and patterns of discrimination, but they are less likely to evoke passion. Qualitative work shows us how power and discrimination get played out in people's lives, and the vividness and immediacy of qualitative reports evoke emotional responses. However, the hard-to-convince can more easily dismiss qualitative work as selective and unrepresentative. To convince the general public and inform social action, we need both the big picture and the textured nuances, both numbers and specific lives.

We need to take down the other barriers that divide us as researchers and develop our collaborations so they include researchers from different social backgrounds, people diverse in gender, race/ethnicity, class biography, and national origin. Both the privileged and the not-so-privileged have important standpoints on which to draw. Researchers who have crossed major social boundaries, such as class and national origin, over the course of their biographies have experienced multiple social locations and have most likely participated in more diverse discourses than have those who have always been in hegemonic groups. To the extent that their social categories are still marginalized within the social organization of knowledge production, these scholars retain distinct social locations. Insiders, by virtue of a lifetime of privilege, better know the workings of a system from the inside; outsiders have a contrasting perspective and sense of alternatives; both are essential.

If we are to work from the standpoint of the disadvantaged, we must bridge the barriers we construct between scholarly life and more public work. Boundary crossing is the privileged strategy for developing knowledge: knowers who participate in contrasting discourses and do work in the everyday world have an epistemological advantage in efforts to go beyond the privileged standpoint. Social researchers should be people who have access to diverse discourses and are involved in their communities, including in the work of meeting people's needs.

Our connections with society begin in our own classrooms and local communities, and we can use them much more effectively if we build on the advice that bell hooks (1994) gives to teachers. Teachers and students bring different resources to the classroom, hooks (1994) says. Teachers bring the conceptual frameworks and accumulated findings of their discipline; students bring the frameworks and accumulated evidence of their lives. The task for teachers and students is to organize a dialogue about what the standpoint of each has to offer the other. We can take down the conceptual wall we tend to construct between classrooms and the rest of the world and extend this model into our various communities. Each of these sites is a place of teaching, where researchers learn about their topics and teachers serve their communities (Sprague 1998).

But if researchers are to change the way we organize our research, we need to change the way we work together as a discipline as well: particularly the way we evaluate one another's work, from the criteria reviewers use to evaluate work products, to those we use as colleagues to evaluate one another's curricula vitae.

CHANGING OUR DISCIPLINE

Scholars tend to talk about their disciplines as an "it," an external social force that organizes the system of constraints and rewards within which we negotiate our work choices. However, representing a discipline as an object out there is a case of abstract individuation. Our disciplines are systems of relations among scholars, maintained by the interrelated practices that each of us as individual scholars engages in with an eye to the standards and expectations of our peers. We are the reviewers, the recommenders, the evaluators, and the coauthors of many of the terms of our employment. If we want to change how we do our own research, without incurring serious economic and professional costs in our careers, we need to change the standards we employ in evaluating one another's work.

The validity of the knowledge we create is the property not of a particular claim to truth, but of an open and critical discourse. We construct a context for rationality by removing the obstacles to thoughtful criticism, Helen Longino (1989) argues, and she has identified several obstacles to true critical discourse. Restricting our audiences to those who share the same background assumptions insulates us against the valuable critical exercise of periodically calling those assumptions into question. At the same time, repetitive debates about background assumptions are unproductive and distracting. Finally, Longino (1989) notes, an overemphasis on novelty and originality can reduce the care with which we critically evaluate existing truth claims.

As members of scholarly communities, we need to construct our discourse as critical conversations among people operating from different standpoints. We have to find the courage to disagree with "politically correct" positions and/or persons, and the commitment to engage one another in dialogue. We must be willing to use our disagreements with other scholars as points of access to improved understanding. Reviewers of scholarly reports need to be more open to innovative forms of writing about research. The standard of a reasonable argument integrated with persuasive evidence remains, but the means for making the case can vary more widely than conventionally appreciated.

Boundary crossing is important, given standpoint epistemology, and to support it we must as a discipline change how we evaluate work. The decreasingly popular practice of assigning greater weight to work that is single-authored than that with multiple authors is a promising sign. Strategic collaborations that build across social and/or methodological differences require considerable additional work that is unrecognized when these projects are discounted.

In evaluating research, the standard practice of using the quantity of publications as a key indicator of scholarly productivity is an obstacle to improving our knowledge base. Equating quantity with productivity undermines possibilities for reading outside one's narrow areas of specialization, participating actively in the world outside the academy, or working with community groups.

The quantitative approach to evaluation reproduces itself—the higher the expectation for productivity, the more researchers will narrow their focus to generate more publications. The narrower our focus, the less competent we are to evaluate the substance of the work of someone with a somewhat different focus. The simpler alternative to actually reading and thinking about someone's research is to count the number of publications and then weigh those by the prestige of the source.

On the other hand, modifying how we do our own research and changing how we as a discipline evaluate one another's work are mutually supportive. If we start reading work generated using contrasting methods and from different standpoints, we will be better able to actually read and assess the substance of the work of colleagues who are in a different substantive area or use a different method. If we stop feeding the escalating rate of publication, we will have time to read and learn from our colleagues' work, and doing this will in turn improve our own knowledge base and conceptual work.

In addition, valuing research over teaching and teaching over community-service work constructs barriers to scholars' taking advantage of how each constitutes distinctive points of access to alternative standpoints. Not taking applied work in sociological practice more seriously creates a barrier that gives the word *academic* its bad connotation. There are many ways to communicate about the findings of scholarly research, and it is the quality of the communication that we should attend to, rather than mindlessly imposing a hierarchy of venues. Otherwise, we support barriers between the academy and the world outside that undermine the effort to circulate research findings broadly.

CHANGING OURSELVES

Many people come to sociology because they want to understand society so they can help improve it. Changing our discipline to facilitate research along the lines that I have been describing will help us make this a job we love to do. All we need to do is take three basic steps: ask passionately, analyze critically, and answer empoweringly.

Asking passionately means asking questions not because they work with the method we know or the data we can easily access, but because people really need the answers to them—questions that will help make a difference, help with a problem, enhance justice. In addition to the strategies throughout this book, outsiders within the academy (and this includes most students, who are themselves new to scholarly discourses) have an additional tactic: use your anger. Like other emotions, anger is an expression of a relationship with someone, one that is wrong in some way (Harrison 1985). Let your anger call your attention to something that needs addressing, and figure out what it tells you about what is missing in our knowledge.

Analyzing critically can be intimidating, because our relationship to our work is often intimidating. Called upon by scholarly discourses to see ourselves as decontextualized knowledge producers, it is easy to fear that our work is irrelevant or outrageously off-course. The way to avoid the fear of irrelevance is by intentionally and strategically recontextualizing our work, grounding it in people's expressed needs or frustrations. The way to avoid the fear that our work is off-course is to recontextualize ourselves in a diversified discourse by reading broadly substantively and methodologically, engaging in discussions with colleagues who are critical by virtue of attitude as well as by methodological and substantive difference, and with people who differ from ourselves in gender, race/ethnicity, and class background. Of course, strategically constructing collaborative research agendas makes these critical conversations more likely.

Answering empoweringly means reporting about our research in ways that will engage others, that is, in ways that are both smart and emotionally compelling. Write so that others will want to read your work. Write so that others can be moved by your ideas (cf. Paget). It increases the scope of your communication to people in other areas, scholars in other academic fields, and activists. But writing is not the only way we provide answers; we teach. Our classrooms are filled with citizens and community members who need our questions and our answers. High school teachers are always looking for interesting and informative guest speakers, as are many civic organizations and those who do continuing professional education for teachers or lawyers. Local newspapers will publish clearly written and engaging op-ed pieces. Reporters need sources for their stories. The right wing has intentionally and successfully exploited scholarly uncertainty to argue that the public should dismiss scientific findings. It is harder for them to easily dismiss collaborative agendas employing diverse researchers in multiple sites using multiple methods. It will be harder for them to dumb down the public if we are participating actively and are effectively engaged in and with the public.

Asking passionately will ensure and sustain our commitment to the work. Analyzing critically will instill confidence in its quality and generalizability. Answering empoweringly will empower others as we empower ourselves. By remaking ourselves, we can make an important contribution to remaking our world into a just, peaceful, and sustainable place. And that is my invitation to you.

References

Abu-Lughod, Lila. 1995. A Tale of Two Pregnancies. Pp. 339–49 in *Women Writing Culture*, ed. Ruth Behar and Deborah A. Gordon. Berkeley: University of California Press.

Acker, Joan. 1988. "Class, Gender, and the Relations of Distribution." *Signs: Journal of Women in Culture and Society* 13, no. 3:473–97.

———. 1999a. Gender and Organizations. Pp. 177–94 in *Handbook of the Sociology of Gender*, ed. Janet Saltzman Chafetz, New York: Kluwer/Plenum.

———. 1999b. Rewriting Class, Race, and Gender: Problems in Feminist Rethinking. Chap. 2 in *Revisioning Gender*, ed. Myra Marx Ferree, Judith Lorber, and Beth B. Hess. Thousand Oaks, CA: Sage.

Acker, Joan, Kate Barry, and Johanna Esseveld. 1983/1991. Objectivity and Truth: Problems in Doing Feminist Research. Pp. 133–53 in *Beyond Methodology: Feminist Scholarship as Lived Research*, ed. Mary Margaret Fonow and Judith A. Cook. Bloomington and Indianapolis: Indiana University Press.

Agar, Michael. 1986. *Speaking of Ethnography*. Beverly Hills, CA: Sage.

Aggarwal, Ravina. 2000. "Tracking Lines of Control: Feminist Anthropology Today." *Analysis of the American Academy of Political and Social Science* 57:14–29.

Alcoff, Linda. 1989. Justifying Feminist Social Science. Pp. 85–103 in *Feminism & Science*, ed. Nancy Tuana. Bloomington: Indiana University Press.

Alway, Joan. 1995. "The Trouble with Gender: Tales of the Still-Missing Feminist Revolution in Sociological Theory." *Sociological Theory* 13:209–28.

American Psychological Association Task Force on Statistical Inference. 1996. Initial Report. www.apa.org/science/tfsi.html.

American Sociological Association Committee on the Status of Women in Sociology. 1980. Sexist Biases in Sociological Research: Problems and Issues. *ASA Footnotes* 8 (January): 8–9. Washington, D.C.

Anderson, Kathryn, and Dana C. Jack. 1991. Learning to Listen: Interview Techniques and Analysis. Pp. 11–26 in *Women's Words: The Feminist Practice of Oral History*, ed. Sherna Berger Gluck and Daphne Patai. New York and London: Routledge.

Anderson, Margo. 1994. "(Only) White Men Have Class: Reflections on Early 19th-Century Occupational Classification Systems." *Work and Occupations* 21, no. 1:5–32.

Angier, Natalie. "Not Just Genes: Moving beyond Nature vs. Nurture." *New York Times*, February 25, 2003.

Aptheker, Bettina. 1989. *Tapestries of Everyday Life: Women's Work, Women's Consciousness, and the Meaning of Daily Experience.* Amherst: University of Massachusetts Press.

Baca Zinn, Maxine. 1979. "Field Research in Minority Communities: Ethical, Methodological, and Political Observations by an Insider." *Social Problems* 27, no. 2:209–19.

Bar On, Bat-Ami. 1993. Marginality and Epistemic Privilege. Pp. 83–100 in *Feminist Epistemologies*, ed. Linda Alcoff and Elizabeth Potter. New York: Routledge.

Barroso, Carmen, and Cristina Bruschini. 1991. Building Politics from Personal Lives: Discussions on Sexuality among Poor Women in Brazil. Pp. 153–72 in *Third World Women and the Politics of Feminism*, ed., Chandra Talpade Mohanty, Ann Russo, and Lourdes Torres. Bloomington: Indiana University Press.

Barzun, Jacques, and Henry F. Graff. 1970. *The Modern Researcher.* NY: Harcourt, Brace & World.

Bechtel, William. 1988. *Philosophy of Mind: An Overview for Cognitive Science.* Hillsdale, NJ: Erlbaum.

Behar, Ruth. 1995. Introduction: Out of Exile. Pp. 1–29 in *Women Writing Culture*, ed. Ruth Behar and Deborah A. Gordon. Berkeley: University of California Press.

Bell, Diane. 1993. Yes Virginia, There Is a Feminist Ethnography: Reflections from Three Australian Fields. Pp. 28–43 in *Gendered Fields: Women, Men and Ethnography*, ed. Diane Bell, Pat Caplan, and Wazir Johan Karim. New York and London: Routledge.

Bem, Sandra. 1983. "Gender Schema Theory and Its Implications for Child Development: Raising Gender-Aschematic Children in a Gender-Schematic Society." *Signs: Journal of Women in Culture and Society* 8, no. 4:598–616.

Benmayor, Rina. 1991. Testimony, Action Research, and Empowerment: Puerto Rican Women and Popular Education. Pp. 159–74 in *Women's Words: The Feminist Practice of Oral History*, ed. Sherna Berger Gluck and Daphne Patai. New York and London: Routledge.

Beoku-Betts, Josephine. 1994. "When Black Is Not Enough: Doing Field Research among Gullah Women." *NWSA Journal* 6, no. 3:413–33.

Bernstein, Basil. 1971. *Class, Codes, and Control*. Vol. 1. London: Routledge.

Bhaskar, Roy, and Christopher Norris. 1999. Roy Bhaskar Interviewed. Questions by Christopher Norris. *The Philosophers' Magazine*, 8. www.philosophers.co.uk/issue8.htm. Accessed July 7, 2003.

Bhavnani, Kum-Kum. 1988. "Empowerment and Social Research: Some Comments," 8, no. 1–2:41–50.

———. 1993. "Tracing the Contours: Feminist Research and Feminist Objectivity." *Women's Studies International Forum* 16, no. 2: 95–104

Bielby, Denise, and William Bielby. 1988. "She Works Hard for the Money." *American Journal of Sociology* 93 (March): 1031–59.

Bielby, William, and Denise Bielby. 1992. "I Will Follow Him: Family Ties, Gender-Role Beliefs, and Reluctance to Relocate for a Better Job." *American Journal of Sociology* 97, 5 (March): 1241–67.

Biernat, Monica, and Kathleen Fuegen. 2001. "Shifting Standards and the Evaluation of Competence: Complexity in Gender-Based Judgment and Decision Making." *Journal of Social Issues* 57, no. 4:707–24.

Birch, Maxine, and Tina Miller. 2000. "Inventing Intimacy: The Interview as Therapeutic Opportunity." *International Journal of Social Research Methodology* 3, no. 3:189–202.

Blee, Kathleen. 1991. *Women of the Klan: Racism and Gender in the 1920s.* Berkeley: University of California Press.

Bleier, Ruth. 1984. *Science and Gender: A Critique of Biology and Its Theories on Women.* New York: Pergamon Press.

Bogdan, Robert, and Steven J. Taylor. 1989. "Relationships with Severely Disabled People: The Social Construction of Humanness." *Social Problems* 36, no. 2: 135–48.

Borland, Katherine. 1991. "That's Not What I Said": Interpretive Conflict in Oral Narrative Research. Pp. 63–76 in *Women's Words: The Feminist Practice of Oral History,* ed. Sherna Berger Gluck and Daphne Patai. New York and London: Routledge.

Bose, Christine E. 1984. "Household Resources and U.S. Women's Work: Factors Affecting Gainful Employment at the Turn of the Century." *American Sociological Review* 49:474–90.

Bowen, Eleanore Smith. 1964. *Return to Laughter.* New York: Doubleday.

Brehm, Sharon, ed. 1988. *Seeing Female: Social Roles and Personal Lives.* New York: Greenwood.

Brines, Julie. 1994. "Economic Dependency and the Division of Labor." *American Journal of Sociology* 100, no. 3:652–88.

Brown, Lyn Mikel, and Carol Gilligan. 1993. "Meeting at the Crossroads: Women's Psychology and Girls' Development." *Feminism & Psychology* 3, no. 1:11–35.

Brush, Lisa. 1990. "Violent Acts and Injurious Outcomes in Married Couples: Methodological Issues in the National Survey of Families and Households." *Gender & Society* 4, no. 1:56–67.

Bulmer, Martin. 1975. *Working-Class Images of Society.* London: Routledge and Kegan Paul.

Burawoy, Michael. 2004. "To Advance, Sociology Must Not Retreat." *Chronicle of Higher Education* 40, no. 49:B24.

Calasanti, Toni M., and Kathleen F. Slevin. 2001. *Gender, Social Inequalities, and Aging.* Walnut Creek, CA: AltaMira Press.

Callero, Peter L., and Judith A. Howard. 1989. Biases of the Scientific Discourse on Human Sexuality. Pp. 425–37 in *Human Sexuality: The Societal and Interpersonal*

Context, ed. Kathleen McKinney and Susan Sprecher. Norwood, NJ: Ablex Publishing.

Campbell, Donald. 1969. "Reforms as Experiments." *American Psychologist* 24:409–29.

Campbell, Marie L. 1998. "Institutional Ethnography and Experience as Data." *Qualitative Sociology* 21, no. 1:55–73.

Campbell, Marie L., and Ann Manicom. 1995. *Knowledge, Experience, and Ruling Relations: Studies in the Social Organization of Knowledge.* Toronto: University of Toronto Press.

Cancian, Francesca M. 1985. Gender Politics: Love and Power in the Private and Public Spheres. Pp. 253–64 in *Gender and the Life Course*, ed. Alice S. Rossi. New York: Aldine.

———. 1992. "Feminist Science: Methodologies That Challenge Inequality." *Gender & Society* 6:623–42.

———. 1996. Participatory Research and Alternative Strategies for Activist Sociology. Pp. 187–205 in *Feminism and Social Change: Bridging Theory and Practice*, ed. Heidi Gottfried. Chicago: University of Illinois Press.

Cancian, Francesca M., and Stacey J. Oliker. 1999. *Caring and Gender.* Thousand Oaks, CA: Pine Forge Press.

Cannon, Lynn Weber, Elizabeth Higginbotham, and Marianne L. A. Leung. 1988. "Race and Class Bias in Qualitative Research on Women." *Gender & Society* 2:449–62.

Carli, Linda L. 1990. "Gender, Language, and Influence." *Journal of Personality and Social Psychology* 59:941–51.

Charmaz, Kathy. 2004. Grounded Theory. Pp. 496–521 in *Approaches to Qualitative Research*, ed. Sharlene Naby Hesse-Biber and Patricia Leavy. New York: Oxford University Press.

Charmaz, Kathy, and Richard G. Mitchell. 1997. The Myth of Silent Authorship: Self, Substance, and Style in Ethnographic Writing. Pp. 193–215 in *Reflexivity and Voice*, ed. Rosanna Hertz. Thousand Oaks, CA: Sage.

Chodorow, Nancy. 1978. *The Reproduction of Mothering: Psychoanalysis and the Sociology of Gender.* Berkeley: University of California Press.

———. 1991. *Feminism and Psychoanalytic Theory*. New Haven, CT: Yale University Press.

Clough, Patricia T. 1993. "On the Brink of Deconstructing Sociology: Critical Reading of Dorothy Smith's Standpoint Epistemology." *The Sociological Quarterly* 34, no. 1: 169–82.

Cohen, Phillip N., and Matt L. Huffman. 2003. "Individuals, Jobs, and Labor Markets: The Devaluation of Women's Work." *American Sociological Review* 68, no. 3:443.

Coleman, James S. 1992. "The Rational Reconstruction of Society." *American Sociological Review* 58:1–15.

Collier, Andrew. 1994. *Critical Realism: An Introduction to the Philosophy of Roy Bhaskar*. London: Verso.

Collins, Patricia Hill. 1986. "Learning from the Outsider Within: The Sociological Significance of Black Feminist Thought." *Social Problems* 33:514–30.

———. 1989. "The Social Construction of Black Feminist Thought." *Signs: Journal of Women in Culture and Society* 14:745–73.

———. 1997. "Comment on Hekman's 'Truth and Method: Feminist Standpoint Revisited': Where's the Power?" *Signs: Journal of Women in Culture and Society* 22, no. 2: 375–81.

———. 2000. *Black Feminist Thought: Knowledge, Consciousness, and the Politics of Empowerment*. 2d ed. New York: Routledge.

Combahee River Collective. 1982. A Black Feminist Statement. Pp. 13–22 in *All the Women Are White, All the Blacks Are Men, but Some of Us Are Brave: Black Women's Studies*, ed. Gloria T. Hull, Patricia Bell Scott, and Barbara Smith.

Connell, R. W. 1987. *Gender & Power*. Stanford, CA: Stanford University Press.

———. 1995. *Masculinities*. Berkeley and Los Angeles: University of California Press.

———. 1997. "Why Is Classical Theory Classical?" *American Journal of Sociology* 102:1511–57.

Conrad, Peter. 1975. "The Discovery of Hyperkinesis: Notes on the Medicalization of Deviant Behavior." *Social Problems* 23:12–21.

Conrad, Peter, and Deborah Potter. 2000. "From Hyperactive Children to ADHD Adults: Observations on the Expansion of Medical Categories." *Social Problems* 47, no. 4:559–82.

Cook, Judith A., and Mary Margaret Fonow. 1986. "Knowledge and Women's Interests: Issues of Epistemology and Methodology in Feminist Sociological Research." *Sociological Inquiry* 56, no. 1:2–29.

Cook, Thomas D., and Donald T. Campbell. 1979. *Quasi-Experimentation: Design and Analysis Issues for Field Settings.* Boston: Houghton Mifflin.

Costello, Cynthia. 1991. *We're Worth It: Women and Collective Action in the Insurance Workplace.* Urbana: University of Illinois Press.

Cotter, David A., JoAnn DeFiore, Joan M. Hermsen, Brenda Marsteller Kowalewski, and Reeve Vanneman. 1997. "All Women Benefit: The Macro-Level Effect of Occupational Integration on Gender Earnings Equality." *American Sociological Review* 62:714–34.

Daniels, Arlene Kaplan. 1987. "Invisible Work." *Social Problems* 34, no. 5:403–13.

Davis, Angela Y. 1993. Outcast Mothers and Surrogates: Racism and Reproductive Politics in the Nineties. Pp. 355–66 in *American Feminist Thought at Century's End: A Reader,* ed. Linda S. Kauffman. Cambridge, MA, and Oxford, UK: Blackwell.

Deacon, Deasley. 1985. "Political Arithmetic: The Nineteenth Century Australian Census and the Construction of the Dependent Woman." *Signs: Journal of Women in Culture and Society* 11, no. 1: 27–47.

Deegan, Mary Jo. 1988. *Jane Addams and the Men of the Chicago School, 1892–1918.* New Brunswick, Canada: Transaction Books.

Denzin, Norman K., and Yvonna S. Lincoln. 1994. Entering the Field of Qualitative Research. Pp. in *Handbook of Qualitative Research,* ed. Norman K. Denzin and Yvonna S. Lincoln. Thousand Oaks, CA: Sage.

DeVault, Marjorie L. 1990. "Talking and Listening from Women's Standpoint: Feminist Strategies for Interviewing and Analysis." *Social Problems* 37:96–116.

———. 1991. *Feeding the Family: The Social Organization of Caring as Gendered Work.* Chicago: University of Chicago Press.

———. 1999. *Liberating Method: Feminism and Social Research.* Philadelphia: Temple University Press.

Dill, Bonnie Thornton. 1983. "Race, Class, and Gender: Prospects for an All-Inclusive Sisterhood." *Feminist Studies* 9, no. 1:131–50.

Dresser, Rebecca. 1992. "Wanted: Single White Male for Medical Research." *Hastings Center Report* (January-February): 24–29.

Eagly, Alice H. 1995. "The Science and Politics of Comparing Women and Men." *American Psychologist* 50, no. 3: 145–58.

Edwards, Rosalind. 1990. "Connecting Method and Epistemology: A White Woman Interviewing Black Women." *Women's Studies International Forum* 13, no. 5:477–90.

Edin, Kathryn, and Laura Lein. 1996. "Work, Welfare, and Single Mothers' Economic Survival Strategies." *American Sociological Review* 61: 253–66.

Edwards, Rosalind, and Jane Ribbens. 1998. Living on the Edges: Public Knowledge, Private Lives, Personal Experience. Pp. 1–23 in *Feminist Dilemmas in Qualitative Research: Public Knowledge and Private Lives,* ed. Jane Ribbens and Rosalind Edwards. Thousand Oaks, CA: Sage.

Ehrenreich, Barbara. 2001. *Nickel and Dimed: On (Not) Getting By in America.* New York: Metropolitan Books.

Eichler, Margrit. 1988. *Nonsexist Research Methods: A Practical Guide.* Boston: Allen and Unwin.

Ellis, Carolyn. 1991. "Sociological Introspection and Emotional Experience." *Symbolic Interaction* 14, no. 1: 23–50.

Ellis, Carolyn, Christine E. Kiesinger, and Lisa M. Tillmann-Healy. 1997. Interactive Interviewing: Talking about Emotional Experience. Pp. 119–49 in *Reflexivity and Voice,* ed. Rosanna Hertz. Thousand Oaks, CA: Sage.

Elster, Jon. 1989. *Nuts and Bolts for the Social Sciences.* New York: Cambridge University Press.

Emerson, Robert M. 2001. *Contemporary Field Research: Perspectives and Formulations.* 2d ed. Prospect Heights, IL: Waveland Press.

England, Paula. 1989. "A Feminist Critique of Rational-Choice Theories: Implications for Sociology." *American Sociologist* 20:14–28.

———. 1999. "The Impact of Feminist Thought on Sociology." *Contemporary Sociology* 28, no. 3:263–68.

England, Paula, Lori L. Reid, and Barbara Stanek Kilbourne. 1996. "The Effect of the Sex Composition of Jobs on Starting Wages in an Organization: Findings from the NLSY." *Demography* 33, no. 4:511–21.

England, Paula, Melissa S. Herbert, Barbara Stanek Kilbourne, Lori L. Reid, and Lori McCreary Megdal. 1994. "The Gendered Valuation of Occupations and Skills: Earnings in the 1980 Census Occupations." *Social Forces* 73, no. 1:65–99.

Enloe, Cynthia. 1990. *Bananas, Beaches and Bases: Making Feminist Sense of International Politics.* Berkeley: University of California Press.

Epstein, Cynthia. 1999. Similarity and Difference: The Sociology of Gender Distinctions. Pp. 45–61 in *Handbook of the Sociology of Gender*, ed. Janet Saltzman Chafetz. Norwell, MA: Kluwer Academic.

Espiritu, Yen Le. 1997. *Asian American Women and Men: Labor, Laws, and Love.* Thousand Oaks, CA: Sage.

Etter-Lewis, Gwendolyn. 1991. Black Women's Life Stories: Reclaiming Self in Narrative Texts. Pp. 43–58 in *Women's Words: The Feminist Practice of Oral History*, ed. Sherna Berger Gluck and Daphne Patai. New York: Routledge.

Farganis, Sandra. 1986. "Social Theory and Feminist Theory: The Need for Dialogue." *Sociological Inquiry* 56:50–68.

Farley, Reynolds. n.d. "Identifying with Multiple Races: A Social Movement That Succeeded but Failed?" PSC Research Report No. 01-491. Ann Arbor: Population Studies Center, Institute for Social Research, University of Michigan.

Fausto-Sterling, Anne. 1985. *Myths of Gender: Biological Theories About Women and Men.* New York: Basic Books.

———. 2000. *Sexing the Body: Gender Politics and the Construction of Sexuality.* New York: Basic Books.

Feagin, Joel. 2000. *Racist America: Roots, Current Realities, and Future Reparations.* New York: Routledge.

Ferguson, Ann Arnett. 2000. *Bad Boys: Public Schools in the Making of Black Masculinity.* Ann Arbor: University of Michigan Press.

Ferree, Myra Marx, Judith Lorber, and Beth B. Hess, eds. 1999. *Revisioning Gender.* Thousand Oaks, CA: Sage.

Ferree, Myra Marx, and Julia McQuillan. 1998. "Methodological and Policy Issues in University Salary Studies." *Gender & Society* 12, no. 1:7–39.

Finch, Janet, and Jennifer Mason. 1990. Decision Taking in the Fieldwork Process: Theoretical Sampling and Collaborative Working. Pp. 25–50 in *Studies in*

Qualitative Methodology: Vol. 2, Reflections on Field Experience, ed. Robert G. Burgess. Greenwich, CT: JAI Press.

Fine, Michelle. 1994. Working the Hyphens: Reinventing Self and Others in Qualitative Research. Pp. 70–82 in *Handbook of Qualitative Research*, ed. Norman Denzin and Yvonna Lincoln. Thousand Oaks, CA: Sage.

Fine, Michelle, and Susan Merle Gordon. 1989. Feminist Transformations of/Despite Psychology. Pp. 146–74 in *Gender and Thought: Psychological Perspectives*, ed. Mary Crawford and Margaret Gentry. New York: Springer-Verlag.

Fine, Michelle, and Lois Weiss. 1996. "Writing the 'Wrongs' of Fieldwork: Confronting Our Own Research/Writing Dilemmas in Urban Ethnographies." *Qualitative Inquiry* 2, no. 3:251–74.

Flood, Michael. 1999. "Claims about Husband Battering." *DVIRC Newsletter* (Summer): 3–8. Melbourne: Domestic Violence and Incest Resource Centre. www.anu.edu.au/~a112465/XY/husbandbattering.htm (accessed June 6, 2001).

Foucault, Michel. 1972. *Power/Knowledge: Selected Interviews and Other Writings, 1972–1977.* Ed. Colin Gordon. New York: Pantheon.

———. 1975/1979. *Discipline and Punish.* New York: Random House.

———. 1976/1978. *The History of Sexuality.* Trans. Robert Hurley. New York: Pantheon Books.

Frankenberg, Ruth. 1993. *White Women, Race Matters: The Social Construction of Whiteness.* Minneapolis: University of Minnesota Press.

Fraser, Nancy. 1989. *Unruly Practices: Power, Discourse and Gender in Contemporary Social Theory.* Minneapolis: University of Minnesota Press.

Fraser, Nancy, and Linda Nicholson. 1988. "Social Criticism without Philosophy: An Encounter between Feminism and Postmodernism." *Communication* 10:345–66.

Fraser, Nancy, and Linda Gordon. 1994. "A Genealogy of Dependency: Tracing a Keyword of the U.S. Welfare State." *Signs: Journal of Women in Culture and Society* 19, no. 2:1–29.

Friedl, Erika. 1989. *Women of Deh Koh: Lives in an Iranian Village.* Washington and London: Smithsonian Press.

Friere, Paulo. 1970. *Pedagogy of the Oppressed.* New York: Herder and Herder.

Geertz, Clifford. 1973. *The Interpretation of Cultures.* New York: Basic Books.

Genova, Anthony C. 1983. "The Metaphysical Turn in Contemporary Philosophy." *Southwest Philosophical Studies* 9:1–22.

Gilkes, Cheryl Townsend. 2003. Discourses of Psychic Survival: Women, African American Sacred Music, and the Politics of Voice and Safety. Distinguished Feminist Lecture presented at the annual meeting of the Sociologists for Women in Society, August 18, Atlanta, GA.

Gill, Sandra, Jean Stockard, Miriam Johnson, and Suzanne Williams. 1987. "Measuring Gender Differences: The Expressive Dimension and Critique of Androgyny Scales." *Sex Roles* 17, no. 7–8: 375–400.

Gilligan, Carol. 1982. *In a Different Voice.* Cambridge, MA: Harvard University Press.

Ginorio, Angela B. 2004. When N = 1–2: Justice, Privacy and Women of Color in Science. Paper presented at conference, Feminist Epistemologies, Methodologies, Metaphysics, and Science Studies. University of Washington.

Ginsburg, Faye. 1997. The Case of Mistaken Identity: Problems in Representing Women on the Right. Pp. 283–99 in *Reflexivity and Voice,* ed. Rosanna Hertz. Thousand Oaks, CA Sage.

Glaser, Barney G., and Anselm L. Strauss. 1967. *The Discovery of Grounded Theory: Strategies for Qualitative Research.* Chicago: Aldine.

Glass, Jennifer. 2000. "Envisioning the Integration of Family and Work: Toward a Kinder, Gentler Workplace." *Contemporary Sociology* 29, no. 1:129–43.

Glass, Jennifer, and Valerie Camarigg. 1992. "Gender, Parenthood, and Job-Family Compatibility." *American Journal of Sociology* 98:131–51.

Glenn, Evelyn Nakano. 1992. "From Servitude to Service Work: Historical Continuities in the Racial Division of Paid Reproductive Labor." *Signs: Journal of Women in Culture and Society* 18:1–43.

———. 1999. The Social Construction and Institutionalization of Gender and Race: An Integrative Framework. Chap. 1 in *Revisioning Gender,* ed. Myra Marx Ferree, Judith Lorber, and Beth B. Hess. Thousand Oaks, CA: Sage.

Glucksmann, Miriam. 1994. The Work of Knowledge and the Knowledge of Women's Work. Pp. 149–65 in *Researching Women's Lives from a Feminist Perspective,* ed. Mary Maynard and June Purvis. London and Bristol, PA: Taylor and Francis.

Gordon, Deborah A. 1988. "Writing Culture, Writing Feminism: The Poetics and Politics of Experimental Ethnography." *Inscriptions* 3/4:7–24.

———. 1995. Border Work: Feminist Ethnography and the Dissemination of Literacy. Pp. 373–89 in *Women Writing Culture*, ed. Ruth Behar and Deborah Gordon. Berkeley: University of California Press.

Gornick, Janet C., and Jerry A. Jacobs. 1998. "Gender, the Welfare State, and Public Employment: A Comparative Study of Seven Industrialized Countries." *American Sociological Review* 63, no. 5:688–710.

Gray, Ross, and Christina Sinding. 2002. *Standing Ovation: Performing Social Science Research about Cancer.* Walnut Creek, CA: AltaMira Press.

Griffith, Allison. 1995. Mothering, Schooling, and Children's Development. Pp. 108–21 in *Knowledge, Experience, and Ruling Relations: Studies in the Social Organization of Knowledge*, ed. Marie Campbell and Ann Manicom. Toronto: University of Toronto Press.

Griswold, Wendy. 2004. *Cultures and Societies in a Changing World, 2nd Edition.* Thousand Oaks, CA: Sage.

Groce, Nora Ellen. 1985. *Everyone Here Spoke Sign Language: Hereditary Deafness on Martha's Vineyard.* Cambridge, MA: Harvard University Press.

Gupta, Akhil, and James Ferguson. 1997. Discipline and Practice: "The Field" as Site, Method, and Location in Anthropology. Pp. 1–46 in *Anthropological Locations: Boundaries and Grounds of a Field Science*, ed. Akhil Gupta and James Ferguson. Berkeley: University of California Press.

Gusfield, Joseph R. 1976. "The Literary Rhetoric of Social Science: Comedy and Pathos in Drinking Driver Research." *American Sociological Review* 41, no. 1:16–34.

Hale, Sondra. 1991. Feminist Method, Process, and Self-Criticism: Interviewing Sudanese Women. Pp. 121–36 in *Women's Words: The Feminist Practice of Oral History*, ed. Sherna Berger Gluck and Daphne Patai. New York: Routledge.

Hamilton, Richard F. 1972. *Class and Politics in the United States.* New York: Wiley.

Hammersley, Martyn. 2003. "Recent Radical Criticism of Interview Studies: Any Implications for the Sociology of Education?" *British Journal of Sociology of Education* 24, no. 1:119–26.

Haraway, Donna. 1978. "Animal Sociology and a Natural Economy of the Body Politic, Part 1: A Political Sociology of Dominance." *Signs: Journal of Women in Culture and Society* 4:21–36.

———. 1988. "Situated Knowledges: The Science Question in Feminism and the Privilege of Partial Perspective." *Feminist Studies* 14:575–99.

———. 1990. A Manifesto for Cyborgs: Science, Technology, and Socialist Feminism in the Last Quarter. Pp. 580–671 in *Feminism and Postmodernism*, ed. Linda Nicholson. New York: Routledge.

———. 1993. The Biopolitics of Postmodern Bodies: Determinations of Self in Immune System Discourse. Pp. 199–233 in *American Feminist Thought at Century's End: A Reader*, ed. Linda S. Kauffman. Cambridge, MA: Blackwell.

Harding, Sandra. 1983. Why Has the Sex/Gender System Become Visible Only Now? Pp. 311–24 in *Discovering Reality: Feminist Perspectives on Epistemology, Metaphysics, Methodology, and Philosophy of Science*, ed. Sandra Harding and Merrill B. Hintikka. Dordrecht, Holland: D. Reidel Publishing Company.

———. 1987. Introduction: Is There a Feminist Method? Pp. 1–14 in *Feminism and Methodology*, ed. Sandra Harding. Bloomington: Indiana University Press.

———. 1991. *Whose Science? Whose Knowledge? Thinking from Women's Lives*. Ithaca, NY: Cornell University Press.

———. 1998. *Is Science Multicultural?: Postcolonialisms, Feminisms, and Epistemologies*. Bloomington: Indiana University Press.

Harkess, Shirley, and Carol A. B. Warren. 1993. "The Social Relations of Intensive Interviewing: Constellations of Strangeness and Science." *Sociological Methods and Research* 21, no. 3:317–39.

Harknett, Kristen, Irwin Garfinkel, Jay Bainbridge, Timothy Smeedling, Nancy Folbre, and Sara McLanahan. 2003. "Do Public Expenditures Improve Child Outcomes in the U.S.: A Comparison across Fifty States. Center for Research on Child Wellbeing." Working paper #03-02 (March).

Harrison, Beverly Wildung. 1985. The Power of Anger in the Work of Love: Christian Ethics for Women and Other Strangers. Pp. 3–21 in *Making the Connections: Essays in Feminist Social Ethics*, ed. Carol S. Robb. Boston: Beacon.

Hartmann, Heidi. 1981. "The Family as the Locus of Gender, Class, and Political Struggle: The Example of Housework." *Signs: Journal of Women in Culture and Society* 6:366–94.

Hartsock, Nancy C. M. 1983. The Feminist Standpoint: Developing the Ground for a Specifically Feminist Historical Materialism. Pp. 283–310 in *Discovering Reality:*

Feminist Perspectives on Epistemology, Metaphysics, Methodology and Philosophy of Science, ed. Sandra Harding and Merrill B. P. Hintikka. Dordrecht, Holland: D. Reidel Publishing Co.

———. 1985. *Money, Sex, and Power: Toward a Feminist Historical Materialism.* Boston: Northeastern.

Hauser, Robert M., Howard F. Taylor, and Troy Duster. 1995. "The Bell Curve." *Contemporary Sociology* 24, no. 2:149–61.

Hawkesworth, Mary E. 1989. "Knowers, Knowing, Known: Feminist Theory and Claims of Truth." *Signs: Journal of Women in Culture and Society* 14, no. 3:533–57.

Hertz, Rosanna, ed. 1997. *Reflexivity and Voice.* Thousand Oaks, CA: Sage.

Hillyer, Barbara. 1993. *Feminism and Disability.* Norman: University of Oklahoma Press.

Hochschild, Arlie R. 1983. *The Managed Heart: Commercialization of Human Feeling.* Berkeley: University of California Press.

———. 1989. *The Second Shift: Working Parents and the Revolution at Home.* New York: Viking.

Holland, Janet, and Caroline Ramazanoglu. 1994. Coming to Conclusions: Power and Interpretation in Researching Young Women's Sexuality. Pp. 125–48 in *Researching Women's Lives from a Feminist Perspective,* ed. Mary Maynard and June Purvis. London: Taylor and Francis.

Holmstrom, Lynda Lytle, and Ann Wolbert Burgess. 1983. "Rape and Everyday Life." *Society* (July/August): 33–40.

Honey, Maureen. 1984. *Creating Rosie the Riveter: Class, Gender, and Propaganda during World War II.* Amherst, MA: University of Massachusetts Press.

hooks, bell. 1981. *Ain't I a Woman? Black Women and Feminism.* Boston: South End Press.

———. 1990. *Yearning: Race, Gender, and Culture Politics.* Boston: South End Press.

———. 1994. *Teaching to Transgress: Education as the Practice of Freedom.* New York: Routledge.

Howard, Judith. 1984. "Societal Influences on Attribution: Blaming Some Victims More Than Others." *Journal of Personality and Social Psychology* 47:494–505.

———. 1987. "The Conceptualization and Measurement of Attributions." *Journal of Experimental Social Psychology* 23:32–58.

Howard, Judith, and Jocelyn A. Hollander. 1997. *Gendered Situations, Gendered Selves: A Gender Lens on Social Psychology*. Thousand Oaks, CA: Sage.

Howard, Judith, and Kenneth C. Pike. 1986. "Ideological Investment in Cognitive Processing: The Influence of Social Statuses on Attribution." *Social Psychology Quarterly* 49:154–67.

Hughes, Donna M. 1995. "Significant Differences: The Construction of Knowledge, Objectivity, and Dominance." *Women's Studies International Forum* 18, no. 4:395–406.

Jacobs, Jerry A., and Kathleen Gerson. 1998. The Endless Day vs. the Flexible Office: Working Time, Work-Family Conflict and Gender Equity. Paper presented at the annual meeting of the American Sociological Association, August.

———. 2000. Do Americans Feel Overworked? Comparing Ideal and Actual Working Time. Pp. 71–95 in *Work and Family: Research Informing Policy*, ed. Toby L. Parcel and Daniel B. Cornfield. Thousand Oaks, CA: Sage.

Jarrett, Robin L. 1993. Focus Group Interviewing with Low-Income Minority Populations: A Research Experience. Pp. 184–201 in *Successful Focus Groups: Advancing the State of the Art*, ed. David L. Morgan. Newbury Park, CA: Sage.

Jay, Nancy. 1981. "Gender and Dichotomy." *Feminist Studies* 7:38–56.

Jayaratne, Toby Epstein, and Abigail J. Stewart. 1991. Quantitative and Qualitative Methods in the Social Sciences. Pp. 86–106 in *Beyond Methodology: Feminist Scholarship as Lived Research*, ed. Mary Margaret Fonow and Judith A. Cook. Bloomington and Indianapolis: Indiana University Press.

Jordan, June. 1985. *On Call: Political Essays*. Boston: South End Press.

Jussim, Lee. 1991. "Social Perception and Social Reality: A Reflection-Construction Model." *Psychological Review* 98:54–73.

Keller, Evelyn Fox. 1982. "Feminism and Science." *Signs: Journal of Women in Culture and Society* 14:42–72.

———. 1983. *A Feeling for the Organism: The Life Work of Barbara McClintock*. New York: Freedman.

Kelly, Liz, Sheila Burton, and Linda Regan. 1994. Researching Women's Lives or Studying Women's Oppression: What Constitutes Feminist Research? Pp. 27–48 in *Researching Women's Lives from a Feminist Perspective*, ed. Mary Maynard and Jane Purvis. London: Taylor and Francis.

Kessler, Suzanne. 1998. *Lessons from the Intersexed*. New Brunswick, NJ: Rutgers University Press.

Kessler, Suzanne, and Wendy McKenna. 1978. *Gender: An Ethnomethodological Approach*. New York: Wiley.

Kilbourne, Barbara, Paula England, George Farkas, Kurt Beron, and Dorothea Weir. 1994. "Returns to Skills, Compensating Differentials, and Gender Bias: Effects of Occupational Characteristics on the Wages of White Women and Men." *American Journal of Sociology* 100:689–719.

King, Deborah K. 1988. "Multiple Jeopardy, Multiple Consciousness: The Context of Black Feminist Ideology." *Signs: Journal of Women in Culture and Society* 14:42–72.

Kollock, Peter, Philip Blumstein, and Pepper Schwartz. 1985. "Sex and Power in Interaction." *American Sociological Review* 50:34–46.

Krieger, Susan. 1983. *The Mirror Dance: Identity in a Women's Community*. Philadelphia: Temple University Press.

———. 1985. "Beyond Subjectivity: The Use of the Self in Social Science." *Qualitative Sociology* 8, no. 4:309–24.

Lakoff, George. 1995. "Metaphor, Morality, and Politics, Or, Why Conservatives Have Left Liberals in the Dust." *Social Research* 62, no. 2: 177(37).

Lakoff, George, and Mark Johnson. 1980. *Metaphors We Live By*. Chicago: University of Chicago Press.

Langer, Ellen. 1989. *Mindfulness*. Reading, MA: Addison Wesley.

Laslett, Barbara, and Rhona Rapoport. 1975. "Collaborative Interviewing and Interactive Research." *Journal of Marriage and the Family* (November): 968–77.

Lather, Patti. 1988. "Feminist Perspectives on Empowering Research Methodologies." *Women's Studies International Forum* 11, no. 6:569–81.

Latour, Bruno, and Steve Woolgar. 1979. *Laboratory Life: The Social Construction of Scientific Facts*. New York: Sage.

LeClere, Felicia B., Richard G. Rogers, and Kimberley Peters. 1998. "Neighborhood Social Context and Racial Differences in Women's Heart Disease Mortality." *Journal of Health and Social Behavior* 39:91–107.

Lofland, John, and Lyn H. Lofland. 1995. *Analyzing Social Settings: A Guide to Qualitative Observation and Analysis*. 3d ed. Belmont, CA: Wadsworth.

Longino, Helen E. 1989. "Feminist Critiques of Rationality: Critiques of Science or Philosophy of Science?" *Women's Studies International Forum* 12:261–69.

Lorber, Judith. 1994. *Paradoxes of Gender*. New Haven: Yale University Press.

Lorber, Judith, Rose L. Coser, Alice S. Rossi, and Nancy Chodorow. 1981. "On the Reproduction of Mothering: A Methodological Debate." *Signs: Journal of Women in Culture and Society* 6:482–514.

Lovibond, Sabina. 1989. "Feminism and Postmodernism." *New Left Review*, no. 178 (Nov./Dec.).

Luff, Donna. 1999. "Dialogue across the Divides: 'Moments of Rapport' and Power in Feminist Research with Anti-Feminist Women." *Sociology* 33 (Nov.):687–703.

Lukacs, Georg. 1971. *History and Class Consciousness*. Cambridge, MA: MIT Press.

Luxton, Meg. 1980. *More Than a Labour of Love: Three Generations of Women's Work in the Home*. Toronto: Women's Press.

Madriz, Esther I. 1998. "Using Focus Groups with Lower Socioeconomic Status Latina Women." *Qualitative Inquiry* 4, no. 1:114–128.

Mandle, Joan D. 1999. "Sisterly Critics." *NWSA Journal* 11, no. 1: 97–109.

Mann, Michael. 1973. *Consciousness and Action among the Western Working Class*. New York: Humanities Press.

Mannheim, Karl. 1936. *Ideology and Utopia*. New York: Harcourt Brace.

Marcus, George E. 1994. What Comes (Just) After "Post"? The Case of Ethnography. Pp. 563–74 in *Handbook of Qualitative Research*, ed. Norman K. Denzin and Yvonna S. Lincoln. Thousand Oaks, CA: Sage.

Markus, Hazel, and Shinobu Kitayama. 1991. "Culture and the Self: Implications for Cognition, Emotion, and Motivation." *Psychological Review* 98:224–53.

———. 1998. "The Cultural Psychology of Personality." *Journal of Cross-Cultural Psychology* 29, no. 1:63–87.

Martin, Emily. 1992. *The Woman in the Body: A Cultural Analysis Of Reproduction*. Boston: Beacon Press.

Martin, Patricia Yancy. 1996. Gendering and Evaluating Dynamics: Men, Masculinities, and Managements. Pp. 186–209 in *Men as Managers, Managers as Men*, ed. Dave Collinson and Jeff Hearn. Thousand Oaks, CA: Sage.

———. 2003. "'Said and Done' versus 'Saying and Doing': Gendering Practices, Practicing Gender at Work." *Gender & Society* 17, no. 3:342–66.

Marx, Karl. 1867/1976. *Capital: A Critique of Political Economy*. Introduced by Ernest Mandel, trans. Ben Fowkes. New York: Vintage.

Mascia-Lees, Frances E., Patricia Sharpe, and Colleen Ballerino Cohen. 1989. "The Postmodern Turn in Anthropology: Cautions from a Feminist Perspective." *Signs: Journal of Women in Culture and Society* 15:7–33.

Mauther, Natasha, and Andrea Doucet. 1998. Reflections on a Voice-centered Relational Method: Analyzing Maternal and Domestic Voices. Pp. 119–46 in *Feminist Dilemmas in Qualitative Research: Public Knowledge and Private Lives*, ed. Rosalind Edwards and Jane Ribbens. Thousand Oaks, CA: Sage.

Maynard, Mary, and June Purvis. 1994. Introduction: Doing Feminist Research. Pp. 1–9 in *Researching Women's Lives from a Feminist Perspective*, ed. Mary Maynard and June Purvis. London and Bristol, PA: Taylor and Francis.

Mazie, Steven V., and Patricia J. Woods. 2003. "Prayer, Contentious Politics, and the Women of the Wall: The Benefits of Collaboration in Participant Observation at Intense Multifocal Events." *Field Methods* 15, no. 1:25–50.

McCall, Michal, and Judith Wittner. 1989. The Good News about Life Histories. Pp. 46–89 in *Cultural Studies and Symbolic Interaction*, ed. Howard Becker and Michal McCall. Chicago: University of Chicago Press.

McCracken, Grant. 1998. *The Long Interview*. Thousand Oaks, CA: Sage.

McKee, Lorna, and Margaret O'Brien. 1983. Interviewing Men: Taking Gender Seriously. Pp. 147–61 in *The Public and the Private*, ed. Eva Gamarnikov, David Morgan, June Purvis, and Daphne Taylorson. London: Heineman.

Mehan, Hugh, and Houston Wood. 1975. *Reality of Ethnomethodology*. New York: Wiley.

Merchant, Carolyn. 1980. *The Death of Nature: Women, Ecology, and the Scientific Revolution: A Feminist Reappraisal of the Scientific Revolution*. San Francisco: Harper and Row.

Merola, Stacey S., and Roberta Spalter-Roth. Profile of 2001 ASA Membership. ASA Research Program on the Discipline and Profession. www.asanet.org/research/db2001memb.html (accessed May 17, 2004).

Messner, Michael A. 1997. *Politics of Masculinities: Men in Movements*. Thousand Oaks, CA: Sage.

Mies, Maria. 1986. *Patriarchy and Accumulation on a World Scale: Women in the International Division of Labor*. Atlantic Highlands, NJ: Zed Books.

———. 1993. Feminist Research: Science, Violence, and Responsibility. Pp. 36–54 in *Ecofeminism*, ed. Maria Mies and Vandana Shiva. London: Zed Books.

Mills, C. Wright. 1959. *The Sociological Imagination*. New York: Oxford University Press.

Minh-ha, Trinh T. 1993. The Language of Nativism: Anthropology as a Scientific Conversation of Man with Man. Pp. 107–39 in *American Feminist Thought at Century's End: A Reader*, ed. Linda S. Kauffman. Cambridge, MA: Blackwell.

Mohanty, Chandra Talpede, Ann Russo, and Lourdes Torres. 1991. *Third World Women and the Politics of Feminism*. Bloomington, IN: Indiana University Press.

Montell, Frances. 1999. "Focus Group Interviews: A New Feminist Method." *NWSA Journal* 11, no. 1:44–71.

Morgan, David. 1981. Men, Masculinity, and the Process of Sociological Inquiry. Pp. 83–113 in *Doing Feminist Research*, ed. Helen Roberts. London, Boston, and Henley: Routledge and Kegan Paul.

———. 1996. "Focus Groups." *Annual Review of Sociology* 22:129–52.

Mueller, Claus. 1973. *The Politics of Communication: A Study in the Political Sociology of Language, Socialization, and Legitimation*. New York: Oxford University Press.

Nader, Laura. 1969. Up the Anthropologist: Perspectives Gained from Studying Up. Pp. 284–311 in *Reinventing Anthropology*, ed. Dell Hymes. New York: Vintage.

Naples, Nancy. 1996/1997. A Feminist Revisiting of the Insider/Outsider Debate: The "Outsider Phenomenon" in Rural Iowa. Pp. 70–94 in *Reflexivity and Voice*, ed. Rosanna Hertz. Thousand Oaks, CA: Sage.

Norris, Christopher. 1999. Interview with Roy Bhaskar. *The Philosophers' Magazine*, no. 8. www.philosophers.co.uk/issue8.htm (accessed July 14, 2003).

Oakley, Ann. 1974. *The Sociology of Housework*. New York: Pantheon.

———. 1981. Interviewing Women: A Contradiction in Terms. Pp. 30–61 in *Doing Feminist Research*, ed. Helen Roberts. London: Routledge and Kegan Paul.

———. 2000. *Experiments in Knowing: Gender and Method in the Social Sciences*. New York: The New Press.

O'Brien, Mary. 1981. *The Politics of Reproduction*. Boston: Routledge and Kegan Paul.

———. 1989. *Reproducing the World: Essays in Feminist Theory*. Boulder, CO: Westview.

Offe, Claus. 1985. Two Logics of Collective Action. Pp. 170–200 in *Disorganized Capitalism*. ed. John Keane. Cambridge: Polity Press.

Olesen, Virginia. 1994. Feminisms and Models of Qualitative Research. Pp. 158–74 in *Handbook of Qualitative Research*, ed. Norman K. Denzin and Yvonna S. Lincoln. Thousand Oaks, CA: Sage.

Ollman, Bertell. 1972. "Toward Class Consciousness Next Time: Marx and the Working Class." *Politics & Society* 3:1–24.

Omi, Michael, and Howard Winant. 1986. *Racial Formation in the United States: From the 1960s to the 1980s*. New York: Routledge and Kegan Paul.

Ong, Aiwa. 1995. Women Out of China: Traveling Tales and Traveling Theories in Postcolonial Feminism. Pp. 350–72 in *Women Writing Culture*, ed. Ruth Behar and Deborah Gordon. Berkeley: University of California Press.

Paget, Marianne A. 1983. "Experience and Knowledge." *Human Studies* 6, no. 1:67–90.

———. 1990. "Unlearning to Not Speak." *Human Studies* 13:147–61.

Patai, Daphne. 1991. U.S. Academics and Third World Women: Is Ethical Research Possible? Pp. 137–53 in *Women's Words: The Feminist Practice of Oral History*, ed. Sherna Berger Gluck and Daphne Patai. New York: Routledge.

Pateman, Carol. 1983. Feminist Critiques of the Public–Private Dichotomy. In *The Public and Private in Social Life*, ed. Stanley I. Benn and Gerald F. Gaus. New York: St. Martin's.

Phoenix, Ann. 1994. Practicing Feminist Research: The Intersection of Gender and "Race" in the Research Process. Pp. 49–71 in *Researching Women's Lives from a Feminist Perspective*, ed. Mary Maynard and June Purvis. London and Bristol, PA: Taylor and Francis.

Pierce, Jennifer. 1995. Reflections on Fieldwork in a Complex Organization: Lawyers, Ethnographic Authority, and Lethal Weapons. Pp. 94–110 in *Studying Elites Using Qualitative Methods*, ed. Rosanna Hertz and Jonathan B. Imber. Thousand Oaks, CA: Sage.

Powdermaker, Hortense. 1966. *Stranger and Friend*. New York: Norton.

Reinharz, Shulamit. 1997. Who Am I? The Need for a Variety of Selves in the Field. Pp. 3–20 in *Reflexivity and Voice*, ed. Rosanna Hertz. Thousand Oaks, CA: Sage.

Reinharz, Shulamit, and Susan Chase. 2002. Interviewing Women. Pp. 221–38 in *The Handbook of Interview Research: Context and Method*, ed. James Holstein and Jaber Gubrium. Thousand Oaks, CA: Sage.

Reskin, Barbara. 2000. "The Proximate Causes of Employment Discrimination." *Contemporary Sociology* 29, no. 2:319–28.

———. 2003. "Including Mechanisms in Our Models of Ascriptive Inequality." *American Sociological Review* 68, no. 1:1–21.

Reskin, Barbara, and Irene Padavic. 2002. *Women and Men at Work*. 2d ed. Thousand Oaks, CA: Pine Forge Press.

Reskin, Barbara, and Patricia Roos. 1990. *Job Queues, Gender Queues: Explaining Women's Inroads into Male Occupations*. Philadelphia, PA: Temple University Press.

Reskin, Barbara, and Catherine E. Ross. 1992. "Jobs, Authority, and Earnings among Managers." *Work and Occupations* 19, no. 4:342–65.

Ribbens, Jane. 1989. "Interviewing—An 'Unnatural Situation.'" *Women's Studies International Forum* 12, no. 6:579–92.

Rich, Adrienne. 1976. *Of Woman Born: Motherhood as Experience and Institution*. New York: Norton.

Richardson, Laurel. 1988. "The Collective Story: Postmodernism and the Writing of Sociology." *Sociological Focus* 21, no. 3:199–208.

Richtermeyer, Gwen. 2001. *Not One of Them: Women's Experiences of the Middle Class*. Ph.D. dissertation, Department of Sociology, University of Kansas, Lawrence.

Ridgeway, Cecilia L. 1982. "Status in Groups: The Importance of Motivation." *American Sociological Review* 47, no. 1:76–88.

———. 1987. "Nonverbal Behavior, Dominance, and the Basis of Status in Task Groups." *American Sociological Review* 52:683–94.

———. 1993. Gender, Status, and the Social Psychology of Expectations. Pp. 175–97 in *Theory on Gender/Feminism on Theory*, ed., Paula England. NY: Aldine.

Riessman, Catherine Kohler. 1987. "When Gender Is Not Enough: Women Interviewing Women." *Gender & Society* 1, no. 2:172–207.

———. 1993. *Narrative Analysis*. Thousand Oaks, CA: Sage.

Ring, Jennifer. 1987. "Toward a Feminist Epistemology." *American Journal of Political Science* 31:753–72.

Risman, Barbara. 1993. "Methodological Implications of Feminist Scholarship." *American Sociologist* 24:15–25.

Risman, Barbara, and Myra Marx Ferree. 1995. "Making Gender Visible." *American Sociological Review* 60:775–82.

Rosaldo, Michelle Zimbalist, and Louise Lamphere, eds. 1974. *Woman, Culture, and Society*. Stanford: Stanford University Press.

Rose, Gillian. 2001. *Visual Methodologies*. Thousand Oaks, CA: Sage.

Rosenfeld, Rachel A., and Arne L. Kalleberg. 1990. "A Cross-National Comparison of the Gender Gap in Income." *American Journal of Sociology* 96, no. 1:69–106.

Rosser, Sue V. 1988. "Good Science: Can It Ever Be Gender Free?" *Women's Studies International Forum* 11:13–19.

Ruddick, Sara. 1980. "Maternal Thinking." *Feminist Studies* 6:342–67.

Russell, Diana. 1984. *Sexual Exploitation*. Newbury Park, CA: Sage.

Sanday, Peggy. 1992. *Fraternity Gang Rape: Sex, Brotherhood, and Privilege on Campus*. New York: New York University Press.

Schuman, Howard, and Stanley Presser. 1981. *Questions and Answers in Attitude Surveys: Experiments on Question Form, Wording, and Context*. New York: Academic Press.

Shea, Christopher. 1996. "Psychologists Debate Accuracy of 'Significance Test.'" *Chronicle of Higher Education* 42, no. 49 (August 16): A12, A17.

Shelton, Beth Anne. 1992. *Women, Men, and Time: Gender Differences in Paid Work, Housework, and Leisure*. New York: Greenwood Press.

Sherif, Carolyn Wood. 1979. Bias in Psychology. In *The Prism of Sex: Essays in the Sociology of Knowledge*, ed. J. A. Sherman and E. T. Beck. Madison: University of Wisconsin Press.

Sherman, Julia A. and Evelyn Torton Beck, eds. 1979. *The Prism of Sex: Essays in the Sociology of Knowledge*. Madison: University of Wisconsin Press.

Shiva, Vandana. 1993. Reductionism and Regeneration: A Crisis in Science. Pp. 22–35 in *Ecofeminism*, ed. Maria Mies and Vandana Shiva. London: Zed Books.

Shostak, Marjorie. 1981. *Nisa, the Life and Words of a Kung Woman*. Cambridge, MA: Harvard University Press.

Smith, Dorothy E. 1979. A Sociology for Women. In *The Prism of Sex: Essays in the Sociology of Knowledge*, ed. Julia A. Sherman and Evelyn Torton Beck. Madison: University of Wisconsin Press.

———. 1987. *The Everyday World as Problematic: A Feminist Sociology*. Boston: Northeastern University Press.

———. 1990. *The Conceptual Practices of Power: A Feminist Sociology of Knowledge*. Boston: Northeastern University Press.

———. 2005. *Institutional Ethnography: A Sociology for People*. Walnut Grove, CA: AltaMira Press.

Smith, Michael D. 1994. "Enhancing the Quality of Survey Data on Violence against Women: A Feminist Approach." *Gender & Society* 8, no. 1:109–27.

Sorensen, Annemette, and Sara McLanahan. 1987. "Married Women's Economic Dependency, 1940–1980." *American Journal of Sociology* 93, no. 3:659–87.

Spalter-Roth, Roberta, and Heidi Hartmann. 1991. Science, Politics, and the "Dual Vision" of Feminist Policy Research: The Example of Family and Medical Leave. Pp. 41–65 in *Parental Leave and Child Care*, ed. Janet Hyde and Marilyn Essex. Philadelphia: Temple University Press.

———. 1996/1999. Small Happiness: The Feminist Struggle to Integrate Social Research with Social Activism. Pp. 333–47 in *Feminist Approaches to Theory and Methodology: An Interdisciplinary Reader*, ed. Sharlene Hesse-Biber, Christina Gilmartin, and Robin Lyndenberg. New York: Oxford University Press.

Spalter-Roth, Roberta, Felice J. Levine, and Andrew Sutter. 2003. The Pipeline for Faculty of Color in Sociology. ASA Research Program on the Discipline and Profession. www.asanet.org/research/pipeline/text.html (accessed May 17, 2004).

Spradley, James P. 1979. *Participant Observation.* New York: Holt, Rinehart and Winston.

Sprague, Joey. 1988. "The Other Side of the Banner: Toward a Feminization of Politics." Pp. 159–71 in *Seeing Female: Reflections by Women Scholars,* ed. Sharon S. Brehm. Westport, CT: Greenwood Press.

———. 1989. "The Structure of Political Thinking: A Multidimensional Model." *Sociological Focus* 22, no. 3 (August): 191–215.

———. 1991. Gender, Class, and Political Thinking. Pp. 111–39 in *Research in Political Sociology,* Vol. 5, ed. Philo Wasburn. Greenwich, CT: JAI Press.

———. 1996. Seeing Gender as Social Structure. Paper presented at the annual meeting of the American Sociological Association, New York (August).

———. 1997. "Holy Men and Big Guns: The Can[n]on in Social Theory." *Gender & Society* 11:88–107.

———. 1998. "(Re)Making Sociology: Breaking the Bonds of Our Discipline." *Contemporary Sociology* 27, no. 1:24–28.

———. 2001. "Structured Knowledges and Strategic Methodologies: Comment on Walby's 'Against Epistemological Chasms: The Science Question in Feminism Revisited,'" *Signs: Journal of Women in Culture and Society* 26, no. 1:527–36.

Sprague, Joey, and Jeanne Hayes. 2000. "Self-Determination and Empowerment: A Feminist Standpoint Analysis of How We Talk about Disability." *American Journal of Community Psychology* 28, no. 5:671–95.

Sprague, Joey, and David Quadagno. 1989. "Gender and Sexual Motivation: An Exploration of Two Assumptions." *Journal of Psychology and Human Sexuality* 2, no. 1:57–76.

Sprague, Joey, and Mary K. Zimmerman. 1989. "Quantity and Quality: Reconstructing Feminist Methodology." *American Sociologist* 20, no. 1 (Spring): 71–86.

———. 1993. Overcoming Dualisms: A Feminist Agenda for Sociological Methodology. Pp. 255–80 in *Theory on Gender/Feminism on Theory,* ed. Paula England. New York: Aldine de Gruyter.

Stacey, Judith. 1988. "Can There Be a Feminist Ethnography?" *Women's Studies International Forum* 11:21–27.

Stacey, Judith, and Barrie Thorne. 1985. "The Missing Feminist Revolution in Sociology." *Social Problems* 32, no. 4:301–16.

Stanley, Liz. 1990. Feminist Praxis and the Academic Mode of Production: an Editorial Introduction. Pp. 3–19 in *Feminist Praxis: Research, Theory, and Epistemology in Feminist Sociology*. London and New York: Routledge.

Steinberg, Ronnie. 1995. Gendered Instructions: Cultural Lag and Gender Bias in the Hay System of Job Evaluation. Pp. 57–92 in *Gender Inequality at Work*, ed. Jerry A. Jacobs. Thousand Oaks, CA: Sage.

Steinberg, Ronnie, and Lois Haignere. 1987. Equitable Compensation: Methodological Criteria for Comparable Worth. Pp. 157–82 in *Ingredients for Women's Employment Policy*, ed. Chris Bose and Glenna Spitze. Albany: State University of New York Press.

Strand, Kerry J. 2000. "Community-Based Research as Pedagogy." *Michigan Journal of Community Service Learning* (Fall): 85–96.

Straus, Murray A. 1979. "Measuring Intrafamilial Conflict and Violence: The Conflict Tactics Scale." *Journal of Marriage and Family* 45:75–88.

Straus, Murray A., Sherry L. Hamby, Sue Boney-McCoy, and David B. Sugarman. 1996. "The Revised Conflict Tactics Scales (CTS2): Development and Preliminary Psychometric Data." *Journal of Family Issues* 17, no. 3:283–316.

Strauss, Anselm, and Juliet Corbin. 1990. *Basics of Qualitative Research: Grounded Theory Procedures and Techniques*. Newbury Park, CA: Sage.

Szasz, Thomas S. 1971. "The Sane Slave: An Historical Note on the Use of Medical Diagnosis as Justificatory Rhetoric." *American Journal of Psychotherapy* 25:228–39.

Tavris, Carol. 1992. *The Mismeasure of Woman*. New York: Simon & Schuster.

Thapar-Björkert, Suruchi. 1999. "Negotiating Otherness: Dilemmas for a non-Western Researcher in the Indian Sub-Continent. *Journal of Gender Studies* 8, no. 1: 57–69.

Thomas, William I., and Dorothy Swayne Thomas. 1928. *The Child in America: Behavior Problems and Programs*. New York: Knopf.

Thorne, Barrie. 1983. Political Activist as Participant-Observer: Conflicts of Commitment in a Study of the Draft Resistance Movement of the 1960s. Pp. 216–34 in *Contemporary Field Research: A Collection of Readings*, ed. Robert M. Emerson. Prospect Heights, IL: Waveland Press.

———. 1994. "Review of Science and the Self: Personal Essays on an Art Form by Susan Krieger." *Gender & Society* 8, no. 1: 138–39.

———. 2001. Learning from Kids. Pp. 224–38 in *Contemporary Field Research*. 2d ed. ed. Robert M. Emerson. Prospect Heights, IL: Waveland Press.

Tixier y Vigil, Yvonne, and Nan Elsasser. 1976. The Effects of the Ethnicity of the Interviewer on Conversation: a Study of Chicana Women. Pp. 161–69 in *Sociology of the Language of American Women*, ed. Betty L. DuBois and Isabel Crouch. San Antonio, TX: Trinity University Press.

Tokarczyk, Michelle M., and Elizabeth A. Fay, eds. 1993. *Working-Class Women in the Academy: Laborers in the Knowledge Factory.* Amherst: University of Massachusetts Press.

Tomaskovic-Devey, Donald. 1993a. "The Gender and Race Composition of Jobs and the Male/Female, White/Black Pay Gaps," *Social Forces* 92: 45-76.

———. 1993b. *Gender and Racial Inequality at Work: The Sources and Consequences of Job Segregation*. Ithaca, NY: ILR Press.

Treichler, Paula A. 1993. AIDS, Gender, and Biomedical Discourse: Current Contests for Meaning. Pp. 281–354 in *American Feminist Thought at Century's End: A Reader*, ed. Linda S. Kauffman. Cambridge, MA: Blackwell.

Tuana, Nancy. 1983. Re-Fusing Nature/Nurture. *Women's Studies International Forum* 6:621–32.

Vanneman, Reeve, and Lynn Weber Cannon. 1987. *The American Perception of Class.* Philadelphia, PA: Temple University Press.

Vidich, Arthur J., and Joseph Bensman. 1964. Academic Bureaucrats and Sensitive Townspeople. Pp. 313–49 in *Reflections on Community Studies*, ed. Arthur J. Vidich and Joseph Bensman. New York: Wiley.

Visweswaran, Kamala. 1988. "Defining Feminist Ethnography," *Inscriptions* 3/4:27–44.

Walby, Sylvia. 2001. "Against Epistemological Chasms: The Science Question in Feminism Revisited." *Signs: Journal of Women in Culture and Society* 26, no. 2: 485–509.

Walters, Suzanna Danuta. 1999. Sex, Text, and Context: (In) between Feminism and Cultural Studies. Pp. 222–57 in *Revisioning Gender*, ed. Myra Marx Ferree, Judith Lorber, and Beth B. Hess. Thousand Oaks, CA: Sage.

Ward, Kathryn B. 1993. Reconceptualizing World System Theory to Include Women. Pp. 43–68 in *Theory on Gender/Feminism on Theory*, ed. Paula England. New York: Aldine de Gruyter.

Ward, Kathryn B., Julie Gast, and Linda Grant. 1992. "Visibility and Dissemination of Women's and Men's Sociological Scholarship." *Social Problems* 39, no. 3:291–98.

Warren, Carol A. B. 1980. "Data Presentation and the Audience: Responses, Ethics, and Effects." *Urban Life* 9, no. 3:282–308.

———. 2002. Qualitative Interviewing. Pp. 83–175 in *The Handbook of Interview Research*, ed. James Holstein and Jaber Gubrium. Thousand Oaks, CA: Sage.

Warren, Carol A. B., and William G. Staples. 1989. "Fieldwork in Forbidden Terrain: The State, Privatization and Human Subjects Regulations." *American Sociologist* (Fall): 263–77.

Wax, Rosalie. 1979. "Gender and Age in Fieldwork and Fieldwork Education: No Good Thing Is Done by Any Man Alone." *Social Problems* 26, no. 5: 509–22.

Weedon, Chris. 1987/1997. *Feminist Practice and Poststructuralist Theory*. 2d ed. Oxford: Basil Blackwell.

Weiss, Robert S. 1994. *Learning from Strangers: The Arts and Method of Qualitative Interview Studies*. New York: Free Press.

Williams, Christine. 1991. Case Studies and the Sociology of Gender. Pp. 224–43 in *A Case for the Case Study*, ed. Joe R. Feagin, Anthony M. Orum, and Gideon Sjoberg. Chapel Hill, NC: University of North Carolina Press.

Williams, Christine, and E. Joel Heikes. 1993. "The Importance of Researcher's Gender in the In-depth Interview: Evidence from Two Case Studies of Male Nurses." *Gender & Society* 7, no. 2: 280–91.

Wolf, Diane L. 1996. Situating Feminist Dilemmas in Fieldwork. Pp. 1–55 in *Feminist Dilemmas in Fieldwork*, ed. Diane L. Wolf. Boulder, CO: Westview Press.

Wolf, Margery. 1992. *A Thrice-Told Tale: Feminism, Postmodernism, and Ethnographic Responsibility*. Stanford, CA: Stanford University Press.

———. 1996. Afterword: Musings from an Old Gray Wolf. Pp. 215–21 in *Feminist Dilemmas in Fieldwork*, ed. Diane L. Wolf. Boulder, CO: Westview Press.

Wolfensberger, Wolf. 1983. "Social Role Valorization: A Proposed New Term for the Principle of Normalization." *Mental Retardation* 21, no. 6: 234–39.

Yeatman, Anna. 1984. "Gender and the Differentiation of Social Life into Public and Domestic Domains." *Social Analysis* 15:32–49.

Zavella, Patricia. 1996. Feminist Insider Dilemmas: Constructing Ethnic Identity with Chicana Informants. Pp. 139–59 in *Feminist Dilemmas in Fieldwork*, ed. Diane L. Wolf. Boulder, CO: Westview Press.

Zerubavel, Eviatar. 1991. The Social Lens. Pp. 61–80 in *The Fine Line: Making Distinctions in Everyday Life*. New York: The Free Press.

Index

About the Author

Joey Sprague is a professor in the Department of Sociology at the University of Kansas, where she teaches feminist theory, research methods, social psychology, and the sociology of gender. Her research focuses on the ways gender, class, and race structure social understanding, particularly the organization of knowledge and the academy. Recent publications include "Structured Knowledges and Strategic Methodologies" (2001) and "Self-Determination and Empowerment: A Feminist Standpoint Analysis of How We Talk about Disability" (with Jeanne Hayes, 2000). She is coeditor of the Gender Lens book series. She tries to balance her work as a sociologist with life in a family that includes a partner, two children, a dog, a cat, and a garden, and with active involvement in organizations working for social equality. She received her Ph.D. in sociology at the University of Wisconsin, Madison.